Herbs Of The Earth

A Self-Teaching Guide To Healing Remedies

Using Common North American Plants and Trees

Mary Carse, M.N.I.M.H
Registered Herbalist

Upper Access Publishers
Hinesburg, Vermont

Upper Access Publishers
One Upper Access Road
P.O. Box 457
Hinesburg, Vermont 05461
802-482-2988
1-800-356-9315

Cover art and line drawings by Amber Foote.

Library of Congress Cataloging-in-Publication Data

Carse, Mary, 1919-
Herbs of the earth: a self-teaching guide to healing remedies : using common North American plants and trees / Mary Carse : [illustration by Amber Foote].
Includes biblographies and index.
ISBN 0-942679-04-0 (alk. paper) : $17.95. — ISBN 0-942679-05-9 (pbk. : alk. paper) : $10.95
1. Herbs—North America—Therapeutic use. I. Title.
RM666.H33C367 1989
615'.321'097—dc20

89-8951
CIP

Printed on acid-free paper.

Second printing

Herbs Of The Earth

"The Most High hath created
Medicines out of the Earth.
And the wise man will not scorn
the use of them."

Sirach 38:4

solomon's seal

Herbs of the Earth

Contents

Part Three
Appendices

MEADOWSWEET

Foreword

Twelve years ago, when I was a beginning family physician, I saw an elderly French Canadian woman whose indigestion and abdominal discomfort clearly pointed to a case of gastritis, if not an early peptic ulcer. I advised her to avoid all caffeine, aspirin, alcohol, and spicy foods, and told her I had the perfect remedy for her. I instructed her in the brewing of an herbal infusion containing dried comfrey and meadowsweet leaves. Before I could finish with the dose schedule of the tea, she looked at me sharply and said, "Doctor, if I wanted to take herbs, I would have gone to my mother's herbalist in Montreal. I come to you because I want a drug."

Her rebuke points out a dilemma in which I have found myself many times since our meeting. Drugs are viewed as strong, modern, and effective. Herbs are seen as old-fashioned, weak, and of dubious value. Yet I view the practice of herbal medicine as one of continuing validity. Herbalism hearkens back to an important branch point in modern medicine. Handed down through folklore by years of empiric knowledge, Herbalism and a caring concern were a physician's main tools until, with the advent of "scientific medicine," doctors began to develop and use strong chemical drugs that altered the biochemistry of specific body processes.

Herbal remedies work more subtly than chemical drugs. While both may effect similar biological reactions, the process of herbal medicines is different. Drugs are part of our fast-paced modern lifestyle. We want results, and we want them immediately. We want to take a pill, end whatever discomfort we may have, and get back to work. Never mind that it is probably our fast-paced lifestyles that are getting us into trouble in the first place.

Herbal treatments force us to stop our routines. A patient must boil some water, make a tea, and drink the tea slowly, for it is hot. The process takes a long time. All the while, however, we are focusing our energies on ourselves. We (and those caring for us) are thinking about our illness, about its relationship to ourselves, and we are channelling love and healing thoughts back to ourselves. This healing process may be as important to the fight against disease as the pharmacological properties of the herb.

If herbalism hearkens back to a time when medicine was less "scientific," it also recalls a time when it was less mysterious and more accessible. Every family had a body of medical knowledge it felt comfortable using when illness struck. Often there was a family or neighborhood resource person with knowledge of herbal remedies handed down over generations. Now, with every illness having potentially terrible and unknown consequences, people visit their doctors sooner. Medical tests done to rule out these unlikely sequellae, like the drugs used to treat them, are often expensive, unnecessary, and may have risks that can lead to further illness. Families that have lost the common knowledge of herbal treatments a generation or two back have lost an important first line of defense against all illnesses.

Incidentally, the knowledge I was trying to impart to my unwilling gastritis patient was a gift to me from Mary Carse. Mary has been teaching and practicing Herbalism for many years. She grows and collects herbs at and around her Vermont farm. This book is a natural outgrowth of that work. She has filtered the Herbalism course syllabus she developed for her students through her years of study and practice. In doing so, she has created one of the best herbal resource books I have seen. Authoritative and broad, it extends from basic information about plant families that helps one identify useful herbs in the field, to techniques for gathering herbs and making herbal preparations, and then to various medical conditions and the herbs that treat them. Extremely well organized, this book allows the reader to approach the study of herbalism from either a medical or botanical point of view. Her work is a great contribution to the field of herbal medicine.

Richard H. Bernstein, M.D.
Charlotte Family Health Center
Charlotte, Vermont
March 20, 1989

About This Book

The body under natural conditions is a self-recuperative organism. Herbs are used to arouse, assist, and cooperate with the vital forces when ill health results from not obeying nature's laws. To this end, we make use of herbal remedies, natural foods, diets and fasting, exercise, and hydrotherapy—in conjunction with the body's own cleansing and eliminative processes. In an emergency, we favor any means necessary for the saving of life. Any person has a right to choose any system of treatment to which his condition will respond. The public welfare demands the co-existence of various forms of therapy which are not competitive but complementary.

In many European countries, herbal remedies, or "simples," are still used by country people for ordinary family illnesses and emergencies. Even doctors in these areas choose these remedies first, saving the more drastic modern drugs for situations of greatest need.

In England there is the Institute of Medical Herbalists, which not only registers herbal practitioners among its members, but conducts training schools, clinics, and public relations activities to acquaint the public with the virtues of natural remedies. In the United States, on the contrary, herbal knowledge has been lost, except for isolated pockets in Appalachia, Pennsylvania Dutch country, and Indian reservations. With interest in natural life styles as an alternative to modern technological society, many are seeking to add natural remedies to their natural foods, to enhance their quality of life. It is for those seeking a simpler and more natural way of life that this course is offered.

Twenty-five years ago, when I started giving courses in herbalism, I found that there were very few books that I could use as a text. Most of those had been published in England and were generally out of print. As a consequence, I had to write my own text to accompany my course, and this is what resulted. It bears the marks of its origin. Because it was initially meant to be only an adjunct to classes, in which the material would be introduced and explained, it is highly condensed.

It always takes more time, effort, and dedication to teach yourself from a book than to learn in a class. What you have here in your hands is essentially a self-teaching course. Each lesson is followed by questions that help to focus on the most important or perhaps the most difficult part of the lesson. Since this course is little more than an index of herbs and conditions in which they can be used, it cannot be skimmed or read hastily. Some things are said only once—blink, and you've missed them!

In another sense, the course is not "self-teaching." It is you who must be self-teaching. You must be willing to fill in what is not contained in this course and what could not be included without making it too unwieldy. Other texts in botany, physiology, anatomy, nursing, first aid, and many other subjects should be located and studied, to flesh out what is given here as a basic outline. It would be risky or even dangerous in the extreme to rely on my brief summaries for diagnosis of certain diseases or conditions of the body. You must also look elsewhere for the actual identification of plants if you intend to collect your own, even though I have included a short instruction for the making of an herbarium of pressed plants. At various places in the course, lists of books are given as the beginning of an essential library for the serious student.

The course is divided into three main sections. Part One is primarily theory, covering botanical families, preparation of herbs, and agents (classification of herbs according to how they work in the body). In general, the material in this first section is to be read "once over once lightly" to get an overview of what it contains and then referred back to frequently during the rest of the course.

Part Two, the main body of the course, is in the form of an alphabetical index. I have included both the herbs (*materia medica*) and the diseases, or physical indications for herbal use.

Part Three consists of several appendices: lists of first herbs to grow or collect, a lesson on how to make an herbarium, and a list of the trees and plants contained in this course. If the reader is beginning this course in the spring, it might be well to turn to the instructions on making the pressed collection in order to begin as soon as the various plants come into flower and to insure proper identification. Specimens that are correctly collected and pressed can be taken or sent (inquire first!) to the botany department of your nearest college or university for identification. It would be well to begin to collect and dry for your own use some of the simplest herbs, listed in Appendix I. For this you will have to pay close attention to the information in Lesson 2.

A substantial amount of the material given in these chapters will be found again, in one form or another, in other places in the course. You will find a great deal of cross-referencing. This is necessary. Do not try to treat any condition by reading just the list of herbs under that condition without referring back to the entries under each specific herb to find out which one would be the best for a particular case.

Above all, keep learning! This is a beginning course in herbalism. Invest in as many of the recommended books as you can. The ones listed here are the best to start with that I've found. But browse through others and add them if they seem useful. Not all herbals are equally good. Try to use the books written by practicing herbalists who have actually used the agents they talk about.

In herbalism, as in everything else, there are fads and fashions that come and go. Try not to be swept away by current novelties. Especially beware of any one system, technique, or herbal agent that is presented as the panacea or cure-all for every human ill. Be aware, too, of the value of other natural therapies such as chiropractic, naturopathy, homeopathy, nutrition, exercise, and massage, as well as the spiritual aspects of human well-being. All of these have their place in a well-balanced lifestyle.

It is my hope that you will not attempt to use this course for profit or gain or power, but only as a means of helping yourself, your family, and perhaps your neighbor to use these simple gifts of the earth—the plants and trees—for the good of people. For those who are faithful and devoted in studying and using these simple remedies, the satisfaction of knowing you have helped yourself or others to better health will be your major reward.

Mary

Mary's Garden
Hinesburg, Vermont

Cautionary Note

Nothing contained in this course is intended to substitute for professional medical diagnosis and treatment. None of the plants recommended is narcotic, poisonous, or dangerous when used as directed.

The completion of this course does not qualify anyone to practice herbalism professionally or for remuneration, nor to diagnose nor perform any clinical procedures, nor to dispense substances that are restricted to medical doctors or pharmacists.

Herbs of the Earth

Part One

General Information and Theory

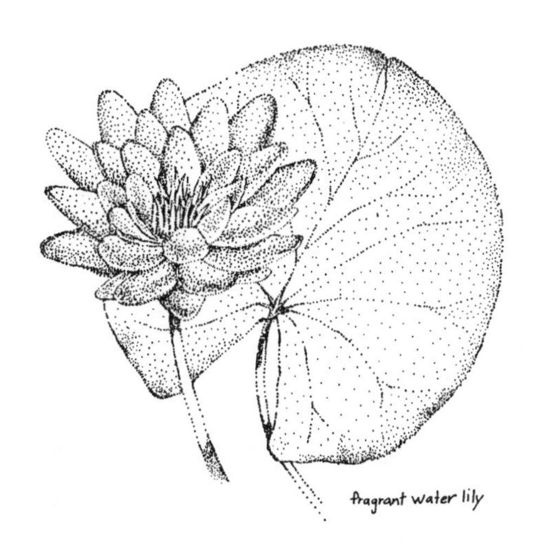

LESSON 1: Botanical Families of Interest to Herbalists

Popular guidebooks differ in their approach to plant identification. Some focus on the color of the flower or flower formation. But those are difficult to use in seasons when the plant is not in bloom. Others place great emphasis on leaf formation. Yet leaf formation is complex and diverse.

I have chosen to cover only the most basic distinctions—monocot and dicot—with a general overview of the common families in each. The ensuing discussions are strictly for exposing the reader to common botanical terms and details. The lesson is intended to serve as an outline, not a text, on plant identification.

For the purpose of precise verification, the student is expected to pursue further study. An experienced botanist or ecologist from a nearby university might be persuaded to take one or two field trips with you. Failing this, continued field trips on your own, guidebook in hand, checking and rechecking, are necessary. (See suggested list at end of lesson.)

In this lesson, I have included few trees and shrubs. Although some of the deciduous trees and shrubs botanically belong to some of the following families, identification for amateurs is along somewhat different lines for trees. Where needed, the identification details for specific trees and shrubs—also ferns, lichens, and mosses—will appear under each entry.

Monocots. This is a large group of plants with the following distinguishing characteristics:

- The seed embryo contains a single kernel (as in corn) instead of two (as in beans).
- The stems are often hollow (corn, bamboos, and some grasses), or at least the wood bundles are separate and scattered in the stem.
- The leaves are usually parallel-veined, with veins that lead up independently, side by side, from the stem.

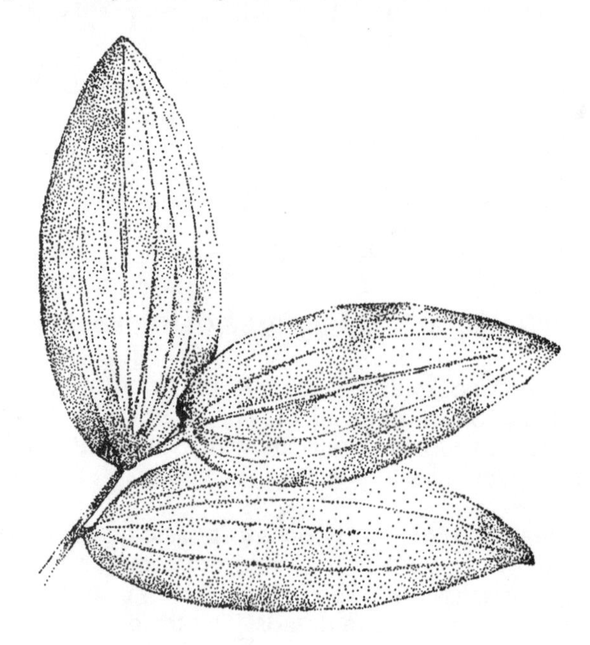

solomon's seal - parallel veins

• The flower parts—the sepals, petals, and stamen—are usually in threes or sixes

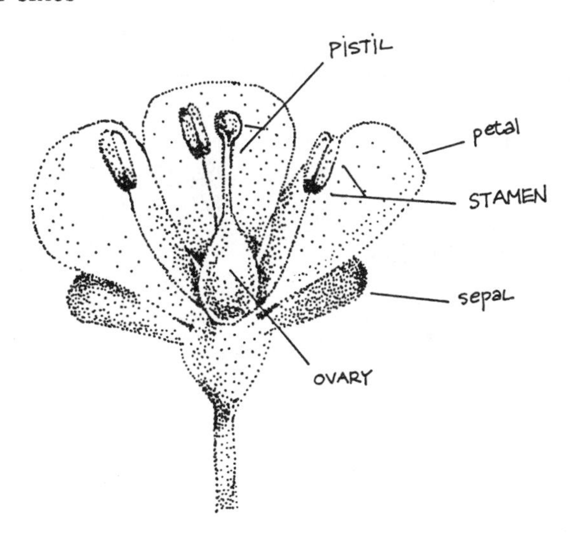

The monocots account for about one-fifth of the flowering plants. Most are grasses that are important for cereal, carbohydrate foods, and livestock feed. They are not too important medicinally. In addition to grasses, there are other families among the monocot group that occur wild or cultivated and are of interest:

- Cattail (*Typhaceae*)—edible.
- Arrowhead (*Alismataceae*)—edible.
- Arum (*Araceae*)—including jack-in-the-pulpit and skunk cabbage—some edible, but with caution.
- Pickerelweed (*Pontederiaceae*)—edible.
- Lily (*Liliaceae*)—a very large family, including not only the obvious lilies but also onions, garlic, and asparagus.
- Amaryllis (*Amaryllidaceae*)—including the daffodils; many bulbs are *poisonous*.
- Iris (*Iridaceae*)—including crocuses and gladioli.
- Orchid (*Orchidaceae*)—including the lady's-slipper, a useful but endangered species in many areas.

Many of these families have some useful and some dangerous members, which should be learned individually.

Dicots. All other flowering plants, including most trees and shrubs, belong to the dicot group.

• The embryo or seed has two kernels (as in beans).

• In the stem or trunk, the wood bundles are usually united into a ring surrounding a central pith.

• The leaves are usually net-veined, branching off from a central vein. (There are, however, some exceptions to this.)

• The leaves adorn the stem in alternating or opposite locations, or in a whorl.

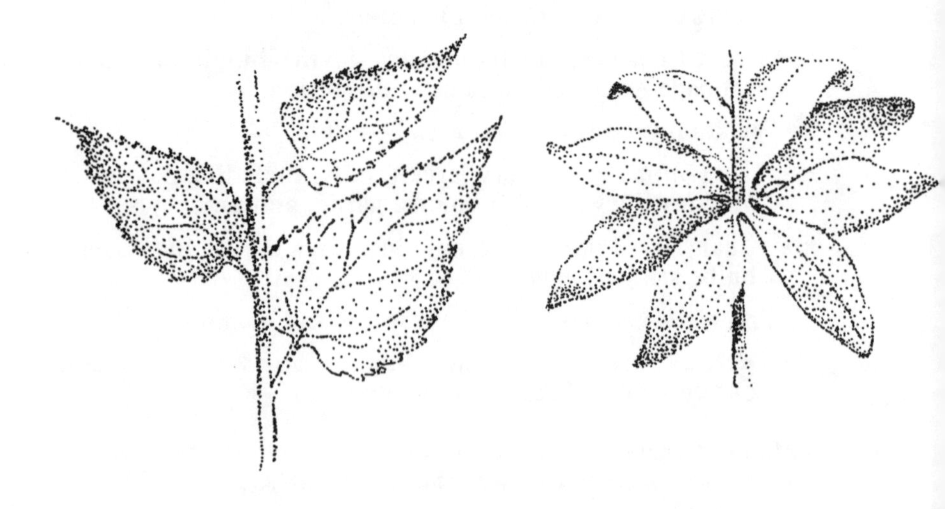

• The parts of the flower (again, with exceptions) are usually in multiples of four or five.

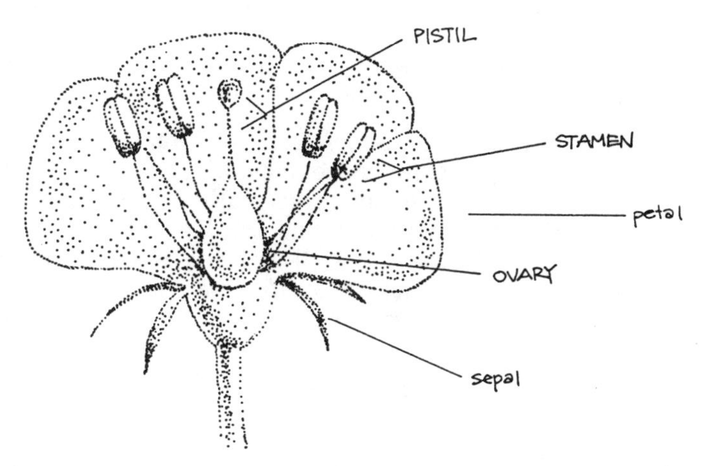

About four-fifths of our flowering plants belong to the dicot group, including tree families such as willows, poplars, birches, nuts, alders, oaks, elm, and mulberries. Plant families of interest are:

- Nettle (*Urticaceae*)—medicinal.
- Birthwort or Dutchman's-pipe (*Aristolochiaceae*)—a small family of twining or low herbs whose flower is a cup or vase-like structure without petals—including wild ginger, Dutchman's-pipe, and Virginia snakeroot—some medicinal, edible.
- Buckwheat (*Polygonaceae*)—a large and very important family containing few, if any, dangerous species. Plants of this group have alternate toothless leaves and swollen joints on the stems, with small inconspicuous flowers lacking petals. Includes the docks, such as yellow dock, rhubarb, buckwheat, and sheep sorrel.
- Goosefoot family (*Chenopodiaceae*)—a large number of weeds, many of them introduced from Europe, often used as greens. Garden beets and spinach belong to this family. Many of them are called pigweed, but so are members of the next family. This family includes lamb's quarters, Jerusalem oak, and wormseed. Mostly wholesome in all parts.
- Amaranth family (*Amaranthus*)—weeds, again, mostly imported. Some cultivated, such as the prince's feather. The common pigweed of this family, found in waste places, is good for greens when young, and the black seeds are good for grain when mature.

- Pokeweed family (*Phytolaccaceae*)—stout-smelling perennial in waste places, stalks reddish, 4-8 feet tall. Young shoots in spring are commonly used for greens, *but the berries, root, and stems—any red parts of this plant—are dangerous.* An ingredient in some medicines, but not recommended for casual use. Used for dyes.
- Pink family (*Caryophyllaceae*)—annual or perennial plants generally characterized by smooth stems and swollen joints, with opposite-growing leaves without teeth. Flowers in fives. Includes bouncing Bet and garden flowers such as sweet William and pinks, as well as many weeds. One of the most useful is the chickweed. *However, some members of this family, such as corn cockle and bouncing Bet, can be dangerous if misused.*
- Water Lily family (*Nymphaeaceae*)—the yellow (also called spatterdock) and the white. Both are useful for food and medicine.
- Crowfoot family (*Ranunculaceae*)—a large family, containing many different species, some useful medicinally but rather potent, *and others rather dangerous.* In general, the flowers tend to be in fives, sometimes with no petals but with showy sepals. Leaves look like crows' feet. Weeds or less-used members of the family include virgin's bower (clematis), anemones, rues, thimbleweed, larkspur, and buttercups of all kinds. *The last two named are poisonous, as are baneberry (both red and white), monkshood (aconite), and perhaps columbine.* Medicinal members, when used with care, include hepatica, goldenseal, and black snakeroot. Members of this family had best be learned one at a time, as few generalities can be made.
- Barberry family (*Berberidaceae*)—includes not only the barberry shrub, useful for both food and medicine, but also blue cohosh and mandrake (*Podophyllum*), both medicinal.
- Poppy family (*Papaveraceae*)—herbs with a milky or yellow sap (but so have some other families). Irregular flowers with four to twelve petals, spurred at the base of the petals. Includes a number of plants cultivated for their flowers, such as the oriental poppy, the seeds of which are used in cooking. *The juice of the plant is narcotic, however.* Bloodroot and celandine are both medicinal.
- Mustard family (*Cruciferae*)—a very large and useful family, most of which are either edible or medicinal or both. None are dangerous. The oil of mustard, which most of this family

contains, can be dangerous when abstracted or ingested in very large doses, but not when these plants are used according to usual methods. The garden vegetables of the cabbage family, radishes, and turnips also belong here. The flowers consist of four petals across from each other in the shape of a cross, thus the Latin name of the family. Cresses are edible raw; the greens of horseradish and the various mustards can be cooked. The main medicinal member of the family is shepherd's-purse. A cultivated garden flower, candytuft, is both medicinal and edible. Nasturtiums, too, are both edible and medicinal.

- Rose family (*Rosaceae*)—one of the largest (over 3,000 species) and most useful and safest of all plant families. Besides the roses, which bear the family name, there are others which we sometimes do not recognize as members of the family: apples, pears, plums, raspberries, blackberries, and strawberries. A thoughtful study of the blossoms of any of these will reveal their relationship—all are in fives or multiples of five. Also, the members bear the common characteristic of being generally astringent when medicinal. The mildest, for infants, are the strawberry plants; then, in ascending order of astringency, raspberry leaves, blackberry, meadowsweet, steeplebush, and tormentil. Some little herbs, such as agrimony, lady's mantle, and burnet, are not easily recognized as belonging to this family. They also possess astringent and medicinal properties. Rose leaves make a good tea to replace commercial tea, and the rose fruits (hips) are one of the best sources of vitamin C. The hawthorns, another prolific and varied group in this family, have edible berries that are also medicinal.
- Pulse family (*Leguminosae*)—include our garden peas and beans and also the various clovers. Medicinally, the red clover, sweet clover, and melilot are the most important. The flowers look like butterflies, and the leaves are usually compound with three leaflets. Some, like the ground nut and hog peanut, have edible tubers. There are *perhaps one or two dangerous or suspected members*, but by sticking to the easily recognized common ones, no one should go wrong.
- Rhus family (*Anacardiaceae*)—included here because *it contains some plants that are poison to touch: poison ivy, poison oak, and poison sumac.* It also, however, contains one very useful plant, the staghorn sumac. It is necessary to be able to distinguish the dangerous members of the family in order to feel free to use the safe member. Poison ivy is a low plant or vine, usually growing in sandy soil, with three leaflets on a

twig. ("Leaves three, leave it be!") The leaflets are not especially toothed and are usually shiny. It has inconspicuous droopy white flowers and white berries that are relished by game birds and animals. Some people appear to be immune to poison ivy, but this seems to change from time to time, and they may find themselves victims. Even the sap, when carried in smoke from burning the plant, can be dangerous. Poison sumac is a small tree or shrub with feathery compound leaves but with flowers and berries droopy and white, like poison ivy. It grows in swamps or bogs. The common sumac of hills and upland pastures is the staghorn sumac, with its showy cones of red berries in fall and winter. The twigs and branches are like a stag's horn in velvet, hence the name. There is also a smooth variety. The red berries of both of these contain vitamin C and can be made into a pleasant acidulous drink. The bark and leaves contain tannin and are a source of dyes and medicine.

- Staff Tree family (*Celastraceae*)—includes the twining shrubby vine called bittersweet, effective medicinally.
- Grape family (*Vitis*)—All wild grapes are safe and useful. However, *two other vines resemble grapes and can be dangerous. One is the Virginia creeper that has five leaflets, and the other is moonseed that has purplish fruits with a single crescent-shaped seed, no tendrils, and leaves with few lobes.*
- Mallow family (*Malvaceae*)—wild mallows, hollyhocks; medicinal.
- Violet family (*Violaceae*)—a very large family, easily recognized both in leaf and flower. Medicinal and has edible leaves and flowers.
- Ginseng family (*Araliaceae*)—includes the ginseng of commerce (medicinal, but much overrated by the Chinese who paid large prices for it in former years). Other members are also medicinal and useful, including the aralias or wild sarsaparillas. *The only cultivated member, the English ivy, is dangerous in all its parts.*
- Parsley family (*Umbelliferae*)—one of the largest and most difficult families to deal with, both botanically and medicinally. It contains at the same time some of the world's most useful food and seasoning plants (carrots, parsnips, parsley, dill, anise, caraway) but *also the world's most dangerous plants (poison hemlock, Fool's parsnip, etc.). Some of these plants are so poisonous that a single seed can kill a child. "Wild caraway" and the like must be very carefully identified.*

Most are rank weeds, with hollow stems, generally deeply cut or ferny compound leaves, and tiny flowers mostly in broad, flat-topped clusters (like little umbrellas, hence the Latin name). Unfortunately, this description would also fit some other plants such as yarrow, boneset, and Joe-Pye weed of the Composite family (which is one reason why the student must not rely only on the facts in this lesson for identification). The difference is in the tiny flowers: in the *Umbelliferae*, the flowers are perfect; in the Composites, the central flowers are usually imperfect, sometimes lacking petals entirely, like the dandelion, or with the outside flowers sometimes showy, like the daisy. Also, the pattern of the flower head on the stem is different. It is necessary to become familiar with these things in the field. The safest rule for the *Umbelliferae* is to use no wild ones but to buy one's seed of caraway, dill, etc., from reputable seed companies. The only wild member I recommend for medicinal use is the wild carrot (Queen Anne's lace), which is easily recognized.

- Heath family (*Ericaceae*)—includes some flowering shrubs not too common in the north (rhododendron, laurel, etc.). *Most of them are poisonous in part, especially to livestock.* We have some small plants, some edible (blueberries, huckleberries, cranberries), and some medicinal (trailing arbutus, wintergreen, bearberry). Most of the medicinal ones in this family influence the urinary apparatus.

- Gentian family (*Gentianaceae*)—includes some garden flowers. Smooth herbs with generally opposite, toothless leaves—some medicinal.

- Dogbane family (*Apocynaceae*) and Milkweeds (*Ascelepiadaceae*)—These two families are combined because they have much in common and were formerly considered one. They are milk-juiced plants with large smooth opposite leaves and five-part flowers with segments turned back. *Some of the species are very dangerous*, others quite useful. The common milkweed is one of the most useful plants we have, for food, medicine, fiber, etc. The butterfly weed (pleurisy root) is *specific* for most ailments of the lungs. *Dogbanes can be dangerous although helpful in some conditions.* The Indian hemp belongs in this family.

- Vervain family (*Verbenaceae*)—small flowers in terminal spikes. The showiest of our wild members has deep blue candelabra, grows in swamps with Joe-Pye weed and boneset in August—medicinal.

- Mint family (*Labiatiae*)—so named because the blossoms have droopy bottom petals like little lips. Some are very aromatic and used in cooking. They also generally have medicinal uses, mostly influencing the nervous system. Besides the characteristic shape of the flowers (that range in color from white through blues to purple), this family can be distinguished by its square stems. Best known cultivated members of the family are the mints, catnip, sage, rosemary, horehound, and thyme.

- Nightshade family (*Solanaceae*)—*a family containing many poisonous members*, of which our potato and tomato are exceptions, although *all green parts of potato plants are dangerous.* Other non-poisonous members of this family include the garden huckleberry, eggplant, green pepper, and Japanese lantern. One wild member called bittersweet should not be confused with the woody vine of the staff tree family that bears the pretty orange berries used for winter decorations. *The nightshade called bittersweet is common in woods and fields, has purple star-shaped flowers with a yellow beaked center, producing in late summer or autumn red berries that are toxic. Jimson weed, sometimes called thorn apple, is an evil-smelling poisonous weed found in waste heaps and dumps. It bears a prickly fruit, and should not be confused with the very safe hawthorn tree*, the fruit of which is also called thorn apple.

- Figwort family (*Scrophulariaeceae*)—a rather diverse family, little known to most people. Two members that are cultivated in the garden are foxglove (*Digitalis*) and snapdragon. The former is a well-known cardiac agent. *The family as a whole has rather dangerous tendencies*, but one member that is safe when used as directed is mullein. Easily recognized by its flannel-like leaves, it grows in dry pastures and roadsides, has a tall spike with yellow flowers.

- Madder family (*Rubiaceae*)—a very diverse family including tropical plants such as coffee and cinchona (quinine). Low herbs with opposite toothless leaves and little bell-like flowers. Medicinally, squawvine (partridgeberry) is the most useful. Others are bedstraw and cleavers.

- Composite or Sunflower family (*Compositae*)—one of the largest families and usually the last listed in botanical texts. The flowers are really compound bunches, either with or without strap-like petals surrounding the whole. The daisy and dandelion are typical. The largest groups within the family are the goldenrods and the asters, both of which are represented by one species each in our materia medica. *Only one member, arnica, is potentially dangerous.* Other composites in use medicinally are the chamomiles, yarrow, and the absinthes.

I am omitting several other families that have only one or two useful members. Specific plants will be described in the alphabetical section of the course.

Useful Texts for This Lesson

Botanical texts that combine clear illustrations with nontechnical descriptions, plus convenient sizes, are almost impossible to come by. The following are the ones I use most:

• *Illustrated Flora of the Northern United States and Canada* by Nathaniel Britton & Addison Brown. (Three-volume paperback.) New York, NY: Dover Publications, 1970. This is the most complete and the best illustrated, but rather large and somewhat technical for beginners.

• *Newcomb's Wildflower Guide* by Lawrence Newcomb. Boston, MA: Little Brown Co., 1977. This has excellent drawings of the majority of the wild flowers, plus flowering shrubs and vines. It has an ingenious key system for tracking them down.

• *Trees of North America: A Golden Guide* edited by Frank Brockman. New York, NY: Western Publishing, 1968, 1979. This covers the whole country, and has good illustrations. Arrangement by tree families makes it a little hard to use unless you consult the introductory material in the front, or just leaf through the pictures until you find what you're looking for.

Also take a look at various field guide series—Peterson's, Audubon, and others—until you find the one with which you are comfortable.

Self-review Questions for Botanical Families

1. The trillium has three petals and three sepals. The veins of its leaves are parallel to each other. To which of the two major classes of plant families do you think it belongs—monocot or dicot?

2. Which three large plant families of many species would you consider the safest for a beginner?

3. Which three, similarly, are the most dangerous medicinally? (Do not include the Rhus family here.)

4. Although no one plant family can claim a monopoly of any of the various classes of herbal agents, to which one, according to this lesson, would you look for an appropriate astringent?

5. To which one would you look for a nerve tonic (nervine)?

6. In which family would you find an agent for the urinary system?

7. If you heard someone talking about wanting some "bittersweet" and also some "thorn apple," what four different plants might be referred to?

8. What is the value of using Latin names for plants?

9. Vocabulary words to define:

annual
biennial
cress
dicot
legume
monocot
perennial
rank (adj.)
shrub (both meanings)
species
tubers
weed

(Answers on page 202.)

Suggested additional project: Using another sheet (and additional books), draw and label:

a. A flower showing petals, sepals, stamen, and pistil
b. Leaves
  — compound and simple
  — entire, toothed, lobed, and divided
  — dicot, and monocot

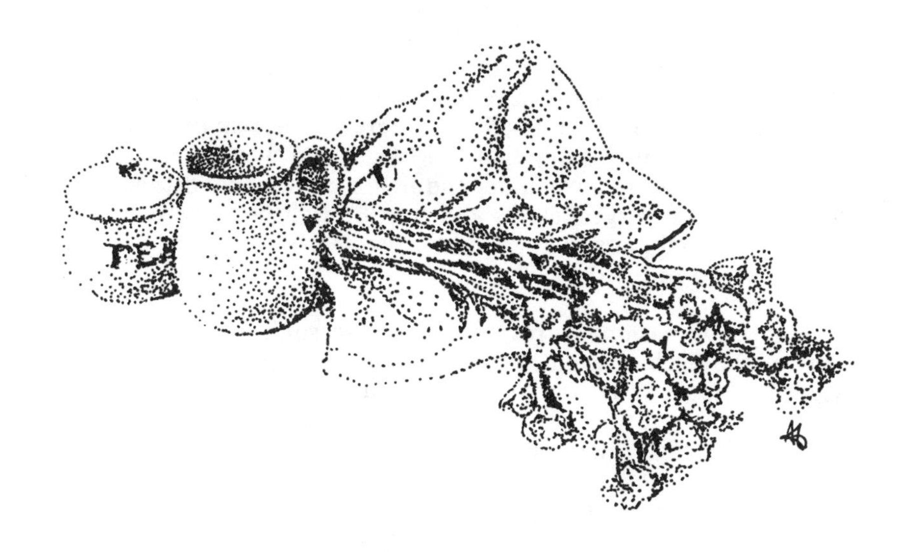

LESSON 2: Gathering and Preparing Herbs

Aside from the positive botanical identification, the first step in preparation is the actual collecting of the herbs. This depends upon the part of the plant that is to be used and the manner in which it is to be used.

Gathering

Whole Plants or Herbs. When a herbal preparation calls for the whole plant (or sometimes refers to it as "the herb"), it usually refers to the leafy above-ground parts, including the flower heads. Most herbs are collected and used in this way. They should be gathered just when the plant is coming into full flower. The herb has attained its full growth at this time and has not yet expended its strength in setting seeds or fruit.

Always collect herbs for drying on a sunny day, not after a long rainy spell, and after all dew or dampness has dried off the plants. Early afternoon is best. Tie the herbs loosely in small bunches and hang in a hot, dry, shaded place such as a well-aired attic or shed where no traffic will kick up dust. Do not collect herbs from power line rights-of-way or sides of the road where poison sprays might have been used, or where constant exhaust from motors leaves a residue. When so much dust remains on the plant that it will have to be washed before being dried, you increase the risk of molding.

When herbs are so dry that the twigs snap when bent (this will take several days to a week depending on weather conditions), strip leaves from the largest stems and store in tightly covered cans. Do not use covered glass jars, as light causes herbs to deteriorate faster than they do in the dark.

Seeds. Occasionally (especially for seasoning in cooking) the part of the herb wanted is the seed. In this case, collect when the seeds are ripe and before they have begun to shatter. Hang the seed-heads downward in a paper bag, so that as the seeds dry they will fall into the bag. When the seeds are dry, store them in jars or bags.

Roots. These are usually dug in the fall, after the plant has had time to store its valuable properties in the root for the winter. Usually I wait until the plant has withered back. If I can't get roots in the fall, the next best time is early spring, before the growing plant begins to take nourishment away from the root. Roots are usually taken from biennial plants and perennial plants.

Biennial plants are those that grow from seed one year, store food in roots over the winter, and the next year send up a larger plant that will flower and set seeds. Then the plant dies. Hollyhocks are biennials. Usually the roots are best taken at the end of the first year, flowers and seeds at the end of the second year.

Perennials are plants that grow up from the same root year after year. In this case, the older the plant is, the larger and better the roots will be. Yellow dock is an example of such a perennial.

Barks. Usually trees or shrubs are used for bark. Sometimes the bark of the root is specified; otherwise the bark on younger twigs is more easily stripped. The best time to take bark is in the spring when rising sap makes bark easier to peel off the branch. Bark should be dried carefully in a hot dry place and then stored as herbs. However, if one has time, it is best to grind up the bark before storing so as to have it ready for use when needed.

Fruits. Sometimes juicy fruits are the parts used (hawthorn berries, for example). These are usually picked when ripe. They may be washed, if necessary, then made up directly into formulae as given under the species, or dried carefully on a cookie sheet in the oven.

Juices. In some cases, herbal preparations of remarkable potency can be made up from the expressed juice of the green plant. This process has become more feasible with the availability of appliances known as "juicers" or "juicerators." If this process is recommended, the herbs are best picked—contrary to the general rule—right after a rain, so they will have as much juice as possible. They can be washed, with a little water left clinging to the leaves, which aids in making up the preparation immediately after collecting. These specialized machines will separate the solid herb mass from the extraction.

If a juicer is unavailable, a blender or food processor can be used. Run the herbs through a chopping cycle. Add only as much additional water as might be needed to keep the machine running smoothly. Press the juice from the shredded mass using cheese cloth or a strainer.

Juices should be used or preserved quickly to retain potency and avoid spoilage.

Now that you have your botanicals safely collected and stored away, the next step is preparing them for use.

Preparing Herbal Agents

Using Water. The easiest, most common, and by far the best manner of preparing herbal agents is the **infusion** or **tea**. This is made by placing the required amount of *dried botanical* in a china teapot (or large china cup with a saucer to cover it) and pouring over it the required amount of boiling water. It is especially important to cover when using agents that have volatile oils that would escape in the steam.

The standard herbalist formula:

⅓ cup of loose leaves or 1-2 tablespoons coarsely ground roots and barks; less for fine, powdered material (1 teaspoon)
2 cups of boiling water

Steep 15-20 minutes, covered. Unless otherwise stated, serve hot, according to recommended dose. Usual dose: ½ cup, 3-4 times daily

The same procedure is used for *fresh, raw herbs* but double the herbal amount to account for the greater bulk and water content of green herbs.

A **decoction** is just like an infusion except that the material (usually roots and bark) is boiled in the water. Infusions are never boiled. Roots and barks are dense material and do not yield their properties as well in infusion. A few herbs are rather dense, too, and do not infuse well. Sometimes the properties needed are the minerals rather than the more volatile oils. In those situations, directions for preparation will call for a decoction.

(*Note on herbal teas and coffees*: These are sometimes recommended for beverage use, in connection with a natural diet. The herbal teas and coffees do not contain any caffeine. The terms "tea" and "coffee" refer to the manner of preparation. Teas are infused, and coffees—usually roasted chicory or dandelion roots, sunflower or pumpkin seeds—are prepared in the same manner as decoctions.)

Infusions and decoctions should be used within 24 hours.

When it comes to making a preparation that will have some keeping properties, the herbal solutions must be more concentrated to make up for the added vehicle. Furthermore, when the natural properties of herbs are subjected to heat, distillation, or other treatment, some potency is lost.

Syrups. The best syrup is pure **honey**. This has the advantage of being a natural preservative since honey is antiseptic and will not tolerate the growth of germs or mold (unless it is diluted past a certain point, where it begins to ferment). Add the raw *juice*—about 3 tablespoonsful—of the green herb to 1 cup of raw, liquid honey. Stir the juice into the honey well but don't heat. Pour into a sterilized jar and seal. This works especially well for the mints—catnip, horehound, and motherwort—and probably also with some others such as shepherd's-purse. This yields a concentrated product. Usual dose: 1 teaspoonful in ½ a glass of water.

To make a syrup with dried herbs, you will need a **concentrated infusion**. Follow the previous directions for infusions, using 8 times the usual quantity of herb and ¾ of the usual quantity of water. When strained, add an amount of honey equal to the liquid. Use the same dose as above.

Ginger syrup can be used for some bad-tasting herbs such as shepherd's-purse and valerian: 6 fluid ounces of concentrated infusion of ginger root (as in the paragraph above) added to 14 fluid ounces of honey. If honey is not available, a **sugar syrup** can be made by adding 3 cups of sugar to two cups of water. Stir on low heat until dissolved.

Preparations with alcohol. Herbs can also be preserved with the addition of alcohol. **Wine** may be added, especially when a **tonic** is being prepared. Wines contain iron and other minerals, as well. Make a concentrated infusion, then add an equal quantity of strong, sweet wine. Be sure to shake well before using. Dose for tonics (but not for more specific agents) would be one wineglassful (about 2 fluid ounces) before meals. Even with the wine, these preparations do not keep very long.

Brandy is better for keeping longer periods of time and is also a natural fruit product. The best way to use brandy is to make a **tincture**:

½ to ⅔ of a cup of green herb, fresh bark or root, cut up
1 pint brandy

Macerate (infuse) for 1 week in a closed jar, inverting daily. Press out through a cloth bag. Dose: 1 tablespoon in ½ glass of water.

Vinegars. Some preparations, such as for gargles and shrubs, are preserved by adding vinegar, and sometimes sugar or honey as well. They will be described under the particular agent when used that way. Vinegars tend to get "ropy" after a time, but this does not affect their quality.

Oils. Some resinous or oily plants and seeds do not yield their properties readily to water. These are sometimes boiled or steeped in oil (preferably vegetable oils, not mineral oil). Still others are used in this way to make liniments or **ointments** for external use. Instead of oil, for a firmer ointment any fat may be used, such as lard, suet, or tallow. Lanolin or cocoa butter is preferred by many. When boiled up with an antiseptic herb such as calendula and sealed in sterile jars, the ointment will not mold or spoil for quite some time, if stored unopened.

Poultices. An old-fashioned but sometimes very effective means for treating certain conditions is with a poultice or plaster. A poultice is held in place over an area of the body; a **plaster** has an agent that makes it stick to the skin. Unless you are deliberately seeking a blistering effect, the latter is not so desirable.

Poultices require: a starchy or grainy vehicle (such as oatmeal, slippery elm powder, or flaxseed) that will make a stiff paste; an herbal agent specific for the particular condition; and finally, porous cloth such as muslin or cheesecloth to enclose the paste and hold it over the area to be treated.

The usual formula to be mixed in a warmed bowl:

1 pint of boiling water
a handful of the herbal agent

Steep for 15 minutes. Sprinkle in the vehicle, stirring constantly to make a smooth dough. Oil—2 or 3 tablespoons—can be stirred into this to prevent sticking to the skin. Or the oil can be rubbed on the skin first. Spread the paste quickly on the cloth, fold ends and sides into the center, and apply poultice to the body, securing with pins or adhesive tape. Oiled silk, plastic, or rubber material can be used to cover so as to keep in the heat and moisture.

Poultices are most often used for sprains, neuritis, bursitis, arthritis, and rheumatism. For some of these conditions, the addition of a stimulating agent such as mustard, ginger, or pepper in small amounts hastens the reaction, but watch for blistering. Poultices are also used as drawing agents for open sores, especially boils. In this case, the poultice must be wetter and constantly renewed.

In former times, poultices and plasters were often used for common colds, coughs, and lung ailments—applied to the back or chest. It is doubtful if these are as useful as other methods we can use for these ailments, but a piece of warmed wool or flannel might be used if it gives comfort.

Suppositories. These are medicated cylinders or cones, usually of a very firm substance such as tallow, cocoa butter, or suet, into which a medicinal agent (finely powdered) is mixed. Suppositories can be inserted into the vagina or rectum where they melt with the body heat and are absorbed, along with the medication. Suppositories are used not only for local treatment but sometimes to get stronger medicines into the system when the person is not conscious or cannot tolerate anything by stomach.

To make suppositories at home, a metal mold for baking bread sticks or small lady fingers could be used. Otherwise, take a sheet of heavy aluminum foil and fold it in such a way as to make a series of small troughs, about the size of a little finger—smaller for infant use. Coat with oil.

Suppository formula:

3 ounces (or approximately ⅓ cup) of cocoa butter, tallow, or suet (beeswax does not readily melt at body temperature)
1 ounce (or 2 tablespoons) of very finely powdered herb

Heat the fat in a double boiler until the material is soft enough to work the powdered herb thoroughly into it—soft, but not necessarily all melted. Pour into the prepared molds and refrigerate until firm. Remove and do any final shaping with your fingers, keeping a cone-shape on one end, flat end on the other. Store in a cool, dark place in jars or tins.

Table of Measurements

Note: Most professional herbalists measure in ounces by weight or in metric quantities by weight. In this book we have tried to express all measurements in common household terms—using cup, pint, teaspoon, and tablespoon. These measurements are volume measures, however, that do not translate equally to weight measurements. In reading older herbals, be alert for the difference. The following table may be used as a guide:*

3 measuring teaspoons = 1 tablespoon
1 measuring tablespoon = ½ fluid ounce
1 wineglassful = 2 fluid ounces
½ cup (standard measure) = 4 fluid ounces
1 cup (standard measure) = 8 fluid ounces
1 pint = 16 fluid ounces, or 2 cups
1 quart = 32 fluid ounces, or 4 cups
1 pound = 16 ounces, by weight

A simple postal letter scale can be used for measurements by weight. Remember that dried herbs will weigh a great deal less than fresh, by measure (for instance, a cup of dried herb will weigh less than one cup of fresh herb).

* From Merck Manual, 13th edition. Merck and Co., Rahway, N.J. 1977.

Self-review Questions for Herbal Preparations

1. What determines when and how you will collect an herb?

2. Why are leafy herbs to be gathered when just coming into full flower?

3. What time of year, generally speaking, would you collect the following for herbal use: catnip herb, yellow dock root, sunflower seeds, and slippery elm bark?

4. What are two exceptions to the rule that herbs should be picked dry and stored dry?

5. What is the main difference between infusions and decoctions?

6. When would you need a concentrated infusion?

7. Decoctions are used most often in preparing what parts of a plant?

8. Name four kinds of preservative agents that can be added to herbal preparations.

9. What is the advantage of using brandy instead of wine in some herbal preparations?

10. For what purpose might you choose a vinegar mix?

11. When would you use a poultice?

12. Which preparation method is probably the best way to make use of herbs? Why?

13. Vocabulary words to define:

macerate
plaster
syrup
poultice
tincture
vehicle
wineglassful

(Answers on page 203.)

LESSON 3: Agents — Medicinal Categories

Herbal remedies are divided into several categories according to the way they act upon the body. Sometimes several herbs may be combined for greater effect—or may be substituted for one another, within one category. In other cases, two or more classes of agents that work well together may be combined.

Alteratives. One of the most useful classes of herbs, but difficult to describe, as modern medicine has nothing similar in its repertoire. Alteratives change the character of the blood and gradually *alter* a condition. They act on the blood current, cleansing and toning. Some of them, it is becoming apparent, contain hormones or hormone-like substances that act like the endocrine secretions. Others seem to enable the endocrines to work better in producing their own secretions.

In general, alteratives are used for skin diseases, scrofulous and scorbutic conditions, and also in gout, arthritis, and rheumatism (in combination with other herbs and a regular regime of natural diet and other natural therapies).

Alteratives act slowly and may take some time to show any noticeable effects, as they have to clear the blood gradually of its impurities, or regain a balance of its chemical constitution. Alteratives do not act well in contact with animal proteins. They combine well with aromatics, bitter tonics, and demulcents. The usual dose is a wineglassful, cold, three times daily one hour before meals, i.e., on an empty stomach. See under the various individual herbs for details.

- Some common alteratives: ash leaves, alder bark, bittersweet bark, burdock root and seeds, red clover heads, prickly ash bark and seeds, yellow dock root, gill-over-the-ground herb, spikenard root. (See under each.)

Anodynes and analgesics dull pain without narcosis. They are not often used, as it is better to get at the cause of the pain. I have not included many botanical agents under this class because most are dangerous to use. For nervous troubles, we prefer the agents known as nervines. (See later.)

- Two gentle anodynes: mullein and violet.

Antacids correct too much acid in the stomach, relieving heartburn and indigestion.

- Meadowsweet is a *specific* for acid stomach.

Anthelmintics kill worms in the stomach or intestines. **Vermifuges** expel worms. Certain ones are best for certain kinds of worms. They should usually be taken fasting, at night, followed by a cathartic in the morning to empty the bowels. The treatment may have to be repeated several times, but with a few days' rest in between.

- Some anthelmintics: male fern (tapeworm), turtlehead (children), blue cohosh, gentian, pumpkin seeds (children), butternut bark (children), garlic, wormseed, and wild carrot. Absinthe is also used.

Antiperiodics and **febrifuges** are used for fevers. Also included in this category are quinine substitutes that are superior to quinine in not having side-effects.

- Antiperiodics: cherry bark, ash leaves, prickly ash bark and berries, boneset, yarrow, dogwood bark, chokecherry bark, elder blossoms. Quinine substitutes: aspen bark, apple bark.

Antiscorbutics and **acidulants** combat scurvy (mostly because of their vitamin C content). They can be used as dietary supplements in drinks, juices, and salads (cooking destroys vitamin C). They are also useful in fevers, as pleasantly acid drinks.

- Common acidulants: sumac berries, barberries, rose hips (highest in vitamin C), elderberries, sheep sorrel, nasturtium (seeds, leaves, and flowers), mustard, asparagus, veronica. Also spruce and hemlock tree twigs.

Antiseptics and **disinfectants** kill microorganisms, or cleanse the system so as to render their growth less likely. Some are used externally on wounds or sores, and sometimes combined with demulcents and stimulants in poultices. Most do not sting or burn and so are more acceptable for children's injuries. Others are used internally to combat infections. These do not have the side-effects of antibiotics, although in most cases they serve the same purpose.

- Examples: calendula flowers (internally and externally—our best herbal antibiotic), garlic (must be fresh), herb Robert (externally), white pond lily root, trout lily root (fresh), apple juice, cider, vinegar, wine.

Antispasmodics relieve muscle tension, spasms or cramps.

- Useful antispasmodics: basswood, viburnum, betony, calendula, catnip, chamomile, daisy, lady's bedstraw, lady's-slipper, lemon balm, motherwort, peppermint, rosemary, sage, St. Johnswort, skullcap, valerian, and vervain.

Antithrombotics prevent blood clots. Care should be taken not to use these herbs when there is any evidence of bleeding, as clotting time will be reduced.

- Melilot is a specific antithrombotic.

Aperients, cathartics, and **laxatives** open the bowels, helping the system to cleanse itself. While these agents should never be overused so as to make a person dependent upon them (less likely with herbal laxatives than with chemical ones), they have their place in a rightly ordered natural life, especially as one gets older.

Dose should be lukewarm, in an empty stomach, at bedtime, followed with a half-strength dose three hours later or in the morning. Generally, it is best to fast for 24 hours.

- For adults: barberry bark, buckthorn bark (must be aged one to two years), prunes, dandelion root, rhubarb root (acts on lower bowel only—is followed by an astringent effect). Milder agents: buckthorn berries, yellow dock root.
- For children: butternut inner bark, turtlehead herb, olive oil.

Aromatics and **carminatives** are pleasant tasting. They produce warmth and pungency in the alimentary tract, expel gas, and make other herbs more palatable.

• Useful ones include: alder, caraway, catnip, chamomile, wild ginger, melilot, mustard seed, peppermint, spearmint, wild mint, sweet flag, and wild carrot.

Astringents act to tighten, contract, or increase the firmness of skin, mucous membranes, or eliminative systems. Many functional disorders of the body respond to astringents, especially those of the digestive tract and those of the reproductive system in women. This also is a class of herbal agents not much used by modern medicine which is more likely to take drastic measures such as surgery or cauterization for internal bleeding.

• For bleeding from any system of the body including the uterus: barberry bark, trillium (bethroot), cinquefoil, raspberry leaves, shepherd's-purse, white water lily root, squawvine (partridge-berry), dogwood bark, yarrow, agrimony.

• For diarrhea and dysentery: cinquefoil, raspberry leaves, meadowsweet, strawberry leaves and roots (especially in infants), alder bark, wild cherry bark, sumac bark, blackberry root.

• Externally as mouthwashes, gargles, and skin washes: agrimony, hemlock bark, ragweed, raspberry leaves, oak bark, white pond lily root, solomon's seal, cherry stems and bark, acorns, dogwood bark, sumac bark, witch hazel.

In all cases refer to each entry before using.

Caustics are often used as **fungicides**, externally only.

• The ones covered in this course: bloodroot, celandine, and jewelweed.

Demulcents and **emollients** are useful for any irritation of mucous membranes, coughs, throat irritations, lung disorders, or diseases of the urinary organs. They are bland and often combined with other agents. Demulcents soothe internally. Emollients are used externally as poultices or given by rectum or vagina. They are also good for burns and scalds.

• Examples: honey (excellent for persistent diaper rash), hollyhock (root, leaves, and flowers), comfrey root, mullein leaves, beech leaves.

Diaphoretics and **sudorifics** influence the circulation toward the surface and increase perspiration, usually not greatly or visibly. These may stimulate the menstrual flow somewhat, but sometimes help to suppress a heavy flow by diverting blood to capillaries of the surface. They help to rid the system of large amounts of offensive material, invaluable in eruptive diseases and fevers. Given in hot infusions. Some of the same agents are diuretic when given cold. (See below.)

• This group includes: yarrow, pennyroyal, vervain, calendula, elder flowers, boneset, prickly ash bark or berries, wild ginger (add to any of these others to hasten action).

Diuretics increase urine output through the kidneys and remove irritations in the urinary tract. They also reduce retained fluid in tissues of the body (dropsy, edema). They are often combined with demulcents. Take cold, during the day, on an empty stomach.

• Some diuretics: Joe-Pye weed, elecampane, juniper berries, white birch leaves, wild sarsaparilla, wild carrot, corn silk.

Emetics induce vomiting. Herbalists use these in a wide variety of occasions, not just to expel poisons. They can be very effective in stimulating total body response in a variety of situations and have been successfully used in diphtheria, nervous diseases, arthritis, and some infectious diseases. Do not use to excess, as this may cause exhaustion.

• Use: blue vervain, boneset, and mustard.

Emmenagogues increase the menstrual flow. They are useful in cases of suppressed menses, in young girls or nervous persons, and in some arthritic cases. These also help to get the period started when it is accompanied by cramps or nausea at the start. *These should not be used during pregnancy, especially by persons who are prone to miscarry, as they may induce hemorrhaging that may be difficult to control.* For the same reason—moral issues aside—no person should try to use any herbs as abortifacients.

• Some emmenagogues: pennyroyal, motherwort, and peppermint.

Expectorants are used to relieve the mucous congestion of lungs and bronchia, and may be used with demulcents.

• Examples: balsam poplar, horehound, pleurisy root, and veronica.

Hemostatics and **hemorrhagaics** stop hemorrhaging. Most of these have already appeared under the list of astringents.

• For external hemorrhaging: puff-ball spores (when dry and black), dried sphagnum moss (that is also antiseptic).

Hepatics and **cholagogues** stimulate the flow of bile and strengthen general liver function. Also sometimes called **antibilious** agents, they relieve symptoms of liver disorder, as in jaundice or hepatitis.

• Many antibilious agents have yellow flowers; agrimony, celandine, barberry, turtlehead, St. Johnswort, hickory, ash, dandelion.

Nervines are essentially nerve tonics. They restore the proper action of the nervous system by restoring diseased or exhausted nervous tissue. They are not narcotic or habit-forming and not really understood by modern medicine. Not all "nervous" symptoms are caused by nerves, however, and may not respond to these agents.

• Excellent nervines: catnip, sweet chamomile, skullcap, valerian root, yarrow, motherwort, blue vervain, lady's-slipper root, oats.

Pectoral agents influence the lungs. While demulcents may also be used for lung complaints, their use is more general for a variety of mucous membranes.

• Lungwort is the pectoral agent listed in this course.

Sedatives exert a calming and soothing effect, not exclusively to the nervous system. These should be used infrequently, as restorative tonics and nervines are preferred.

• Sedatives: bugleweed, mullein.

Stimulants temporarily quicken and increase body functions, especially circulation. (I do not include cerebral stimulants such as caffeine.) Persons of a phlegmatic temperament need larger doses than those of a sanguine nature. Stimulants are often used in combination with other agents to hasten the effect. They should not be used to the point of exhaustion.

• Examples: ginger, mustard, pennyroyal, prickly ash, aspen bark, vervain, wintergreen, yarrow.

Tonics differ from stimulants in that they work more slowly to strengthen and improve the tone of various tissues, especially the heart and stomach. Tonics are particularly useful during convalescence.

• Tonics for digestion: calendula, wild cherry, boneset (taken cold), sweet chamomile, gentian, and wild carrot.

• Tonics for convalescence from fevers (may contain iron): meadowsweet, wild cherry bark, sweet chamomile, boneset (cold), barberry, yarrow.

• Tonics for anemia: meadowsweet, raspberry leaves, poplar (aspen) bark, nettles.

Vermifuges. See **anthelmintics.**

Vulneraries aid in healing wounds and can be used in conjunction with hemostatics, demulcents, and antiseptics.

- External wounds: calendula, sphagnum moss dressings, plantain, chickweed.
- Internal wounds, sprains, tears, and hernias: daisy, comfrey.

Some herbs are *specific* and unique remedies for certain conditions, although other herbs also may be used. These are the ones we think of first in these conditions. They are described in more detail in the index section of the book.

Specifics of interest:

- Antacid—meadowsweet.
- Antibiotic—calendula.
- Bedwetting—agrimony.
- Bronchitis—garlic (fresh).
- Coughs—elecampane.
- Diarrhea—blackberry leaves (children), mullein (adults).
- Flu or grippe—boneset.
- Head colds, sinus—costmary.
- Morning sickness—raspberry leaves.
- Nervous heart disorders (arrhythmia)—motherwort.
- Skin eruptions—yellow dock.
- Tuberculosis—elecampane root.
- Uterine fibroid tumors—shepherd's-purse.
- Uterine hemorrhage—trillium (bethroot).
- Whooping cough—red clover blossoms.

This chapter is a general introduction to terms found in this book. For detailed guidelines for each herb, condition, or disease, see Part Two.

Self-review Questions for Agents

1. Name three classes of herbal agents that herbalists find very useful but that modern medicine uses rarely.

2. In what category of agents would you look for herbs for the following: adolescent acne, diarrhea, insomnia, sore throat, flatulence, sprained ankle?

3. List five or six herbs that are especially appropriate for children and the class or category to which each belongs.

4. What three classes of agents do you think would be especially helpful to the elderly?

5. What cautions would you think of if someone asked you for: A laxative? A sedative? A stimulant?

6. What class of agents should not be used in pregnancy?

7. What is the best herbal antibiotic?

8. Give two reasons for avoiding the use of anodynes.

9. Vocabulary to define:

alterative
anodyne
anthelmintic
antidote
antiperiodic
antispasmodic
antithrombotic
antiseptic
aperient
aromatic
astringent
carminative
cathartic
caustic
demulcent
diaphoretic
diuretic
emetic
emmenagogue
emollient
hemostatic
nervine
phlegmatic
sanguine
scorbutic
scrofulous
sedative
stimulant
tonic
vermifuge
vulnerary

(Answers on page 204.)

Useful Texts for Lessons 2 & 3

• *The Herb Book* by John Lust. New York, NY: Bantam Books, 1983. This is the best one-volume book you can buy. Lust comes from a family of practicing herbalists and knows the subject thoroughly. There are all kinds of lists and appendices on various topics. The individual herbs are also fairly well illustrated, alphabetically arranged.

• *Herbal Book for Everyone* by Juliette de Bairacli Levy. Newton, MA: Charles T. Branford, 1960. Mrs. Levy is a famous herbalist, best known for her books on veterinary herbalism. She includes fewer herbs than Lust does, but most are in this course. This book is detailed on uses, dosage, and preparation.

• *Health, Happiness and the Pursuit of Herbs* by Adele Dawson. Brattleboro, VT: Stephen Greene Press, 1980. Selected herbs and in depth, this book contains much folklore, culinary uses, and good illustrations. Adele Dawson is a practicing herbalist in Vermont. She is well-traveled, with a European background and deep knowledge from which she draws in her writing.

• *A Modern Herbal* by Mrs. M. Grieve, edited by Mrs. C. F. Leyel. (Two volumes.) New York, NY: Dover Publications, 1971. In spite of the title, it is now one of the older books but a classic. It gives more information than any of those above.

• *Back to Eden* by Jethro Kloss. Ashland, OR: World Wide, 1984. First published in 1939, this book has gone through more than sixteen printings. It has been very popular among beginners and people living on the land, especially in the Sixties. It is rather old-fashioned, covering herbs, natural remedies, and general health practices. It is not detailed enough for specific herbs and uses, and does not point out the dangers of certain herbs. Its best use is for diet and nursing treatment.

• *Let's Get Well* by Adele Davis. (Paperback.) New York, NY: New American Library, 1988. Adele Davis has long been recognized as an authority on the nutritional aspects of well-being. Since herbal remedies work best in a total program of health, her book will be an invaluable reference to keep on your shelf.

Any health food store or library will undoubtedly have many more books on herbs from which to choose. In addition, advanced students may want to purchase the *Merck Manual* for a comprehensive medical guide. Texts on *First Aid* and *Home Nursing*, both available through the Red Cross, would also be helpful.

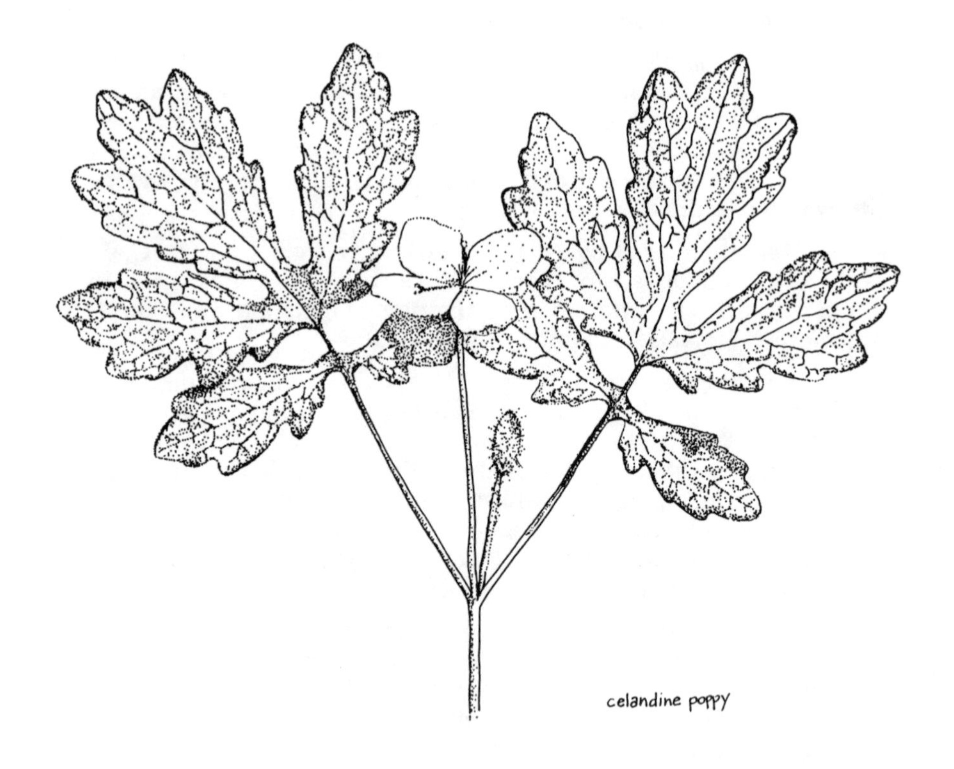
celandine poppy

Part Two

Alphabetical Index of Materia Medica and Physical Symptoms

How to use this index:

Herbal agents are listed by their common names. The Latin name is also given, together with a brief botanical description, parts used, chemical properties, and uses. All conditions under this agent should be consulted, in their proper alphabetical place, for other herbs that might be used. When not otherwise directed, the proper way to prepare an herb is the standard infusion. (See page 31.)

Physical conditions of the body or its parts are also included in the headings. When several remedies are listed, please look under each herb for appropriate preparation and dosage, possible side-effects, and more detailed data that will help you choose which one to use in each instance. Occasionally I have listed herbs not included in detail in this course, if they are particularly common and useful. You can find them and their other uses described in some of the books listed on page 45. Herbs described in this course appear in boldface type.

Latin names are also indexed, so that if an herb is found only by its Latin name in some other book, it may be easily identified here. It is sometimes important to use Latin names to distinguish between two plants with similar or confusing common names.

Occasionally, I have taken the liberty to expand beyond herbs for the treatment of some conditions. While the primary focus of the book is, indeed, on the use of herbs for healing, it seems only prudent to discuss herbs in company with other natural remedies, especially when current medical practice offers little or no help.

You will also notice that I use a great many medical terms as well as a few—such as "catarrh"—that may seem dated. I have tried to use them in contexts where the meaning comes through. There is a glossary in the back of the book for further reference. Since you may be collecting older herbals, without such a guide, I hope this will be useful.

Agrimonia Eupatoria

LESSON 4: "A"

abdomen — pain in. May be caused by:

diarrhea—with frequent and watery stools.
dysentery—with passage of tough mucous tinged with blood.
appendicitis—with vomiting, fever, tenderness.
ulcer or colitis.
(Refer to each.)

abortion — For spontaneous abortion, see **miscarriage**.

Some herbal books present a class of herbs called abortifacients, i.e., herbs that under certain conditions may produce abortion. Some of these herbs are mentioned in this course as being emmenagogues. They tend to bring on the menstrual flow, or increase it. These have a legitimate use in young girls whose periods are slow to start and scanty. It is not prudent to use these herbs, or other substances, in order to produce an abortion in a pregnant woman. They are neither safe nor sure. Most of them got their reputation for producing abortions because some women are particularly sensitive to them and miscarry easily. What they do is to start the menstrual flow and/or uterine contractions. Any such use may quite possibly result in hemorrhaging that may be difficult or impossible to control. This type of activity is not within the province of beginners in herbalism. Abortion—moral and ethical considerations aside—is a modern surgical procedure restricted to hospitals or clinics set up for this practice. There are many "old wives' tales" circulating as to plants or other substances that are reputed to be abortifacient. They are all, without exception, either useless or dangerous. Some are quite toxic.

acne — *Herbal agent:* see **burdock**; also **alteratives.**

afterpains of childbirth — *Herbal agent:* see **raspberry** leaves.

agrimony — (*Agrimonia eupatoria*). Rose family. Small yellow flowers on spikes, later followed by sticky burs. Leaves have curious mixed sizes up the stem.

Part used: whole herb, dried.
Properties and use: astringent, tonic, aromatic, stimulating. Acts on mucous membranes, especially those of the abdomen. Use in mesenteritis, peritonitis, colitis, liver abscesses, dysentery, and diarrhea. Cold infusion for enuresis. Combine with female tonics in leucorrhea. Agrimony would be the agent of choice if appendicitis were suspected but not yet acute. Also, in conjunction with antibiotics, in peritonitis resulting from ruptured appendix. These conditions certainly require medical help when available.
Preparation: infusion.
Dose: ½ cup, 3 times daily.
Seeds used in decoction for eyewash (astringent).

ague — An old-fashioned term for chills and fever; see **fever, flu,** and **malaria.**

AIDS — (Acquired Immune Deficiency Syndrome). A disease in which a virus (or possibly several related viruses) attack the body's immune system, making it unable to combat infections and cancer. This disease has made its appearance world-wide and has reached epidemic proportions among some high-risk groups of the population. Medical science (at this writing) has not been able to find a cure for this disease.

Meanwhile, herbalists and other natural therapists are working in their particular fields to combine what they know about supporting and strengthening the body's own immune system. In this way, they can give the person something to do for himself—beneficial both physically and psychologically.

The natural treatment of AIDS is two-pronged:

• **Nutrition**—with particular emphasis on raw vegetables, whole grains, and fish—provides the body with its important vitamins, minerals, and amino acids. It must be supplemented, however, to reach the optimum. The first line of treatment would be a good vitamin supplement that contains the recommended daily requirement of all the vitamins in their proper ratio. Be sure that inositol and choline, as well as a rich assortment of the other B vitamins —plus A and D—are included. A daily mineral tablet should be taken, also, with selenium and zinc in the formula. In addition to these, *the most important single vitamin supplement would be vitamin C, the anti-infection vitamin par excellence.* AIDS patients are taking what seem like stratospheric amounts of this vitamin, anywhere from 10 to 30 grams daily in divided doses. (One gram equals 1,000 milligrams.) Since an orange may give you only 70-80 milligrams of C, it would be impossible to get this amount of vitamin C in food alone, or even in the one-a-day-type vitamins.

Dose: 1 teaspoon of ascorbic acid crystals (4-5 grams) in a glass of juice or water. Repeat as tolerated. (May cause a burning of the urinary tract or diarrhea if the body is overloaded. In that case, reduce dosage to tolerance level.)

Other supplements might include:

- Vitamin E—up to 1,200 units a day.
- Calcium—total of 2 grams daily, counting dietary intake.
- Magnesium—total of 1 gram daily.
- Potassium—up to 3 grams daily, but should equal or exceed sodium intake.
- Amino acids—glutamic acid, 400 mg; tryptophane, 2 grams; lysine and histidine, 2 grams each.

In addition to vitamin and mineral supplements, some foods are especially helpful: wheatgrass, spirulina, alfalfa, and garlic. Wheat grass can be grown by planting wheat grains in shallow trays of soil placed in a sunny spot. When the grass is 3-4 inches high, it can be cut with scissors. This harvest should then be put through a juicer, extracting only the juice. Since this is very concentrated, start with 1 or 2 ounces per day. More can be harmful. For better taste, add to other juices such as carrot, parsley, celery, and tomato. Alfalfa can be obtained in tea or capsule form; take once a day. Garlic, too, comes in capsule form; take 3-4 a day or, preferably, 1 clove of fresh garlic 3-4 times daily.

Caffeine, alcohol, and smoking consume large quantities of all these nutrients, reducing the body's own healing powers!

• **Herbal.** The second prong of the treatment should consist of herbs that have proven to be especially active in the immune system. *Echinacea* extract may be obtained in most health food stores. **Red clover** is the next herb of choice. The standard infusion is not sufficiently strong, and an herbal supply house may offer the extract. Take according to label instructions.

alder — (*Alnus rugosa*). Or spotted alder. Common shrub or small tree of swamps. Leaves oval, toothed. Bears cones that persist in winter.

Part used: bark.
Properties and use: tonic, alterative, astringent. Influences secretions, glands and lymphatics, skin diseases, diarrhea, sore mouth, sore throat, dyspepsia, catarrh of stomach and bowels, hemorrhages of alimentary tract. General tonic in debilitated states.
Preparation: decoction.
Dose: 1 teaspoon dried powdered bark to 1 pint boiling water. Take 1 wineglassful (cold) several times daily.

aloe — (*Aloe vera*). A cactus-like member of the lily family. Can be grown as a house plant. Sometimes called the first aid plant. (When little shoots appear at the base of the plant, cut them out, leaving as much root attached as possible, and plant them in another pot.)

Part used: gelatinous interior of the leaf. Take a leaf or part of a leaf from the sides or bottom of the plant, leaving top leaders to grow.
Properties and use: emollient, antiseptic; first aid for scalds and burns. Slit leaf open, broadside, to expose gel. Cut off any sharp spines. Bind gel side of leaf against burn and cover with gauze or cloth for 12 hours. Also good for fungus infections, ringworm, and some eczemas. Good for radiation burns and radiation sickness. Made into shampoos and face creams. Good for heartburn and stomach upset: cut a leaf into pieces, soak in 1 quart of cold water overnight and drink as desired. Aloe leaves, dried and powdered, have a cathartic action and are an ingredient in many laxative compounds.

alteratives — This group of herbs gradually alters the blood chemistry. Some common alteratives include **ash** leaves, **alder**

bark, **bittersweet** bark, **burdock** root and seeds, **red clover** heads, **prickly ash** bark and seeds, **yellow dock** root, **gill-over-the-ground**, **spikenard** root. See Lesson 3.

angina pectoris — A heart disease characterized by severe, sudden pain, sometimes radiating to the left elbow or fingers, with pallor and sweating. May last seconds or hours; death may occur or the person may recover, usually with successive episodes. May be brought on by exertion, especially in cold air. *Herbal agent:* see **hawthorn.**

anodynes — This class of herbs dulls pain without narcosis. Two useful anodynes are **violet** and **mullein** leaves. Many herbal anodynes are dangerous, however. **Nervines** might be used instead. See Lesson 3.

antacids — Herbal antacids correct the acidic content in the stomach. **Meadowsweet** is a *specific* for acid stomach.

anthelmintics — These herbs kill worms in the stomach or intestines. Some herbal anthelmintics are **male fern**, **turtlehead** (children), blue cohosh, gentian, pumpkin seeds (children), **butternut** bark (children), **garlic**, and wormseed. See Lesson 3.

antiperiodics — This class of herbs is used for fevers. Common antiperiodics are **cherry** bark, **ash** leaves, **prickly ash** bark and berries, **boneset, yarrow, dogwood** bark, **chokecherry** bark, and **elder** blossoms. See Lesson 3.

antiseptics — This class of herbs kills bacteria. Herbal antiseptics include **calendula** flowers, **garlic, herb Robert, white water lily** root, trout lily root, **apple** juice, cider, **vinegar**, and wine. See Lesson 3.

antiscorbutics — Are also acidulants. These herbs are high in vitamin C: **sumac** berries, **barberries, rose** hips, **elderberries,** sheep sorrel, **mustard, nasturtium** (all parts), asparagus, **veronica.** Also **spruce** and **hemlock** tree twigs. See Lesson 3.

anus, sore — Especially when caused by diarrhea. *Herbal agent:* **gill-over-the-ground**; standard infusion. Wineglassful before meals. May also be used as an external wash. Also: **chickweed** ointment.

aperients — And cathartics and laxatives open the bowels. For adults: **barberry** bark, buckthorn bark, **dandelion** root, **yellow dock** root. For children: **butternut** inner bark and **turtlehead**. See Lesson 3.

apoplexy — Often associated with high blood pressure or mental or physical excitement, especially in persons of plethoric temperament. Commonly identified as a "stroke" or "shock." See **stroke** and **hawthorn.**

appendicitis — An infection of the coliform appendix, usually acute. Many cases formerly called subacute or chronic appendicitis are now considered to be **colitis**. Symptoms include fever, vomiting, and a severe stomach pain. At first it may occur around the navel but eventually it becomes localized on the lower right side, the patient doubled up. In acute cases, speedy surgery is the only remedy before the appendix ruptures and peritonitis sets in, which can be very dangerous, even fatal. In more chronic or doubtful cases, where the physician chooses to wait, begin herbal treatment at once. *Herbal agent:* **agrimony**. Also see **fasting**.

apple — (*Malus*, any species), cultivated or wild. One of the most useful trees known.

Parts used: fruit, bark.

Properties and use: The fruit contains malic or tartaric acids, and is rich in vitamins, minerals. The acid helps digestion; apple cider prevents kidney or gall stones, and may dissolve them. Apple cider vinegar does the same if taken daily in water. Apples contain a substance said to prevent tooth decay, and an apple should be eaten at the end of the day to cleanse the teeth. Vinegar contains a substance that kills bacteria, even typhoid. Therefore, water of doubtful quality could be treated with a teaspoon of vinegar per cup if boiling is impossible. Concentrated apple juice (made with a juicer) may be used for gastrointestinal disorders, hyperacidity, toxemia, diarrhea, and in convalescence. *Fresh* apple juice or cider is antiseptic and promotes granulation and healing in infected tissues. Apple juice for babies is sometimes better tolerated than orange juice. One of the most palatable ways to use vinegar is in **shrubs** (see listing).

Apple bark is used in decoction as an antiperiodic, for intermittent fevers. *Dose:* 1 wineglassful, 3 times daily.

aromatics — Are usually classed with carminatives. They are pleasant tasting and can be combined with other herbs to make them more palatable. Carminatives produce warmth and expel gas.

Examples are **alder**, caraway, **catnip**, sweet **chamomile**, wild **ginger**, sweet **melilot**, **mustard** seed, **peppermint**, **spearmint**, **wild mint**, and sweet flag. See Lesson 3.

arteriosclerosis — Hardening of the arteries. See **hawthorn** and high **blood pressure.**

arthritis — One of a large group of degenerative diseases affecting the musculoskeletal systems of the body. See also: **rheumatism**, **sciatica**, **neuritis**, **bursitis**, and **gout**. Aside from rheumatoid arthritis, for which some focus of infection is found, osteoarthritis and the other related diseases listed above are believed by herbalists to be caused by a build-up in the tissues of irritant metabolic wastes, especially uric acids. The disease is most common after the age of 40 and in women after the cessation of the menses. Modern medical theory does not recognize the above as the cause for these diseases and considers the cause "unknown." Consequently, it has failed to find a safe and sure cure. Traditional medical treatment begins with rest, local liniments, and salicylates, and proceeds to potentially hazardous medication of gold compounds, cortisone, and other drugs of increasing toxicity. The patient is told the treatment must extend for years, with dubious prognosis.

On the other hand, safe and effective natural treatment of arthritis does exist, but all parts of the treatment must be used at once, not picking and choosing among them. Treatment:

• **Elimination** of metabolic wastes, uric acids through the excretory system: Use a saline laxative (Epsom salts) which thins the blood at the same time, or use cholagogue laxatives, especially **aloe**, **rhubarb**, and **dandelion** root. Check under each herb just mentioned. Additional herbs are mentioned under **diuretics** and **aperients**. In women whose menstrual flow is insufficient, refer to **emmenagogues**. Elimination through the skin: Persons who have arthritis frequently have dry skin and perspire little. When this is coupled with a low metabolism, as it often is, natural thyroid tablets (1 or 2 grains a day) may be indicated. Anything that produces copious sweating, such as sweat baths and saunas, is preferable to dry heat (heating pads or diathermy). *Herbal agents* to produce sweating are found under **diaphoretics**.

• **Counter-irritation**. This is the single most important treatment of arthritic diseases, but it must be pursued not just to the point of a reddening ointment, but to an actual blistering or rash-producing agent. The point is that the exudate of the blister or rash carries off some of the accumulated toxins, and rallies the body's recuperative mechanism at that point. One blistering agent is a stiff **mustard** plaster made with equal parts of flour and dry mustard, mixed with a little hot water, and spread on a gauze pad (covered, if necessary, with another pad). Leave on the afflicted area until it raises a watery blister. Other *herbal agents* for causing rashes or blisters (exanthemas) are fresh green buttercup leaves, fresh **prickly ash** berries, grated horseradish root, **nettles**.

Another very successful treatment for arthritis consists of **bee venom**. This must be administered by a capable practitioner in the form of actual stings from live bees, not as injections. This form of treatment is not as successful with the particular form of arthritis that afflicts women in the menopause, as with the exanthemas mentioned above, but it would be the best for long-standing, badly crippled cases. The treatments may take months to effect a cure.

• **Diet**. In overweight individuals, weight reduction should be pursued at the same time as other treatment, or the disease will recur. (See **diet**). It is advantageous to reduce farinaceous foods; therefore, a diabetic diet with gluten breads can be used to advantage. Use carbonated beverages and vinegar preparations such as sh**rubs** to thin the blood. If a person is highly colored, indicating a plethoric nature, it is important to thin the blood. Coffee and tea are good, within limits, and light white wine. Fasting helps in some forms of arthritis but not all. Excessive use of very acid fruits, especially by people living in cold climates and who do not sweat easily, has been found to aggravate the situation in many people. On the other hand, lactic acids found in buttermilk and yogurt are good, as are the natural ferments produced in sauerkraut and other such preparations. Meat is good, in limits, as it binds the surplus acid. Excessive fruitarian or vegetarian diets carried on too long tend to weaken the individual and upset the digestion. Milk can be overdone and tends to thicken the blood.

A smaller number of arthritics are thin instead of heavy; in their cases the arthritis is caused by build-up of wastes because of a defect in the digestion of food. The defect should be treated with suitable agents (see **stomach**), but the rest of the treatment is the same.

• **Herbal agents:** When used in conjunction with all the above, herbal treatment can aid and support the cure but is not effective by itself. Many herbs classed as **alteratives** have been useful for these diseases. The following formula may be useful:

equal parts—**prickly ash** berries, **yarrow**, **agrimony**

To prepare, place 1 ounce (2 tablespoons) of the mix in 1 pint of water and bring to a boil. Simmer 15 minutes; strain and cool. *Dose:* 1 wineglassful 3 times daily.

• **Massage, exercise, and other treatments**. See **rheumatism**.

aspen — see **poplar.**

ash, white — (*Fraxinus americana*). A large tree, related to the maples, with compound leaves and single-winged (paddle-shaped) seeds. Useful in basket-making, snowshoes, tool handles, etc.

Parts used: root bark and bark of the inner layer of trunk and branches.

Properties and use: a stimulating tonic alterative used in chronic jaundice, chronic hepatic congestion, skin eruptions, dropsy (edema), chronic coughs with biliousness.

Preparation: decoction.

Dose: wineglassful, 3 times daily.

asthma — A chronic disease of the breathing apparatus bringing on sudden paroxysms when it is difficult to inhale and almost impossible to exhale. It is commonly an allergic state, aggravated in cold weather by virus infections. This and bronchial asthma are sometimes the chronic outcome of years of suppression of colds with chemical drugs, so that waste material is kept in the respiratory system. Also aggravated by overacidity caused by wastes. Sometimes due to nervous tension in the environment, especially in children. Asthmatic children use up their blood sugar rapidly. They should have orange juice or fruit juices sweetened with honey, morning and night. Follow up with food that metabolizes slowly. A raw diet is good. It is likely that asthma has increased with the stresses and allergens of modern industrial civilization, beyond anything the old herbalists had to handle. For a promising new approach, books on low blood sugar may be helpful.

Herbal agents: Herbal treatments have usually consisted of rather drastic agents that are not included in this course. The only herbs in this course that might be tried would be **yarrow**, whole herb, either by itself or combined with **elecampane** and **comfrey** roots. *Dose:* in decoction, a wineglassful, 3 or 4 times daily.

astringents — This class of herbs acts to tighten or contract membranes. For bleeding: **agrimony**, **barberry** bark, **cinquefoil**, **raspberry** leaves, **shepherd's-purse**, **white water lily** root, **squawvine**, **dogwood** bark, **trillium**, and **yarrow**. See Lesson 3 for additional astringents, including those used for diarrhea and externally in washes.

athlete's foot — See **fungus diseases.**

Avena — See **oats.**

Self-review Questions for "A"

1. Five herbs in this section were discussed in detail: agrimony, alder, aloe, apple, and ash. For each list the properties and the part(s) of the plant used.

2. Why might abortifacients be dangerous?

3. What is a safe and common substance that prevents dental caries?

4. What two agents included in this lesson are said to have an effect on the liver?

5. What one agent (not listed in this section) was mentioned three times in association with heart disease?

6. For what condition mentioned in this lesson is immediate surgery usually indicated?

7. Under what situations would the same condition be treated herbally? With what?

8. What herb is recommended for bedwetting? In what preparation?

9. What agents stimulate the immune system?

10. List five natural therapies, other than herbs, that were recommended for some of the conditions in this section.

11. Vocabulary to define:

alimentary
catarrh
cholagogue
colitis
dysentery
dyspepsia
edema
enuresis
exanthemas
farinaceous
gluten
granulation
hepatic
leucorrhea
mesenteritis
peritonitis
plethoric
purge

(Answers on page 205.)

LESSON 5: "B"

backache — Symptoms in:

• kidney troubles—pain in middle or lower back, right or left of spine.
• lumbago—confined to lower lumbar region, across the hips.
• articular rheumatism—over whole spinal column.
• gallstone or inflammation of the gall bladder—pain from lower rib on right side to under shoulder blade.

Herbal agents: **veronica, milkweed, trailing arbutus, Joe-Pye weed**; the last two are for kidney disorders. See under each herb.

Balmony — See **turtlehead**.

bandage, emergency — Dried **sphagnum** moss is an antiseptic and hemostatic.

barberry — (*Berberis vulgaris*). A shrub found both wild and cultivated. Simple toothed leaves with thorns in threes at base of leaf. Red berries drooping along the stem persist in winter.

Part used: inner bark of trunk, branches, or root.
Properties and use: stimulating tonic, hepatic alterative for all liver complaints, jaundice; laxative.
Preparation: decoction.
Dose: wineglassful, 3 times a day.

Part used: berries.
Properties and use: antiscorbutic and astringent. Use in fevers.
Preparation: as a cooling drink made like lemonade (squash the berries) and in juice and jelly.
Dose: ad lib.

basswood — (*Tilia americana*). Similar to the linden tree of Europe. A large tree with very large heart-shaped leaves. The flowers and nut-like fruit are borne on a blade-like leaf. The nut has been used as a flavoring. (The inner bark is one of the best sources of rope and cordage in our forests. Strip off in sheets, pound into filaments, and twist by rubbing on thigh or between fingers.)

Part used: flowers.
Properties and uses: gently stimulating tonic, influencing the circulation and mucous membranes; antispasmodic. For colds, coughs, eruptive diseases, bronchitis, acute catarrh, nervous ailments such as hysteria and insomnia.
Preparation: hot infusion.
Dose: ½ cup, 3 times daily.

bedwetting — Especially when this occurs in older children and adults, treat the causes of nervousness or tension if these can be found.
Herbal agents: Between 4 and 6 p.m. (not later), give a strong tea (infusion) of **agrimony**. Results may take some time. Also try **sumac** berries, **yarrow**, or **shepherd's-purse** if agrimony is not available. Agrimony is, however, the herb of choice.

bee venom — A successful treatment for muscular arthritis, neuritis and neuralgia. See under arthritis. Also migraine, eczema, gout, and some chronic inflammatory conditions. *Contra-indicated in:* tuberculosis and gonorrhea. These may mimic arthritis but react to venom seriously. Do not use with kidney or cardiovascular diseases. Arthritis in the menopause does not usually respond to bee venom treatment.

This requires an experienced practitioner. Usually one sting is administered and the effects noted. If all is well, try two stings the first week, then two stings twice weekly, then three stings twice weekly, etc. By the end of the sixth week there should be an improvement. Try to start in early summer. Use dorsal surfaces of arms, legs, back, or shoulder blades. Anesthetize the site by applying ice (or frozen juice can). Make weals one inch apart. Effects: at first, if this is genuine arthritis or related, there will be local symptoms (swelling). Later, general constitutional symptoms (malaise, fever), then a latent stage with no symptoms. For more chronic cases, press on beyond the latent stage to repeat the process. If serious reactions occur on the first treatments, discontinue at once.

beech — (*Fagus americanus*). A large tree with very smooth grey bark. Twin, edible nutlets in bristly cases. (The nuts produce the best natural oil for cooking and lighting. Crush or pound the nuts, boil in a large amount of water, and strain. Let oil come to the top and skim off. The dried leaves can be used in stuffing mattresses while camping and will resist packing down or molding longer than most materials. The wood ashes are good for soapmaking, and the whitest of them can be used as an acceptable baking soda substitute. Use more than with soda and let dough rise a while before baking.)

Part used: leaves (fresh, green).

Properties and use: diuretic, used for cystic catarrh, nephritis, urethritis, scalding urine.

Preparation: infusion.

Dose: ½ cup, 3-4 times daily.

beers — See **birch** and **meadowsweet**. These are good preparations for mineral-rich tonics for convalescence, anemia, etc., and are sometimes well-tolerated when other preparations might not be. In the method of preparation given, a small amount of alcohol may be generated, but not much, similar to homemade root beer.

bethroot — See **trillium**.

betony — (*Stachys betonica*). A cultivated plant of the *Labiatiae* family. Worth buying the seeds or plant to keep near the house.

Part used: whole herb.
Properties and use: gently stimulating tonic to mucous membranes, nervine, antispasmodic. Used for catarrh of nose or stomach or bladder, influenza, neuralgia, prostate gland trouble, dyspepsia, chronic rheumatism, renal and nephritic colic, headaches of all sorts. Any obscure nervous disfunction: "Try betony." Also used for nightmares and severe depression.
Preparation: infusion.
Dose: ½ cup, 3-4 times daily.

Bible leaf — See **costmary.**

birch, black — (*Betula lenta*). Sometimes called cherry birch, as the tight dark bark resembles cherry bark. In the wintertime the two trees can be distinguished by nibbling a twig. Cherry has a burnt-almond flavor; black birch has the wintergreen flavor.

Parts used: same as for **yellow birch**, below.
Properties and use: similar to yellow birch, but has a greater concentration of the oil of wintergreen, and the leaves are more diuretic. Twigs used for birch beer.
Preparation of birch beer: Take 4 gallons of birch sap or water and boil together with 1 gallon of honey for 10 minutes. Pour over 4 quarts of finely cut birch twigs or inner bark of root or branches. Do not boil twigs. Cool. Add 1 yeast cake, or 1 teaspoon of granular yeast, spread on a slice of toast. Let sit for 1 week; bottle and cap.

birch, yellow — (*Betula allegheniensis*). A very common tree in northern and upper elevations. Coppery or brassy bark very curled and good for starting fires, even in wet weather. This tree contains an oil similar to the oil of wintergreen, although not as much as the black birch above.

Parts used: leaves, inner bark, twigs.
Properties and use: The leaves are an alterative and tonic, good for skin, eczema, dropsy (edema). The oil from the bark is used externally for psoriasis and as an antiseptic. A tea can be made from the twigs and a syrup from the sap. A twig frazzled at one end and used as an "Indian toothbrush"—with the wintergreen flavor built right in—prevents tooth decay when used regularly.
Preparation: leaves and twigs—infusion.
Dose: ½ cup, 3-4 times daily.

bittersweet — (*Celastrus scandens*). A shrubby, twining vine of the Staff Tree family found on trees or old stone walls. Flower in fives. Orange berry opens after frost and is much used in indoor winter decorations. *Do not confuse with the herbaceous vine of the Solanaceae family, bearing purple flowers and red berries, which is poisonous, also sometimes called bittersweet.*

Parts used: bark of the root, or twigs in winter.
Properties and use: a slow alterative for the nervous system, nervous irritation with skin troubles such as **eczema**, scaly **skin**, eruptions. Also externally for rectal ulcers and fissures.
Preparation: decoction; 1 ounce (2 tablespoons) of chopped bark to 1 pint of water.
Dose: wineglassful, cold, 3 times daily.

black haw — (*Viburnum prunifolium*). See other **viburnums** for possible substitutes. *Specific* for threatened **miscarriage.**

blackberry — (*Rubus, any species*). Also called black long-berries, as they have a long core and are not thimble-shaped like black raspberries. Many slightly different species; all are similarly useful.

Parts used: whole plant, berries, and root.
Properties and use: astringent, tonic. Used for diarrhea and dysentery, especially "summer complaint" in children.
Preparation: infusion from leaves, decoction from roots, cordial from berries.
Blackberry cordial: Boil blackberries in just enough water to prevent scorching. Strain. To each cup of juice add 2 cups of sugar or honey, 1/2 stick of cinnamon, 2 teaspoons of cloves, 1/4 teaspoon of mace or allspice. Boil for 20 minutes. Strain. Add to each quart of syrup 1 pint of brandy (especially blackberry brandy); bottle.
Dose: 1 teaspoon in 1/2 cup of water every 4 hours until relieved.

bladder, pain — Caused by:
• catarrh of the bladder—spasmodic pains, with frequent painful urination.
• gravel or stone—pain in neck of bladder, extending along urinary tract, stoppage or interruption of urine.
• displacement of uterus—dull, bearing-down pains, constant desire to urinate (for this, **white water lily** suppositories are used).
• gonorrhea—burning pain when urinating, discharge of pus from urinary canal.
Herbal agents: see **diuretics**, then check each suggested herb separately.

bleeding gums — See **gums**.

blood — Thickness of the blood may result in arthritis and other chronic diseases. To thin the blood, take more acid fluids such as **apple** juice, cider, or **vinegar**, **cranberry**, grape or **sumac** juice. *Herbal agents:* any **aperients** and **diaphoretics**.

blood pressure — A simple method of determining relative blood pressure when no equipment is available is to place fingers on the pulse and then gradually increase pressure. After trying this several times with persons of known blood pressure, you can begin to feel whether pressure is high, low, or relatively normal.

blood pressure, high — (hypertension). Many conditions contribute to high blood pressure, such as hardening of the arteries and kidney disease. However, the usual contributing causes are worry, tension, and overeating. Food sensitivities, especially to monosodium glutamate, are an often unrecognized cause.

Treatment: A short fast (see **diet**) several times a year or even once a month if noticeably overweight. Then start with fruit juices, fruit-and-vegetable days, or a vegetarian diet for a time. Use foods high in potassium (such as, orange juice, bananas) to balance any sodium occurring naturally in the diet. Avoid salt or salty foods. Keep bowels open.

Osteopathic or chiropractic treatments are said to help normalize blood pressure in 48 percent of the cases.

Specific herbal agent for high blood pressure is **hawthorn**. Next best is **garlic**.

blood pressure, low — (hypotension). Low blood pressure is often caused by anemia, constitutional diseases, or an operation. Sometimes thyroid is needed, but sports and exercise will help; air, brush, and water baths are helpful. Stimulants, even coffee, are good with moderation. Vitamin E is also useful.

Herbal agent: **yarrow** in cold infusion; stimulants and tonics in general. Herb beers are good, especially **meadowsweet**, for tonic effect.

bloodroot — (*Sanguinaria canadensis*). Poppy family. Early spring flower (white) of deciduous woods, with large lobed leaf, orange or red juice.

Part used: juice.

Properties and use: The juice is caustic and can be used for a smoker's cancer on the lip. Also for warts and fungus diseases.

Preparation: fresh juice applied directly.

blueberries — (*Vaccinium*, any species). Several species of these, as well as related huckleberries, are useful as food.

Part used: root, bark.

Properties and use: stimulating astringent for sore mouth, sore throat, and leucorrhea. Arrests hemorrhages.

Preparation: hot infusion or decoction.

Dose: ½ cup, 3-4 times daily.

Part used: berries.

Properties and use: fresh berries are cooling, diuretic, and astringent. Dried berries are useful in dropsy (edema), gravel, and all bladder ailments.

Preparation: dried berries in decoction (fresh berries as is, ad lib).

Dose: ½ cup, 3-4 times daily.

boils — Usually caused by an impurity in the blood, succeeding each other over a period of time.

Herbal agents: internally, use a good alterative formula, especially containing burdock. Externally, apply a moist poultice of slippery **elm** and **comfrey** or **chickweed**. Keep poultice moist under plastic covering. When the boil comes to a head, press out or incise the core and apply a sterile dressing, using **calendula** ointment or lotion.

bones, aching — See **arthritis** and **rheumatism**. For aching in the joints caused by influenza or grippe, see **boneset**.

bones, broken — To hasten healing, the *herbal agents* are **daisy** or **comfrey** or a combination of both, taken internally. Make a strong decoction, added to equal parts of **daisy wine**. Silica can be added using **horsetail**. Also add calcium to the diet.

boneset — (*Eupatorium perfoliatum*). Composite family. A plant of marshes and wet ground, with rather coarse leaves that seem all in one piece, pierced by the plant's stem. White head of blossoms. *Resembles white snakeroot which is toxic.* The leaves of snakeroot, however, do not wrap around the stem, and snakeroot is found in woods and thickets, not marshes.

Part used: whole herb.
Properties and use: sudorific, diaphoretic, tonic, antiperiodic. *Specific* for **flu, grippe,** or **fevers**. In excess, can cause emesis.
Preparation: infusion.
Dose: ½ cup, 3-4 times daily.

breasts — For "gathered breasts" (mastitis), the *herbal agents* are a combination of **marsh mallow** or **hollyhock** roots, leaves, or blossoms. Include **calendula** for antibiotic. After steeping the herbs, strain them out and use the pulp for a poultice. The infusion is taken internally. *Dose:* 1 cup, every 2-4 hours.

For breast tumors, the *herbal agent* is **St. Johnswort.**

To condition the breasts for lactation, dab on a weak solution of **hemlock** bark daily beginning in the eighth month, and then with oiled fingers, gently draw out the nipples. During nursing, wipe off breasts after each nursing with a solution of **herb Robert**. Use **calendula** ointment if nipples crack.

bronchial asthma or chronic bronchitis. Results from persistent suppression of colds or acid wastes in the system. *Herbal agents:* **pleurisy root, elecampane, comfrey**. See under each. Add as much raw **garlic** in salads as the system will tolerate. Restrict sugar, using honey instead, and a 50 percent raw diet.

bronchitis — *Herbal agent:* a syrup of **garlic**—1 whole bulb, peeled, ground, and blended with 1 cup of honey. Try to take the whole amount, in small doses, within a 24-hour period (but discontinue if stomach rebels). Discard after 24-36 hours as the oil becomes rancid. If bronchitis continues and becomes chronic, use **hollyhock or marsh mallow** and **pleurisy root**.

bugleweed — (*Lycopus virginicus*). A small plant of the Mint family, growing in wet places, with very sharply toothed leaves and white labiate flowers clustered at leaf joints on the stem.

Part used: whole herb.
Properties and use: nervine, sedative; for circulatory disturbances, especially weak rapid heart, and wherever heart and stomach systems interact. *Specific* for heart conditions caused by over-activity of the thyroid. Sedative to sympathetic nervous system. Good for high blood pressure when taken hot. Good combined with cough remedies for sedative effect.
Preparation: infusion.
Dose: wineglassful (usually cold), 3 times a day.

burdock —(*Arctium lappa*). Composite family. Very common large coarse weed of waste places. Excellent source of iron and B-vitamins. Many parts are edible but rather bitter. Main stalk can be peeled, boiled in several waters, and buttered or creamed. Break open burrs to remove seeds when ripe.

Parts used: seeds, leaves, roots.

Properties and use: tonic, alterative, aperient. The seeds are best for skin diseases, especially adolescent acne. The green leaves are used in poultices for sprains, etc. The cold preparation of roots, stems, and leaves yields a liver tonic.The root is *specific* for dry **eczema** and **psoriasis**. Can be combined with **yellow dock** and **red clover**.

Preparation: infusion or decoction.

Dose: 1 cup, 3 times daily.

burns — *Specific* treatment for burns: **aloe** gel directly from cut leaf or grind up leaves in a blender. Apply immediately and leave on at least 24 hours. Also, a poultice of cloth soaked in the tea of **herb Robert**, if aloe is not available. (Crushed aloe can be frozen in an ice cube tray and kept indefinitely. Cubes will be ready for any emergency.)

bursitis — Treatment as for **arthritis** and **rheumatism.**

butternut — (*Juglans cinera*). A large forest tree with compound leaves, many leaflets. Young bark rather green-striped. The green husks of the nuts yield a yellow dye, the dried husks a brownish dye. The green nuts can be pickled; the mature nuts are eaten or used for oil. See **beech** for oil extraction procedure.

Part used: bark of root or inner bark of branches.

Properties and use: a mild and certain cathartic, especially for children; aperient.

Preparation: decoction—1 teaspoon of bark to 1 cup of water.

Dose: 1 cupful per day in frequent, 1-teaspoon doses.

Self-review Questions for "B"

1. Thirteen agents were listed in this lesson: barberry, basswood, beech, betony, birch, bittersweet, blackberry, bloodroot, blueberry, boneset, bugleweed, burdock, and butternut. Identify the properties of each.

2. Under bladder agents, it says to see diuretics. Which agents *in this lesson* were listed as diuretics?

3. Which agent was mentioned as being a specific for headaches of undetermined origin? Where would you find it?

4. Several agents in this lesson were mentioned as being useful in skin diseases which are nervous in origin or caused by disorders of the blood. Which agents?

5. Which agents in this lesson would be good for skin diseases resulting from external causes such as fungus?

6. Which agents in this lesson should be used with *caution*?

7. "The leaves of the trees shall be for the healing of the nations." (Revelations 22:2) The leaves of what trees were mentioned in this lesson for healing?

8. Which plants mentioned in this lesson have useful berries? For what?

9. Vocabulary to define:

ad lib
antibilious
dyspepsia
dysentery
emesis
lumbago
sudorific

(Answers on page 206.)

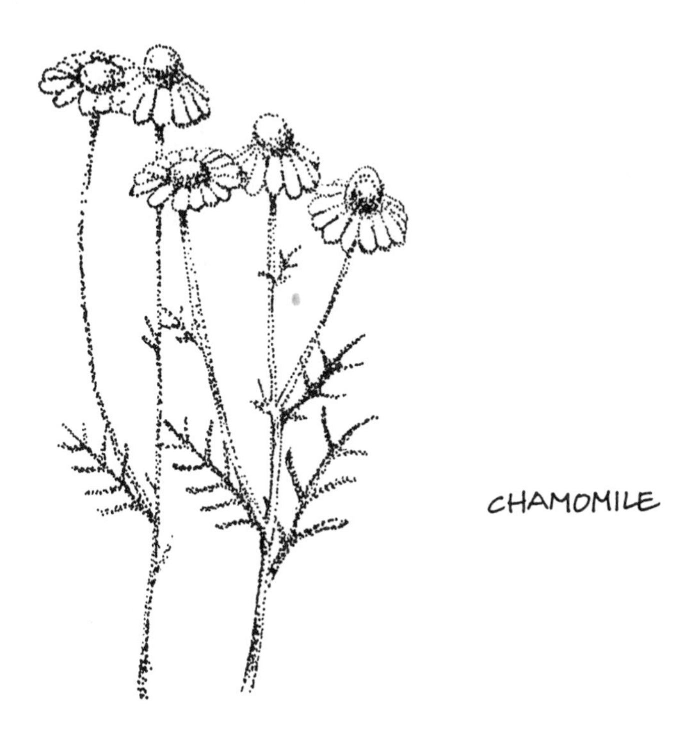

LESSON 6: "C" (part one)

calendula—(*Calendula officinalis*). Composite family. Also called pot marigold. Old-fashioned garden flower, not akin to the more popular African marigolds with their feathery leaves. Calendula has a simple, entire leaf. Seeds can be obtained from any garden store or catalog. They may also be saved year to year.

Part used: flowers.

Properties and use: soothing, antispasmodic, resolvent, antiseptic, antibiotic, vulnerary. An organic source of iodine. In any diseases of children, add a calendula blossom (or 1 teaspoon of the petals) to whatever other herb you are using, usually raspberry. In most cases this will remove fever and illness in 24 hours. It acts especially well on swollen glands in the throat. In a cold infusion, it is used as a wash for sore eyes and on varicose veins; also taken internally. Good for prostate gland enlargement: wineglassful of the standard infusion, cold, 4 times daily for a period of weeks or months. Widely used in ointment for burns, bruises, sprains, etc. Promotes granulation and healing. Calendula is one of our safest and most efficient agents for any instance, inward or outward, where infection is present or threatened.

Preparation: infusion, ointment.

cancer — Cancer is a disease of an affluent society; it is uncommon in areas where there is a deficiency of food. Although it can be caused by even an excess of natural foods, in our society it has become more prevalent lately because of the tremendous quantities of inorganic chemicals that find their way into our foods, water, and air. According to Natural Therapeutics, cancer is caused by diminished resistance of the whole body to cancer-causing factors, mostly because of impaired metabolism and improper functioning of the vital organs, especially the liver.

Modern orthodox medical theory seeks a single source for cancer, possibly a virus. It is also against any experimentation with any but radiation, surgery, or chemotherapy treatments. Consequently, doctors who use unorthodox means of treating cancers are liable to persecution. From time to time some chemical compound or another is widely touted as the long-sought "cure" for cancer, but this enthusiasm is usually short-lived and side-effects may be dire. One of the most unfortunate aspects of our modern approach to cancer is that patients—especially terminal patients—are simply returned to their home environment in which their cancer developed in the first place. A network of special cancer nursing homes or spas that could undertake wide-spectrum treatment—including diet, vitamin and mineral supplements, and herbs, with judicious fasting, careful monitoring and follow-up—would come up with a more reliable, promising cancer treatment.

The natural approach to the prevention and cure of cancer uses all known measures for detoxifying the body, stimulating the vital body functions, improving glandular activity, and improving the body's own healing forces. This includes a mass approach on many fronts simultaneously, and it includes a radical revision of the person's habits *in toto*. The total approach is the most difficult to initiate and maintain, since most persons would almost literally rather die than change their habits, especially their food habits. Yet that is what is involved in the best known and most successful cancer treatments over the last few years.

• **Fasting**. If the person is not too weak, and if the liver and other organs are not destroyed, supervised fasting should be considered. The rationale behind this is that the body, when fasting, will use up its excess fat first and then diseased tissue. This presupposes a place where a cancer patient can be carefully supervised and vital responses monitored. Many famous cancer treatments, such as the Grape Diet, the Carrot Juice diet, and even the Gerson and Hoxsey treatments—by stressing only one fresh fruit or juice—are essentially fasting techniques.

• **Diet**. The importance of dietary deficiencies, especially of protein, B-2, and vitamin A has never been adequately studied by organized medicine. However, experiments with mice have revealed a strong correlation between these deficiencies and susceptibility to cancer. In fact, Adele Davis went so far as to state that she has never seen cancer develop in an adult who habitually drinks a quart of milk daily. In addition, certain food-types seem to have definite anticancer properties: fermented (lactic acid) foods such as sauerkraut, buttermilk, fermented grains, pickled vegetables, etc. In beets (tops and raw juice) or fermented grated beet roots, there seems to be a special substance that prevents or cures cancer, perhaps because it resembles or substitutes for one of the B vitamins, choline; also in cabbage, broccoli, Brussels sprouts, and kale. Vitamin E seems to have a special role in cancer prevention, while large amounts of vitamin C help in the treatment of cancers. Scars from X-rays and symptoms of radiation sickness can be alleviated by vitamin E, according to Adele Davis (*Let's Get Well*, p. 305). Fiber in the diet reduces the risk of colonic cancer.

• **Herbal remedies**. Herbs that have a reputation for usefulness in various forms of cancer treatment are listed here, although modern sophisticated analysis of their effect is not available. Some of these herbs are not included in this course, but are listed for those who may wish to follow up.

General cancer agent: podophyllum (fresh herb)
Skin cancer: *thuja* (Arborvitae)
Breast cancer and for cancer prevention: **red clover**
Cancer of mucous membranes: goldenseal
Cancer of the bowel: **dandelion** root
Cancer of the lymphatics and throat: **violet** leaves
Cancer of the rectum: rue
Cancer of the lip: **bloodroot**

cardiac agents — See also **heart**. *Herbal agents:* **hawthorn** (the *specific* for all cardiac conditions), **candytuft**, **lily-of-the-valley**, **rosemary**, **bugle-weed**, **melilot**, **motherwort**.

carminatives — See **aromatics.**

castor oil — (*Oleum ricini*). May be found as a house plant; available in seed-houses. *Note: seeds are poisonous, to children especially.* Oil would have to be extracted from seeds. *Seed pulp also poisonous.* Oil is usually bought in stores.

Part used: oil from seeds.

Properties and use: cathartic, but may upset stomach. For warts: apply oil 2 or 3 times daily, rubbing into wart very thoroughly each time, and continue over weeks or months. (Try to locate the original wart, and if this is removed, the rest usually leave.) For breasts: to increase the flow of milk, rub into breasts; wipe off before nursing. For navel of newborn: gently swab with oil. For eyes, soreness and irritation: 1 drop in eye daily. For dandruff: rub warmed oil into scalp; apply steaming towels, then shampoo. Papillomas: rub in twice daily, as for warts.

cataracts — Nutritionally, cataracts respond well to increased amounts or supplements of vitamins B-2, E, amino acids, and a general improvement in diet.(Compare the use of fish gall bladder in the Book of Tobias in the Bible.) *Herbal agents:* sterile expressed juices of dusty miller (*cineraria maritima*), a plant that can be grown in the garden, and **celandine** have been used but are rather caustic. Apparently, they cause the film to harden and separate itself from the eye. (The surgical procedure for removal is common and usually successful.)

catarrh — Inflammation of the mucous membrane, usually respiratory. *Herbal agents:* **pleurisy root**, skunk cabbage, **elecampane, boneset, costmary, betony.** Also **demulcents.**

cathartics — See **aperients.**

catnip — (*Nepata cataria*). Labiatiae family. Common near houses and in waste places.

Part used: whole herb.

Properties and use: aromatic, carminative, antispasmodic, relaxing nervine, emmenagogue. For children: colic, restlessness, fevers, convulsions, sleeplessness, nightmares, sleepwalking. Women: hysteria, amenorrhea, dysmenorrhea (cramps).

Preparation: for nervine effect, use at least a handful of the herb to a pint of hot water.

Dose: 1 cup, hot, at bedtime, and another cup an hour later if needed. Less for children (½ cup).

celandine — (*Chelidonium majus*). Poppy family. Light green, divided leaves, four-petal orange or yellow flowers, common in patches.

Parts used: dried herb, raw juice.
Properties and use: purgative, cholagogue, caustic. Contains alkaloids, including chelidonine, in an orange latex. Chelidonine inhibits mitosis and has been used for cancer. In gross excess, it is a cardiac depressant, but in normal therapeutic doses no side-effects are noted. Raw juice has been used for eczema, ringworm, athlete's foot, warts, and malignant tumors of the skin. Also used for gallstones.
Preparation: standard infusion of dried herb; combine with **barberry** and **dandelion.**
Dose: 3 times daily.

Preparation of celandine eye lotion for cataracts: Boil 2 tablespoons of fresh-cut celandine herb, including flowers, in 2 cups of water. When cold, add an equal amount of milk. Bathe eye with lotion 3 times daily. Make a fresh batch each day.

chamomile — (*Matricharia chamomilla*). Composite family. Also called pineapple weed. Small plant of dooryards and gravelly driveways with feathery leaves and small yellow blossom with no white rays. The small daisy-like weed of barnyards and roadsides, another chamomile, is sometimes referred to as stink weed and should not be used internally. The German or Hungarian chamomile, obtainable from herbal supply houses, does have white rays but is yet another species.

Part used: whole herb.
Properties and use: soothing, gastric, nervine; for infants and children: teething and colic; adults: for nervous stomach disorders; antispasmodic, carminative.
Preparation: standard infusion; do not sweeten or boil.
Dose: 1 cup, 3-4 times daily.

chapped hands — *Herbal agents:* **elder** flower ointment, **chickweed** ointment. Lanolin is the vehicle of choice.

cherry — (*Prunus*, any species). Several are used: wild (rum) cherry, fire cherry, **chokecherry**. The bark and winter twigs are used, mostly in combination with other agents, for coughs. *All cherry leaves and seeds are dangerous, containing prussic (cyanide) acid.* All berries are edible.

chest pains —

• in **pleurisy**: pain is sharp and stinging, especially on taking a deep breath; low fever.

• in **pneumonia**: dry, painful, hacking cough; high fever and chills.

• in **neuralgia** and **rheumatism**: pressure increases pain, breathing sometimes painful.

• in **shingles**: severe neuralgic pain with bright red eruptions on inflamed skin.

chicken pox — Rash comes first, with small red papules, later with a watery fluid; several successive crops. *Herbal agents:* dust with antiseptic powder (slippery **elm** powder). Internally: **raspberry**, **yarrow**, and **calendula** tea.

chickweed — (*Stellaria media*). Pink family. Common dooryard weed, creeping on ground, with white star-like flowers.

Part used: whole herb.

Properties and use: antiseptic, vulnerary; influences skin and mucous membranes; excellent for chapped skin, sores, eczema, erysipelas.

Preparation: boil up a double handful of herb in 1 pound of lard or suet; strain into jars and seal. Use hot poultices externally for abscesses, inflammation. Infusion for eye wash, sore throat.

Self-review Questions for "C" (part one)

1. What would you advise friends who are told they have inoperable cancer? What would you say of an herbalist who made up a compound of podophyllum, red clover, and dandelion, and advertised it as a "cancer cure"?

2. What herb in this lesson is better cultivated in the garden rather than sought in the wild?

3. Which herbs mentioned in this lesson should not be used in pregnancy? What one word in their descriptions leads you to think so?

4. The herbal agents listed in this lesson were calendula, castor oil, catnip, celandine, chamomile, and chickweed. Identify the properties of each.

5. Of the agents listed above, which is the most universally useful?

6. Vocabulary to define:

amenorrhea	gastric
dysmenorrhea	papules
erysipelas	resolvent

(Answers on page 207.)

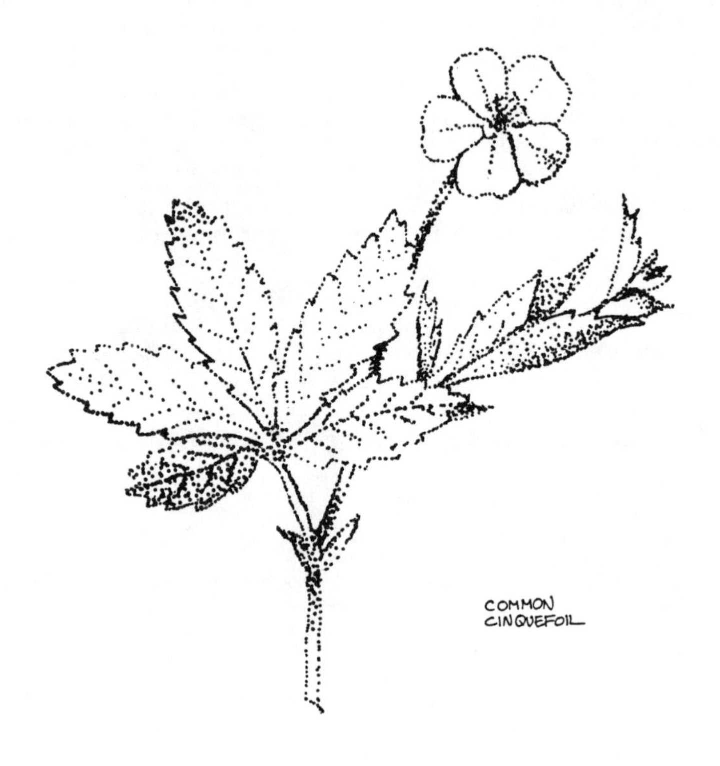

LESSON 7: "C" (part two)

chilblains — *Herbal agents:* **herb Robert** decoction on cloths; **aloe gel**. Also see **chapped hands.**

childbirth — During pregnancy and lactation, *herbal agents:* **raspberry** leaves. To anticipate flooding during last stage of labor (to expel the placenta): **trillium** (bethroot). See also **pregnancy** and **afterpains.**

children's diseases —

Symptoms (especially for infants and very young children who cannot tell you how they feel):

• brain diseases and head trouble—forehead and eyebrows contracted.
• bronchitis—cry is brassy and metallic, with crowing inspiration.
• colic—legs drawn up, abdomen feels hard, hands shut tightly, toes bent.
• earache—hands to ear, pulls ear, rolls head side-to-side, cries if you press front or rear of ear.
• headache—hands to head.
• kidney involvement (especially following scarlet fever)—puffiness around eyelids.
• pleuritic—louder, shriller cry, with cough when child is moved.
• pneumonia—cough with phlegm, labored breathing during which nostrils sharply dilate and contract.
• sudden, profuse vomiting—often indicates onset of any disease of children and has little significance by itself.
• teething—fingers in mouth, drooling.

Treatment:
• general: **chamomile**, **raspberry** leaves, **calendula** (with a mild or unidentifiable illness).
• colds: **calendula**, **raspberry**.
• colic: **chamomile**, **catnip**, **peppermint**.
• convulsions; hot **mustard** bath, **catnip** tea.
• coughs, bronchitis: **horehound** syrup, **elecampane** syrup, **calendula**, **pleurisy root**.
• diaper rash: **honey**; black walnut bark or hulls, or **butternut** bark or hulls (as a wash); slippery **elm** or cornstarch powder; **chickweed** decoction.
• diarrhea: **strawberry** leaves (infants), **meadowsweet**, **raspberry**, **blackberry**.
• earaches: poultice of **camomile** or coltsfoot.
• eruptive diseases— scarlet fever, chicken pox, measles (all kinds): **raspberry**, **yarrow**, **calendula** (add hyssop for measles).
• fevers: **yarrow** (use less than for adults), **calendula**.
• laxatives: rhubarb, prunes, **violet** flowers, **butternut** bark, **turtlehead**, pumpkin seeds, **dandelion**. (These also for worms.)
• mumps: the *specific* is **white clover** blossoms (prophylactic); **everlasting** may also be used.
• nervous disorders: **catnip**, **chamomile**.
• skin eruptions in babies: pansy (external wash).
• stomach disorders: **chamomile**, dill.
• vomiting: **raspberry** leaves, **peppermint**.
• whooping cough: lilac flowers, **wild cherry** bark.

chokecherry — (*Prunus virginiana*). Shrub or small tree; fruit very puckery until ripe. Makes good jelly. **Caution: cherry leaves and seeds contain dangerous concentrations of prussic acid (cyanide).**

Parts used: bark, winter twigs.
Properties and use: antiperiodic. Use also for coughs, sciatica.
Preparation: decoction, or use fresh powdered bark in a syrup.
Dose: 1 teaspoonful in ½ glass of hot water.

chorea — (St. Vitus' Dance). A nervous spasmodic affliction usually occurring before puberty, associated with rheumatic fever.

Herbal agents: nervines, especially **skullcap**, **valerian**, blue **vervain, motherwort**, peony, **lady's-slipper**. Also 10-60 mg daily of vitamin B-6 and magnesium, together with a high total of vitamin and mineral supplements.

cinquefoil — A genus of herbs belonging to the Rose family that are characterized by usually having five leaflets (toothed) on a leaf and yellow five-petal flowers. Some are creeping, some more upstanding. One that usually has seven leaflets is called septfoil or **tormentil**.

cleavers — (*Galium aparine*). Madder family. Similar to lady's bedstraw, but has little hooks on stems to aid in climbing. Common in woods and fields. Sometimes listed as clivers.

Part used: whole herb.
Properties and use: diuretic, diaphoretic. For scalding urine.
Preparation: infusion.
Dose: ½ cup, 3-4 times daily.

clover, red — (*Trifolium praetense*) Legume family. Large, three-part leaf has a white triangle traced across all three. The large magenta blossoms of this common clover are collected at full flower and spread carefully on screens to dry in the shade.

Part used: blossoms.
Properties and use: contains calcium, potassium, and silicon. Alterative and slow-acting blood purifier; *specific* for whooping cough and for spasmodic, dry coughs. Combined with burdock and yellow dock, it is useful in adolescent skin disorders. In cancer, red clover is undoubtedly of value and proves some help in delaying the progress of malignancy and metastasis. Useful also in AIDS.
Preparation: infusion, or briefly simmered as a decoction; syrup.
Dose: 1 cup, 3-4 times daily; in syrup, 1 teaspoon ad lib.

clover, white — (*Trifolium repens*). Smaller than the above, pale pink or white blossoms. *Use:* prophylactic against mumps.

colds — According to herbalist principles, a cold is nature's safety valve for eliminating accumulated poisons through free discharge from mucous membranes and through fever. The best treatment is not complete suppression through potent drugs that bring their own cumulative effects but through helping nature do its job. Begin a short **fast** at first sign of cold. Allow only fruit juices and herbal teas for 24 hours or until fever leaves.

Herbal agents: **costmary** (*specific* for sinus head colds), **yarrow** (early stages with fever), **boneset** (for the flu, aches, and pains in the joints), **elder** flowers, **peppermint**. Add vitamin C, 500-1,000 mg or more per day.

colic — *Herbal agents:* **catnip, chamomile, peppermint**, calamus (sweet flag), marjoram. See **childhood diseases**.

comfrey — (*Symphytum officinalis*). Borage family. Much grown for human and cattle dietary supplement, sometimes found wild. Fantastic healing reputation.

Parts used: leaves and root.

Properties and use: demulcent, vulnerary; contains many minerals and vitamins, as well as allantoin for healing. Used for mucous membranes and respiratory system in cough syrups and combined with other agents such as **pleurisy root**. Also used for internal ulcers, ruptures, and in knitting broken bones, torn ligaments.

Preparation: decoction from root, infusion from leaves for internal use; also in poultice application externally.

Dose: follow standard for each preparation.

constipation — See **aperients**. Do not give these if possible symptoms of appendicitis exist.

convalescence — See **tonics**, also **diets**.

convulsions — Occur in many diseases and conditions: uremia, epilepsy, eclampsia, brain injuries or diseases, heart block, tetany, tetanus, and so on. In children they may occur at the onset of an infectious disease or for trifling causes.

First aid for gross motor seizures: Lay the person flat and roll on side to allow a clear breathing passage. Loosen clothing, if necessary. Do not restrain but protect from injury (i.e., sharp nearby corners or projections). *Do not attempt to place anything in the person's mouth.* When the seizure has passed, the person may choose to rest or sleep.

Herbal agents: nervines, especially **skullcap** and **blue vervain.** Hot **mustard** bath to feet. Be sure diet is rich in calcium, magnesium, and vitamin B-6. The amino acid L-Taurine also has anticonvulsant properties.

corn oil — Use internally for eczema, granulated eyelids: 1 tablespoon, 3 times daily. Externally, use for scalp. See **castor oil.**

corn silk — Spread out thinly on screens in a dry place. Dry carefully, as it molds easily.

Properties and use: diuretic, antiseptic to urinary tract. Used in many urinary diseases and infections.
Preparation: infusion.
Dose: 1/2 to 1 cup, 3-4 times daily.

costmary — (*Tanecetum balsamita*). Composite family. Often found cultivated in gardens of old houses. Hardy perennial. Sometimes called Bible leaf because the fragrant leaf was used to mark pages of the Bible. Also used in drawers for moth prevention. Yellow button-like flowers.

Part used: whole herb.
Properties and use: astringent, demulcent. For colds, especially sinus head colds.
Preparation: hot infusion—use only a small amount (1/2 teaspoon to 1 pint of hot water) at start, as it can get bitter. Sweeten with honey.
Dose: 1/4 to 1/2 cup, ad lib.

coughs — See also **demulcents**. *Herbal agents:* wild cherry bark, **violet** flowers, sunflower seeds, **white pine** needles, maidenhair fern, **lungwort**, hyssop, horehound, **elecampane, pleurisy root, polypody, hemlock** tree twigs, balsam fir, **chokecherry bark** and winter twigs, red **clover**.
Suggested preparations:

Boil up 1/3 cup fresh or dried red clover blossoms in 1 cup of thin syrup or honey. Take 1 tablespoonful, 2-3 times daily.

or

Two cups of chopped white pine twigs (fresh and green) and ½ cup of chopped chokecherry twigs (winter only), boiled together in 2 cups of water until reduced to ½ cupful of liquid. Strain. Add to 2 cups of honey and bottle.

or

One whole bulb of garlic, peeled, ground up in the blender with 1 cupful of honey. Take teaspoonful doses frequently, over 24-hour period. Especially good for bronchitis.

crampbark — See **Viburnum**.

cranberry — (*Vaccinium*, any species). Grows in boggy places, more commonly on coast. High-bush cranberry is a viburnum species.

Part used: berry.
Properties and use: Contains quinic acid that is converted in the body to hippuric acid, a strong antibacterial agent. Used in kidney disorders, in pyelonephritis, in painful and frequent urination, diuretic. Good for kidney stones.
Preparation: simmer 2 cups of ground cranberries in 1 quart of water; add honey or sugar if desired. (Commercial drink will do, also.)
Dose: 6 ounces of juice, 2-3 times daily.

croup — a common ailment of children: breathing is labored and noisy. *Treatment:* steam inhaler (vaporizer) by bedside. Add to the liquid a strong decoction of **costmary** or thyme. For internal use: see **pleurisy root**.

cystic catarrh — *Herbal agent:* see **beech** leaves.

Self-review Questions for "C" (part two)

1. The herbs mentioned in this lesson were chokecherry, cleavers, red clover, comfrey, cornsilk, costmary, and cranberry. List the parts used and the properties of each.

2. What herbs in this lesson are mentioned as prophylactic?

3. How many kinds of flowers are mentioned for use in children's diseases?

4. Which herbs appear most frequently in the treatment of children?

5. Chokecherry is listed as an antiperiodic. Therefore, it can be used for what? What caution do you need to remember?

6. What three herbal agents in this lesson are listed as diuretic or good for kidney diseases?

7. Vocabulary to define:

   prophylactic

(Answers on page 207.)

LESSON 8: "D"

daisy — (*Chrysanthemum leucanthemum*). Composite family. Common in fields and roadsides in summer.

Part used: whole herb.

Properties and use: contains oil and ammoniacal salts, antispasmodic, diuretic, tonic, resolvent, vulnerary. Soreness is an indication for its use. Acts on muscle fiber of blood vessels. For venous congestion due to mechanical causes: varicose veins, ruptures, strained ligaments.

Preparation: decoction.

Dose: wineglassful, cold, before meals. Or make daisy wine that has some of the medicinal properties of the whole herb, and add it in equal parts to a strong decoction of the herb.

Daisy Wine: Pour 1 gallon of boiling water over 4 quarts of daisy blossoms. Let stand in a crock or enamelware vessel overnight. In the morning, drain and squeeze out the daisies. Boil the liquid 10 minutes. Cool to lukewarm. Add 1 yeast cake spread on a slice of toast to float on liquid, or add 1 tablespoon dry yeast dissolved in a little warm water. Also add 2 sliced oranges, 2 sliced lemons, 1 cup of raisins, and 3 pounds of sugar. Let stand in crock at room temperature (covered with a towel) for three weeks. Skim and strain. Bottle but cork loosely until it has stopped working (bubbling). Then put cork down hard. Can be used in *1 month.*

dandelion —(*Taraxacum officionale*). Composite family. Common weed of lawns, fields, and waysides. In addition to medicinal use, the roots can be roasted, ground for a caffeine-free coffee substitute (although chicory roots are preferred). The greens can be eaten raw or cooked, while tender in spring; they contain iron and other useful substances, including high amounts of vitamin A. The blossoms can be made into wine using the same recipe as for daisy wine, but age the wine for *one year.*

Part used: roots.
Properties and use: aperient, tonic, hepatic, mild laxative. Assists digestion and assimilation, assists the liver in its functions. Used for dropsy (edema), jaundice, indigestion, irritation of the gastric membrane, constipation, diabetes.
Preparation: gather the roots in late summer after they have completed their growth and before the ground freezes. Dry and store carefully. Boiling impairs its strength, so even with roots use an infusion rather than a decoction (2 tablespoons to 1 cup of water).
Dose: ½ cup, 3-4 times daily.

dandruff — *Herbal agent:* strong infusion of **rosemary** rubbed into the scalp. Also, massage scalp with warmed olive oil at bedtime. Wrap in warmed towel and shampoo the next day.

delirium tremens — *Herbal agent:* A wineglassful of strong **vinegar** is said to restore sense and locomotion at the start of attack.

demulcents and emollients — Demulcents soothe mucous membranes internally; emollients are used externally. Examples include **honey**, **hollyhock** (all parts), **comfrey** root, **mullein** leaves, and **beech** leaves. See Lesson 3.

diabetes — A disease caused by a deficiency of the insulin produced in the pancreas. Insulin is essential for burning glucose in the muscles. When insulin is deficient, the blood-sugar level remains excessively high, spilling sugars into the urine. Fatty acids are not burned, and accumulated poisons eventually cause severe complications—cataracts, retinitis, gangrene, and advanced arteriosclerosis.

Type I diabetes strikes most often during childhood, and until recently was referred to as juvenile diabetes. Insulin injections at least once a day, and often three times a day, are a necessary component of therapy. Type II diabetes, which is far more common, usually strikes adults after age 40. It can often be controlled by diet and by oral medications prescribed by a physician. There is a marked familial tendency toward diabetes, although that has been better documented with Type II than with Type I.

Some studies (especially as reported in Adele Davis's *Let's Get Well*, Chapter 9) indicate a definite correlation between diet and the onset of diabetes when there is a B-6 and magnesium deficiency. Therefore, it seems possible that a vitamin-and-mineral-rich diet begun before diabetes develops might effectively prevent it. There are also indications that an improved natural diet lowers the need for insulin and reduces complications in both kinds of diabetes. Such a diet should include high amounts of vitamin A, vitamin E, and B vitamins—particularly B-6, choline, and inositol, as well as magnesium. Natural whole-grain foods with high fiber content slow the absorption of glucose, decreasing the need for insulin. Additions of bran, wheat germ, brewers' yeast, plus liver, fish, and fortified milk are also healthful.

Indications for diabetes: increased thirst; increase in quantity of urine passed—2 to 15 pints in 24 hours; pale urine—acid and sweet-smelling; constipation; muscular weakness; skin dry; tongue very red.

Herbal agents that have had a reputation for treating diabetes in the past are: **sumac** berries (cold infusion, no sugar added), **beech** bark, and **dandelion**. It is not certain how effective these agents actually have been. At present, scientists at a university in Israel are engaged in sophisticated research on herbal remedies for diabetes. While no one should be taken off insulin on the grounds that "a natural therapy will do it," any beneficial results will show up in a gradual lessening of the need for insulin.

The diabetic must balance blood sugar and insulin. If blood sugar is too high, the result may be diabetic coma. If it is too low in relation to the insulin in the person's system, the result may be insulin shock. It is important to know the difference, as the remedy for one condition is deadly to a person suffering from the other. Many diabetics carry equipment for a finger-prick blood test. This is the simplest, most accurate assessment.

Insulin shock may come on very quickly, with the person exhibiting dizziness, speech difficulty, confusion, acute apprehension, wide-eyed staring, clammy sweating, muscle tremor or weakness, loss of consciousness. If not treated, convulsions, delirium, and death may ensue. Treatment requires immediate ingestion of sugar. A diabetic usually carries candy or glucose tablets. When the person is unconscious, small but frequent spoonfuls of maple syrup, honey, or raw sugar can be tried until the ambulance arrives. Remember that the unconscious person has no muscular control, and any form of sugar that could cause choking may be dangerous.

Similar symptoms may occur in nondiabetics who experience a sudden drop in blood sugar (such as athletes) or in persons prone to low blood sugar (hypoglycemia).

Diabetic coma, from excess sugars, usually develops more slowly but has serious side-effects, including death within two or three days if not treated. Breath is sweet, like apples, new-mown hay, or chloroform. There is drowsiness with great gasping for breath. The treatment requires insulin injection, with bed rest and close monitoring to return the body to a condition of balance.

diaper rash — *Herbal agents:* **honey**, **calendula** lotion, cornstarch, **lycopodium** spores.

diaphoretics and sudorifics — Increase surface circulation and perspiration. Some examples are **yarrow**, **pennyroyal**, **vervain**, **calendula**, **elder** flowers, **boneset**, **prickly ash** bark or berries, and wild **ginger**. See Lesson 3.

diarrhea — *Herbal agents:*

In infants—**strawberry** leaves.
In children—**blackberry** roots or leaves.
In adults—**mullein**.

Also see **astringents** and Lesson 3.

diets — See also **fasting**. Careful attention to diet (especially natural, organic instead of processed, chemical-laden foods) and to fasting will be seen in many cases to mark the difference between success and failure of many herbal treatments. Modern medicine tends to ignore diet—except in certain obvious situations such as diabetes or pernicious anemia—and to rely on drugs or surgery. Not only are many human ills traceable to eating too much food or too much of the wrong kinds of food, but most diseases can be, if not cured, at least substantially helped by attention to diet, elimination, breathing, exercise, and other natural means of maintaining health, combined with the proper herbs *to help the body help itself.*

The Short Fast or Cleansing Diet. This is recommended for normal adults at least once a year during a long weekend or vacation. For obese or plethoric persons, it can be done more often. Also recommended in fevers and certain acute and chronic illnesses.

Day 1. Morning (or night before): herbal laxative tea; glass of weak orange juice (½ juice/ ½ water) with 1 teaspoon of honey and 1 teaspoon of lemon juice. Midmorning: repeat the juice. Noon: vegetable infusion (4 ounces of carrots, 6 ounces of beets, 2 ounces of parsley, 4 ounces of celery, 1 clove of garlic, all chopped fine or put through the blender; add 1 quart of water and let stand overnight in the refrigerator). Take 1 or 2 glasses, ad lib. Note: do not cook this mixture. Midafternoon: alfalfa tea, no sugar. Evening: vegetable broth (above), may be warmed slightly but do not boil. Bedtime: more of fruit juice mix, herbal laxative tea.

Day two. Morning: fruit juice mix and herbal dandelion coffee. Midmorning: alfalfa tea. Noon: vegetable broth as on first day, but simmer vegetables in the water and add beef or chicken bouillon cube if desired. Midafternoon: fruit juice of any kind, full strength. Supper: broth as at noon. Bedtime: Fruit juice mix. Herbal laxative tea only if still needed.

Day three. Morning: fruit juice, wholemeal cereal (cooked), herbal coffee. Midmorning: fruit or vegetable juice, full strength. Noon: any kind of thin soup or chowder, two or three wheatmeal crackers or Ry-Krisp. Mid-afternoon: herbal tea. Supper: poached egg on toast or Ry-krisp.

Day 4. Morning: fruit juice, wholemeal cereal (cooked), herbal coffee. Midmorning: broth as before. Noon: regular soup, small salad without dressing, wholemeal bread, milk pudding or fruit. Midafternoon: herbal tea or juice or vegetable broth. Evening:

light meat or fish, baked or steamed; steamed or baked vegetables including a potato; wholemeal bread and butter; herbal tea or herbal coffee.

Now go on with the standard natural diet below. If one has been on a typical modern refined and synthetic diet heretofore, this would be an excellent time to switch permanently to a better diet.

General Natural Foods Diet. Check out labels for chemical additives. Sausage, bacon, and ham, for example, are high in chemicals unless home-butchered and cured. Almost all processing, especially that which changes a food item from its original appearance, also reduces its nutritive value or adds harmful substances. Be especially cautious about using foods that contain monosodium glutamate (MSG).

Avoid	*Use*
mixes and "instant" foods	fruits and vegetables—raw, steamed, baked
"convenience" foods	fish and meats without additives, naturally fed
bleached flour	unbleached or whole-grain
bakery products	homemade bread, muffins
commercial cereals	whole-grain cooked cereals, granola
white sugar	honey, molasses, raw sugar
margarine	corn or olive oil, unsalted butter
tea, coffee	herbal teas and coffees, vegetable and fruit juice

Use especially those foods native to your own environment. Apple, cranberry, grape, pear, elder, barberry, currant, and other berries make excellent juice. Many of these actually contain more vitamin C than citrus fruit.

Building Diet (for children, teens, or convalescents). Children need more replacement foods, and adolescents need minerals. Adolescent girls especially need iron to store in their bodies for menstruation and for childbearing, and this is the item most lacking in a typical teen diet of cola drinks and potato chips.

Beverages: fruit juices of all kinds; **shrubs;** milk shakes with molasses, maple syrup, or honey; eggnog (shake egg, honey, and nutmeg in a glass jar or blender, then add milk and shake again); alfalfa tea, and other vitamin- and mineral-rich herbal teas, such as meadowsweet.

Snacks: raisins, dates, dried apricots, prunes, homemade popcorn, carrot and celery sticks, cheese, nuts (not oiled or salted, preferably in the shell); goodies baked with whole-grain flours, such as corn-molasses bread, gingerbread, raisin-applesauce cake, hermit cookies, or gingersnaps. Additional carbohydrates should be obtained from the whole grains in breads and from granola or cooked cereals.

For protein, serve at least one egg daily; organ meats (that are high in iron and B vitamins) such as liver, kidneys, and heart, at least once a week; fish, especially shellfish (to supply the iodine for teenage thyroid needs), often.

diet supplements — Even with the best of natural food diets, it is often necessary to add high vitamin-mineral supplements in some way. Remarkable results are being obtained in some otherwise incurable diseases, even epilepsy and schizophrenia, by administering exceptionally high doses of certain vitamins and minerals. It is suspected that with the general degeneration and deterioration of our environment, even "natural" foods are no longer as complete or free from taint as they used to be. Certainly in chronic or acute diseases it is advisable to inquire into the high-vitamin- and-mineral therapies now being utilized. However, in general, a few principles seem to be advisable in using these supplements:

The more natural and complete the supplement, the better. Highly vitamin- and mineral-rich foods such as brewer's yeast, liver, wheat germ, brown rice, alfalfa, molasses, eggs, natural oils, and milk appear again and again at the top of any vitamin analysis list.

When taking high doses of synthetic or highly concentrated vitamin or mineral products, take them on a base of the above-mentioned high-value foods. Instead of taking such vitamin supplements on an empty stomach, take them with a balanced meal or at least with a glass of milk or juice.

Be very careful in taking individual vitamin supplements. The B vitamins are especially tricky. Too much B-1 (thiamin) will be excreted and will take with it useful B-2 and B-6. It is important that B-3 (niacin) be at least four or five times the amount of other B's. It is not enough to take equal amounts of each of these vitamins—it's the percentage that's important. It is better, if taking individual vitamins, to seek the formula of an expert nutritionist or doctor skilled in this form of therapy. Also, some vitamins like vitamins A, D, and E (that are not water-soluble and are stored in the body fat) are harmful when taken in excess.

diuretics — These increase urine output and reduce retained fluid. Some diuretics include: **Joe-Pye weed, elecampane, juniper** berries, **white birch** leaves, **wild sarsaparilla, wild carrot, corn silk**. See Lesson 3.

dizziness — May be a symptom of: bowel, stomach, or liver disorders; obstruction of bile ducts; nervous headache (migraine); blood pressure disorder; some poisons; menopause. *Herbal agents:* in elderly, **daisy**; in general, **rose** leaves, **rosemary**.

dock, yellow — (*Rumex crispus*). Buckwheat family. A rank weed in waysides and gardens, having long leaves somewhat curled at the edges. Flowers are inconspicuous and greenish, in tall shoots, very much like rhubarb, which belongs to the same family. Reddish seeds persist all winter. The root has a distinctive yellow-orange center that contains chrysophanic acid, a *specific* in skin diseases. The young leaves can be boiled for greens.

Part used: roots; harvest in fall to dry.
Properties and use: alterative, *specific* for skin diseases.
Preparation: for acne, eczema, psoriasis—use ground root as a powder; also for these and other eruptions (rashes, swellings, and itching), boil fresh root in fat, oil, or water to use as a lotion or wash. Make fresh every 24 hours.

dogwoods — (*Cornus*, any species). Shrubs or small trees, ornamentals or in hedgerows. The flowering dogwood is not so frequent in northern areas. The shrubs of several species are common and mostly interchangeable in use.

flowering dogwood (*Cornus florida*). Small tree with large white-bract flowers May-June.

Parts used: bark and flowers.
Properties and use: bark is astringent, influencing mucous membranes, as in laxity of the bowels (combined with rhubarb); sore mouth and tender gums (dried powdered bark for open ulcers); also antiperiodic. Flowers are a mild tonic for after-fevers, soothing and sustaining to the nervous system. Berries are a mild, bitter tonic for convalescence.
Preparation: decoction.
Dose: wineglassful, 3 times daily.

red osier (*Cornus sericea*). Bushy shrub, with shoots and stems bright red even in winter. Common along roadsides. Fruit: small white or lead-colored berries, black-dotted at tips.

Part used: bark.

Properties and use: astringent. Used for hemorrhages threatened at childbirth, and other bleeding of uterus, lungs, bowel, and nose.

Preparation: decoction.

Dose: as before.

dropsy — See **edema**.

dysentery — See **diarrhea**. Also see under **astringents** and Lesson 3. The term dysentery is usually reserved for those forms of diarrhea that are caused by bacterial or other organisms common in hot countries and that may carry disease of an epidemic nature. Herbal treatment of true dysentery would include not only the astringents to combat the diarrheal symptoms but should also include a bacteriocidal or fungicidal agent, such as **garlic** or **calendula**, to combat the organisms involved.

dyspepsia — "Upset stomach," sometimes of a chronic nature, especially in older individuals; indigestion. *Herbal agents:* dill, wild **ginger**, **raspberry** leaves, **peppermint**, and other carminative agents. (Make sure it is not due to some more serious cause.)

Self-review Questions for "D"

1. Herbal agents covered in this lesson are daisy, dandelion, yellow dock, and two dogwoods. List the properties and parts used of each.

2. Which of the above agents could be used for diarrhea or for dysentery?

3. Which herbal agent in this lesson is a *specific* for skin diseases?

4. What herb or herbs in this lesson would you use in convalescence from an operation?

5. What is the remedy for insulin shock?

6. What is the remedy for diabetic coma?

7. Which of the above symptoms could occur in a nondiabetic?

8. What are the extra dietary needs of teenage young women?

9. Vocabulary words to define:

acute
chronic
dropsy
edema
hyperglycemia
hypoglycemia

(Answers on page 208.)

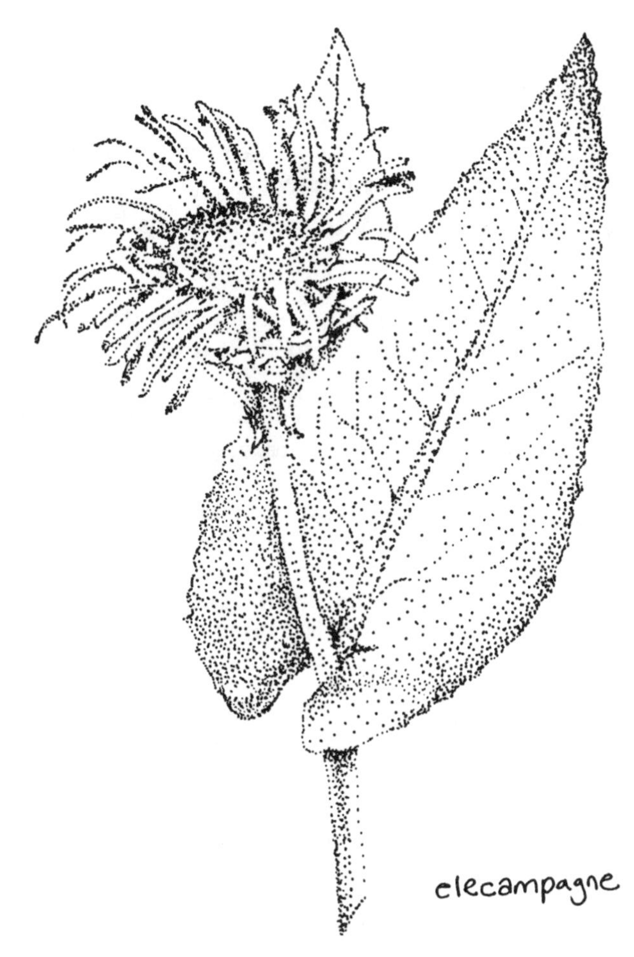

LESSON 9: "E"

earache — *Herbal agents:* apply a warm poultice of **chamomile** or coltsfoot to the ear.

ears — *Herbal agents for:*

• noises in the ear (*tinnitus*)—**violets, valerian, thyme**, tansy, **gill-over-the-ground**. (Cause also may be an iodine-potassium deficiency.)

• middle-ear infections—infusions of **rose** leaves, **mullein**; poultice steeped in hot **vinegar**; high doses of vitamin C, 2-3 grams every 4 hours.

• tearing pains in the ear—infusion of **chamomile**, tansy.

• deafness, caused by neuritis, iodine deficiency—B vitamins, yeast, liver, and kelp.

• wax—a few drops in the ear of warm olive oil, **castor oil**, or strong warm decoction of **agrimony**.

Measles should be carefully treated, as a possible complication may be ear troubles.

eczema — Eczema is a condition of the skin similar to that in allergies. It can be very stubborn to cure. It is presently treated by doctors with cortisone.

Herbal agents: alteratives, especially **burdock**, **yellow dock**, **celandine** ointment; also beets, juice or grated.

edema — In older books, it is referred to as dropsy. Edema is a condition characterized by an accumulation of fluid in the tissues, especially in the legs, hands, abdomen, and lungs. It may be due to an alteration in the blood itself (such as in anemia, lead poisoning, etc.), but usually it is caused by interference in circulation in the kidneys (renal edema) or in the heart (cardiac edema).

Treatment: hot-air baths, hot packs. Light, nourishing diet with restriction of fluids and salt. Take great care to avoid bedsores or any abrasion of the skin; use a sheepskin under the body.

Herbal agents: **diaphoretics** and **diuretics**. **Juniper** berries are used largely for renal and cardiac edema, and are perhaps the safest agent for beginning, but even these in large amounts can be highly irritating to the kidneys. **Lily-of-the-valley** also for cardiac edema.

(Digitalis has been used widely for edema, but its effect can be cumulative and dangerous. This is even more so if abdominal tapping of fluid is used, with the sudden withdrawal of fluid giving symptoms of overdose.)

elder — (*Sambucus canadensis*). The common elder is a medium-sized shrub that grows best in damp places. It bears a flat-topped cluster of white blossoms and later purple berries. There is another variety, the red-berried elder, that bears a cone-shaped blossom followed by red berries and that comes into bloom very much earlier than the common elder. *The red-berried elder is poisonous.*

Part used: young leaves.
Properties and use: The bark and twigs can be purgative; the young leaves are milder. Used as a diuretic for edema. (*Caution!*)
Preparation: infusion as wash for sores; strong decoction (bark and leaves) used *externally* on cattle for gadfly or blowfly and maggots on hide; green bark boiled in vaseline for old sores.

Part used: berries when ripe. (Do not use raw. Cook at least slightly, or use in **shrub**.)
Properties and use: aperient, diuretic; very high in vitamin C.
Preparation: for jelly, pie, **shrub**, wine. Juice for fevers. The wine or **shrub** is *specific* for sciatica.
Dose: ad lib.

Part used: flowers.
Properties and use: flowers contain a volatile oil stimulant, sudorific and diaphoretic.
Preparation: Boiled in lard or suet, as ointment for sore nipples, cracked lips, chapped hands. Infusion of dried flowers, combined with peppermint, for colds. Infuse flowers in wine for fevers.

elecampane — (*Inula helenium*). Composite family. A tall plant with wide stalkless leaves and yellow composite flowers, smaller than sunflowers. Grows in damp places.

Part used: roots; dig 2- to 3-year-old roots in fall, then dry and store.
Properties and use: contains inulin, helenin, and alantol. Demulcent, pectoral, antibiotic. Also contains a substance that is *specific* in combatting the tuberculosis bacillus. Used for chronic coughs, catarrh, bronchitis.
Preparation: 1 tablespoon of powdered root in 1 cup of honey; heat slightly but do not boil; strain. Or wash, peel, and grate the fresh roots into honey in a blender; bottle and store.
Dose: small spoonful, 3-4 times daily, for coughs or lung congestion.

Fresh, peeled roots may be candied by boiling in sugar syrup or honey. (Follow cookbook recipe.) Strain and save the syrup for cough syrup. Dry the candied pieces on wax paper and roll in sugar or slippery elm powder to use as lozenges.

elm, slippery — (*Ulmus fulva* or *rubra*). A common tree, but different from the American elm whose umbrella shape lined many roads. Slippery elm can be distinguished by feeling the leaf which is like sandpaper underneath, and by noting that the leaves are folded upward along the midrib. When chewed, the twigs and new leaves have a pleasant nutty flavor that allays hunger for some time.

Part used: inner bark.

Properties and use: demulcent, emollient, pectoral, nutritive. The inner bark is mucilaginous. This bark, when cut into pieces or ground, then dried and carefully stored, is one of our most soothing and nutritious demulcents. As an emergency food or a gruel for convalescents: boil up a 2-inch piece of bark in 1 pint of water. As it stands, it gets rather gelatinous, with a pleasant flavor that needs no addition, but honey or lemon may be added. For diseases in which no other food can be tolerated, especially diarrhea and vomiting, this food is often accepted and very nutritious. For infants who cannot tolerate a milk formula, this could serve as temporary nourishment.

Externally, the ground bark is used as a vehicle in poultices (combine with oil for burns and scalds). Use dry powdered bark in ulcers, wounds, boils.

Veterinary uses are many: for scours in young stock and also in lung diseases of cattle and horses, combined with **elecampane** (above).

embolism — A clot in a blood vessel. *Herbal agent:* Sweet clover (**melilot**) is *specific* for prevention and cure of this. Check entry.

emetics — Produce vomiting. See **mustard**, **boneset**, blue **vervain**, and **Solomon's seal**.

emmenagogues — Increase the menstrual flow. Some emmenagogues include **pennyroyal**, **motherwort**, and **peppermint**. See Lesson 3.

emollients — See **demulcents**.

enuresis — See **bedwetting**.

English ivy — Ginseng family. Cultivated, especially on walls of buildings and in some gardens. *Dangerous because it contains a strong alkaloid that even exudes from the underside of the leaves. The berries are also poisonous.*

epilepsy — See **convulsions**. *Treatment:* As for convulsions, prevent the person from harm. Grand mal has always been considered incurable. However, modern trials with various high-mineral and vitamin combinations—especially magnesium, L-taurine, and B-6—have kept the person seizure-free, without the side-effects of prescription drugs.

Herbal agents: **nervine** tea, to build up the nervous system (possibly these also contain high amounts of the needed nerve mineral, magnesium); **lady's bedstraw, valerian, skullcap, blue vervain, lady's-slipper**. Indiana Botanic Company's *Viro Tea* contains most of these.

eruptive diseases — See under **children's diseases**. For adults, use the same treatments but guard against possible aftereffects even more carefully. Measles, mumps, and scarlet fever can have more serious consequences in adults.

erysipelas — Erysipelas is an acute and infectious skin rash caused by a streptococcus. It usually begins in connection with a wound but may occur alone. Complications such as pneumonia and kidney diseases may follow. Occasionally, chronic skin tumors or other skin diseases have been cured or improved after an attack of erysipelas that apparently brings on, in an acute form, a cleansing of the poisons in the system that were causing the chronic diseases.

Treatment: During acute stage, treat as for any severe infectious disease—bed care, **fasting** followed by light diet, sponge baths if fever goes too high.

Herbal agents: see **alteratives**.

Suggested formula:

30 parts **bittersweet** twigs
30 parts **burdock** seeds
15 parts **yellow dock** root
1 part **prickly ash** berries

Mix dry and store. This can be made up in a concentrated infusion, as in Lesson 3; then add an equal amount of honey or ginger syrup.

Dose: 1 tablespoon, 3-4 times daily.

Externally (wash or poultice), walnut bark and leaves, **chickweed, plantain, bittersweet**, corn oil.

everlasting — (*Gnaphalium, Atennaria,* and *Anaphalis*). Composite family. So-called because the flowers dry on the stalk and are used in winter bouquets. The everlastings bloom in late summer. Any of several species are used interchangeably.

Part used: whole herb.

Properties and use: astringent, demulcent, soothing to mucous membranes. In decoction, as a mouthwash for sore mouth, cleansing wash (douche) for leucorrhea. Internally, infusion is used for bronchial catarrh, colds with bronchial congestion, croupy cough, laryngitis, mumps. The dried plant (including flowers) is sometimes smoked in a pipe for asthma or bronchitis.

Preparation: decoction or infusion.

Dose for infusion: 1-2 cups daily.

eyes — *Herbal agents:*

- for general eyewash, red eyes—**hollyhock**, **raspberry** leaves, **waterlily** root, **melilot**, **witch hazel** (infusion, *not* the commercial alcoholic preparation!), **elder** flowers, quince seeds, **cinquefoils**, rose water, swamp maple, red maple, **chickweed**.
- for granular conjunctivitis—**chickweed** infusion, as eyewash.
- for inflammation—ragweed (wash).
- for irritation—**castor oil** or corn oil, 1 drop in eye at night.
- for black eye—poultice of fresh roots of **Solomon's seal**.
- for eye injuries—**comfrey** (both internally and externally).
- for eyestrain—**yarrow** (wash).
- for eye complaints in general—the hawkweeds (wash).
- for cataracts—dusty miller, **celandine** (*caution: check entry under herb and follow directions; see caution under* **cataracts**).

Nutrition has a great effect on the eyes. Lack of vitamin A results not only in night blindness, but many uncomfortable symptoms. Lack of various B vitamins can result in dryness, inflammation, enlarged capillaries, corneal ulcers, and even blindness. The most essential B vitamin for eyes is riboflavin, B-2, but it must be taken in balance with others. (See **diet supplements**.) Chromium is essential in avoiding retinopathy in diabetics. Follow recommended dose for supplements. Chromium also can be found in brewers' yeast, clams, corn oil, whole grains, and mushrooms.

Self-review Questions for "E"

1. The herbal agents covered in this lesson were elder, elecampane, elm, and everlasting. List the properties and parts used for each.

2. What three plants are mentioned as *specifics* and for what conditions?

3. What remedy would you recommend to persons with poor hearing?

4. What remedy would you try if an invalid had trouble keeping down anything eaten?

5. What plant is mentioned in this lesson only as a warning that it is dangerous?

6. How is erysipelas different from eczema?

7. In one entry you are directed to make a concentrated infusion. How does that procedure differ from the standard infusion?

8. Some older herbals call for "1 dr." of a dried herb. Consult a dictionary to see how much that would be.

9. Vocabulary to define:

mucilaginous
pectoral

(Answers on page 209.)

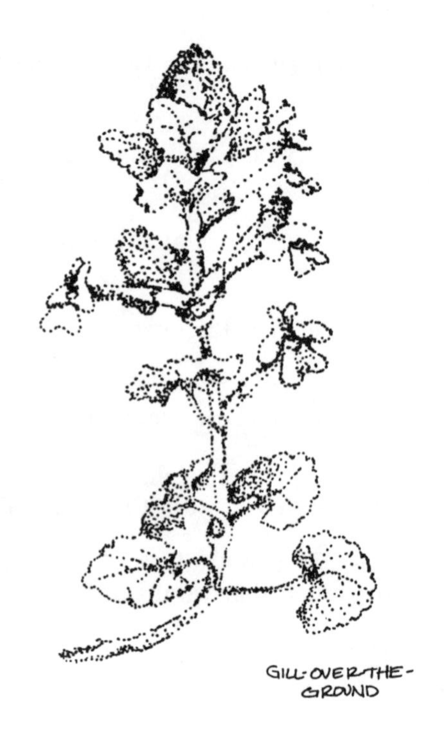

LESSON 10: "F" and "G"

fasting — One of the most important therapies to be considered in any diseased condition of the body is fasting. Strictly speaking, fasting is taking no food at all. (The short fast that was given under **diet** is not a true fast.) Even if herbal remedies did not exist, many diseases could be cured by fasting alone. Take an example from the animals: when they are sick, they go "off their feed," crawl off by themselves, and take only water. The body is a tremendously self-recuperative organism, given half a chance, but it cannot fight off disease when it is significantly engaged in coping with a new load of food every few hours. Most of the major degenerative diseases of our day, especially cancer, heart trouble, and adult diabetes, are characteristic of affluent societies where there is too much food and too rich food available. Aside from allowing the body a rest from assimilation, fasting is of special value when administering herbal remedies, as it enables the herb to get right to work in the body without having to counteract other substances present at the same time.

Fasts of varying durations should be used in acute illnesses, especially colds and fevers, for at least as long as the acute stage lasts. Fasting for other conditions, such as chronic diseases, depends somewhat upon the specific conditions of patients, their type of work, their family situations, and their degree of cooperation. It is axiomatic that most persons in our society would almost rather die than change their way of eating, or even fast. But fasting in certain chronic conditions, and in obesity, is of almost no use if the person returns to old habits immediately afterward.

The fast can best be used at times when one is entering a new way of life and will be able to take up a new diet and regime once it is over. For this and other reasons, any extended fast is best undertaken at a naturopathic clinic or spa that has experience in such matters and can supervise the patient's progress.

Certain types of fasting can acquaint a person with the procedure and can be of great assistance.

No-lunch plan. Eating only breakfast and supper gives the stomach about 12 hours rest. This is preferable to a no-breakfast plan, as the body, in most circumstances, needs some food on which to start the day.

One-meal-a-day plan. (For a limited time only) This gives the stomach a 24-hour rest. Nonmilk drinks are permitted, especially herbal teas, and fruit and vegetable juices.

Alternate-day plan. Eating three meals one day, and fasting the next, is excellent for diseases of the digestive tract. (Again, for a limited time only.) Drinks permitted as above.

Fasting one day a week. For those who have to work, this might be on a day off. This can be kept up almost indefinitely and would amount to 52 fast days a year, which is not to be scorned.

Three-day fast. Taken while on vacation. If this results in a coated tongue, it usually indicates that a longer fast would be beneficial, as it indicates the body is beginning to eliminate surplus or toxic substances. The preferred drink for this fast is water. See **short fast** on page 87.

Seven-day fast. This should be done only when one does not have to work or take responsibility for family. After the first three days, hunger symptoms usually subside. It is best to be under the care of a doctor or at a spa or clinic in case untoward symptoms develop. Water and fruit or vegetable juices are usually permitted.

The long fast of 30 or 40 days is recommended only in exceptional cases, and then only under strict supervision. It most often has been undertaken for religious or political reasons. It is somehow most attractive to those who need it the least, faddists or fanatics who tend to go to excess in anything they do, especially among young people. There are and have been, of course, undoubted instances where such extended fasts have been of physical and or spiritual benefit, and I have seen these. I have also seen more occasions on which it was abused, having been undertaken without sufficient understanding or without adequate preparation and supervision.

Any long fast is definitely contra-indicated in cases of terminal cancer (especially where the liver has been affected), in lead poisoning, diabetes requiring insulin, organic heart disease (especially when on digitalis), tuberculosis, emaciation, postoperative conditions, in nervous exhaustion (neurasthenia) and depressive or melancholia, and in the elderly (over 70).

female tonics — are useful for building up the female reproductive system, especially for women who have scanty or irregular periods, difficulty in conceiving, or repeated miscarriages. *Herbal agents:* **squawvine** (partridgeberry) is a *specific* for regulating the female system, cramp bark (**viburnum**), **motherwort**, **raspberry**. See each.

flatulence — intestinal gas. *Herbal agents:* **peppermint**, dill, **chamomile**, **ginger**, **juniper** berries.

flu — See **influenza**. Use **antiperiodics**. *Herbal agents:* **peppermint**, **boneset**, **yarrow**.

food poisoning — If contaminated food is suspected, take one teaspoon of **vinegar** in a glass of water and sip every five minutes until the glass is empty.

In all circumstances, avoid food containing milk, cream, or eggs, and that has been allowed to sit around at room temperature for many hours (at church suppers, for example). Avoid home-canned foods of nonacid type (corn, beans, or meats) unless they have been boiled at least 15 minutes or canned by pressure methods. The dangerous organism in these cases (that causes botulism poisoning) is odorless, tasteless, and deadly. Be cautious, too, about all wild mushrooms, "wild caraway," and all unknown plants.

food values of common herbs and wild foods—See **minerals** and **vitamins.**

fumigation — For insect infestations: burn dried cedar or **juniper** branches tied into smudge sticks or in a safe container, allowing smoke to remain in the closed room as long as possible. Then air out.

fungus diseases — *Herbal agents:* for ringworm and athlete's foot, fresh raw juice of **bloodroot** or **jewelweed** in external application, or a wash from reindeer moss (**lichens**). For fungoid types of vaginal infections, douche with a decoction of reindeer moss. Check each listing.

"G"

gargles — See **astringents** and also Lesson 3. *Herbal agents:* **sage**, **raspberry** leaves, **oak** bark, **everlasting**, **hollyhock**, **cinquefoil**, **alder** bark, **sumac** berries, cranesbill. Sometimes combined with hot vinegar. Various kinds of **shrubs** are good when used as gargles. See entry.

garlic — (*Allium sativum*). Lily family. Usually the cultivated type, although wild garlic is found in many areas.

Part used: whole bulb.
Properties and use: antibiotic, pectoral. The bulb contains a bacteriostatic factor (an antiseptic) as well as important trace minerals. Best used fresh, as it loses its effect rapidly. Most often used for bronchitis; also to lower blood pressure, or as a diuretic.
Preparation: 1 whole bulb, each section peeled and ground up very fine; beaten together with 1 cup of honey (or put through a blender).
Dose: teaspoonful, ad lib; use up in 24 hours.

geranium — (*Geraniaceae*). Geranium family. All geraniums are wholesome. Many of the cultivated houseplants have scented leaves used in flavoring teas, jellies, and frosting. Two wild varieties, cranesbill and herb Robert, are astringent and used medicinally. See **herb Robert**.

German (or Hungarian) chamomile — (*Anthemis nobilis*). This has the same properties as our pineapple weed. See **chamomile**. Seeds can be bought at some seed houses and raised in the garden. This species has white petals and is the kind usually sold as commercial chamomile by botanical houses.

German measles — Symptoms: swelling, tenderness, enlargement of lymph glands; rash of slightly elevated red spots that may run together; slight fever. Avoid exposure during pregnancy, especially the first three months. *Prophylactic:* **red clover** heads combined with **raspberry** leaves. *Herbal agents:* in addition to rest, short fast, liquids and juice, use cornstarch or powdered **slippery elm** on rash; also **calendula** water externally. Internally, use infusion of **yarrow, calendula, raspberry** leaves —alone or in combination. If stomach is upset, use **slippery elm** gruel.

gill-over-the-ground — (*Nepata hederacea*). Labiatiae family. Pronounced "Jill;" also called ground ivy. Small heart-shaped leaves, purple flowers at juncture of leaves and stem. Very common ground cover in many places, especially lawns and gardens.

Part used: whole herb.

Properties and use: alterative, tonic, pectoral, antiscorbutic. Very high in vitamin C. Cold infusion used for blood tonic, wash for eyes; hot infusion for colds, coughs, chronic bronchitis, communicable diseases. *Specific* for lead poisoning due to its high vitamin C content.

Preparation: both hot and cold infusions.

Dose: ½ cup, 3-4 times daily.

ginger — Commercial product available in the produce section of most grocery stores.

Part used: whole root.

Properties and use: aromatic, carminative, stimulant. Used in syrup as a vehicle for bad-tasting agents. Used in poultices instead of mustard as it is not so irritating to the skin. Internally for gas, dyspepsia, etc. Added to many herbal agents to hasten their effect. Hot ginger tea is an excellent stimulant to those chilled or exhausted after exposure.

Preparation: syrup, infusion (1 teaspoon powdered ginger to 1 cup of water).

Dose: ½ cupful dose; 1 dose only, then wait to see if symptom subsides.

ginger, wild — (*Asarum canadensis*). Birthwort family. Small plant of deciduous woodlands. Heart-shaped flannel leaves (usually two) with a small purplish-brown flower at the base of leaf on the ground. This is a very early spring flower. Rootstalks under leaf mold.

Part used: root. Dig in late spring or early summer. Wash or brush dirt off roots, split if thick, and dry in sun or slow oven until snap-dry.

Properties and use: are the same as for commercial ginger, but wild ginger is stronger, so use less.

glands, endocrine — See **alteratives.** *Herbal agents:* see each.

- for pituitary—**yarrow.**
- for pituitary or thyroid—**motherwort.**
- for thyroid—seaweeds.
- for adrenals—borage.
- for testes—**spikenard.**
- for estrogenic hormones—aletris, alfalfa, and **squawvine** (partridgeberry).

glands, lymphatic — *Herbal agents:* **alder**, **bittersweet**, **lemon balm**, spleenworts (ferns). See each.

goiter — A disorder of the thyroid gland resulting in a great enlargement of it. It can be prevented by use of seafood, vegetables grown near the sea, or iodized salt in areas where the soil is iodine deficient. *Herbal agents:* seaweed, **calendula.**

gonorrhea — An infectious disease of the genitourinary system. *Herbal agents that were used in the past:* great willow herb, **trailing arbutus, hollyhock.** See **diuretics** and **demulcents.**

gout — A disease characterized by inflammation of the joints, most often in the feet, caused by deposits of urates of soda or kidney disorders. It is often associated with overindulgence in food and drink and a deficiency of exercise. Acute attacks are sudden, with much pain, heat, and inflammation, but which subside usually after a few hours. The joint (often the big toe) is swollen and inflamed; the person is feverish with coated tongue; and urine is scanty and highly colored. Thirst, constipation, and loss of appetite are noted during an attack. In chronic gout, attacks are frequent and sometimes result in joint deformity.

Treatment: Rest in bed during acute attack. Elevate affected part; protect from weight of bedclothes.

Herbal agents: colchicum (a dangerous plant not included in this course) has been the only *specific* known for gout. It is one of the few botanicals still commonly in use in the medical profession. Other herbs that have been used with success are sassafras, **gill-over-the-ground**, bur marigold, **Joe-Pye weed** (gravel root), **ash** leaves, cider. Use a foot bath of mixed herbs infused in water and cooled to 86°, soaking feet for 12-15 minutes, three times weekly. These herbs, especially Joe-Pye weed, may be used internally, but check each entry.

Between acute attacks would be an excellent time to conduct a strict fasting regime ending up with a special diet of purine-free foods—those not forming uric acids—such as milk, strong natural cheese, eggs, barley, rice, tapioca, oatmeal, cucumbers, carrots, onions, apricots, apples, bananas, oranges, pears, peaches, plums, grapes, tomatoes, pineapple, wholewheat bread. Limit meats. Fresh air, regular exercise, and regular habits help.

gravel and stone — (of kidneys and bladder). The cause is unknown but probably similar to gall stones. It also has much in common with **gout**, above. This ailment is relatively unknown in areas where apple cider is the staple drink or in households where much vinegar is used. Symptoms are renal colic, becoming very acute; person may vomit, lie doubled up, faint, or collapse; crystals may be found in urine.

Treatment: during attack, a hot bath or hot poultices will help to relieve the pain, but strong nervines or even opiates may be required in very bad attacks. In between attacks, liquids are in order, and a **short fast** would be beneficial.

Herbal agents: **Joe-Pye weed** (also called gravel root) must be taken over a long period of time but is *specific* for this condition. Also use **apple** juice, cider, or **vinegar** as a dietary staple. Additional remedies:

• equal parts of **marsh mallow** or **hollyhock** and **wild carrot** in infusion; take 1 wineglassful (cold) every 2 hours.

• cook and eat 2 ounces each of **plantain** and **hollyhock** (the fresh green leaves and cooking liquid) daily.

• a sitz-bath of warm **horsetail** decoction (86-90°) for 15 minutes, followed by a quick (1-2 minute) cold bath of the decoction 3 hours later. Repeat 2 or 3 times weekly.

grippe — an old term for influenza or flu, characterized by fever, chills, and aching bones. *Specific* is **boneset**, usually combined with **yarrow** and **peppermint**. For formula, see under **influenza**.

ground ivy — See **gill-over-the-ground.**

gums, sore or spongy — Sore gums are often a symptom of vitamin C deficiency; see **antiscorbutics.** Also check **astringents.** *Herbal agents:* **plantain**, goldthread.

Self-review Questions for "F" and "G"

1. The herbal agents covered in this lesson are garlic, geraniums, gill-over-the-ground, and ginger. List the properties and parts used for each.

2. Vinegar appears as an important agent for which three conditions?

3. What substance mentioned in this lesson is best used fresh?

4. Identify one reason why fasting may be of importance when using herbal remedies.

5. Which agents in this lesson were identified as *specifics* and for what conditions?

6. What remedy might you suggest for athlete's foot?

7. Which agent listed in this lesson is probably most appropriate for bronchitis?

8. Which agent in this lesson may speed the action of other agents?

9. Vocabulary to define:

   bacteriostatic
   purine
   renal

(Answers on page 209.)

LESSON 11: "H"

hawthorn —(*Crataegus*, any species). Small trees of the rose family characterized by long thorns on the branches and small, red, apple-like fruit. There are many species of hawthorns barely distinguishable from each other, except by an expert botanist, and sometimes the botanists don't agree.

It may be that native American hawthorns are equally as good in medicine as the English variety, *C. oxycantha*, that is sometimes found cultivated or escaped from cultivation, but sufficient work has not been done on this question. For use in food, jellies, and juices, the fruits of the native varieties are fine. While none of the hawthorns is dangerous, they are sometimes (and properly) called thorn apples. Unfortunately, a plant of the nightshade family (*Solanaceae*) is also, but improperly, called thorn apple. Since the nightshade is poisonous, be sure to know the difference.

Part used: berries.

Properties and use: hawthorn (*C. oxycantha*) is *specific* for all types of heart disease. It apparently has an active principle that works on the musculature of heart tissue in such a way as to normalize its action from both extremes. When used over a period of time, the effects are not only palliative but curative. Used in angina, valvular deficiency, palpitation, vertigo, apoplexy, cardiac edema, arrhythmia, arteriosclerosis, high blood pressure, functional derangements of the heart.

Preparation: 16 pounds of ripe, fresh berries; 2 pints of water; 3 pounds of sugar or honey. Dissolve sugar or honey in heated water, pour over berries in enamelled or glass vessel, and cook very slowly for 3-4 hours. Press out all the fluid (through muslin) and measure. Add boiling water until liquid measures 1 gallon. (Or evaporate down to 1 gallon.)

Dose: 2-10 drops, 4 times daily. Start with lower dose and work up. This agent works best when used for two weeks, then rest for a day or two, then start again. The fresher the preparation the better.

hay fever — *Herbal agents:* **mullein** and **yarrow**. See **asthma**.

headache — Usually not a disease itself, but a symptom of a variety of other disturbances in the body. Therefore, just to "take something" is usually not effective; the cause should be traced down and treated. Headaches are frequently symptoms of: stomach disorders, constipation, anemia, eyestrain, sinus colds, menstrual disorders, lung and heart diseases, blood pressure disorders, low blood sugar, endocrine disorders. See also **migraine**.

Herbal agents: for any undifferentiated headache, try **betony**. Also **chamomile**, **dogwood**, **valerian**, and **nervines** in general.

head cold — See **colds**.

heart — An old herbalist used to say: "When they complain of the stomach, suspect the heart; when they complain of the heart, suspect the stomach." Of course, diagnosis should be done by a competent physician.

Herbal agents for heart complaints:

- weak, rapid pulse—**bugleweed**.
- irritable heart—**motherwort**.

- valvular diseases—**hawthorn, lily-of-the-valley**.
- myocarditis—**hawthorn**.
- weak, enlarged heart—candytuft.
- endocarditis—**hawthorn, lily-of-the-valley**.
- coronary thrombosis—**melilot** (sweet clover).
- angina—**hawthorn**.
- pain around the heart—**daisy**.
- heart stimulants—capsicum (red pepper), **rose** leaves.
- heart tonics—**hawthorn, motherwort**.
- palpitation, arrhythmia—**motherwort, hawthorn, cherry** bark, tiger lily root.
- cardiac edema—**hawthorn, corn silk, juniper** berries. See **diuretics**.

heatstroke and sunstroke –

Symptoms:

heat exhaustion prostration	sunstroke or heatstroke
sudden or gradual onset	sudden onset
headache, exhaustion	
low temperature	high temperature (up to 107°)
nausea	nausea
moist, cool, clammy skin	flushed, hot, dry skin
	little sweating
weak, soft pulse	increased pulse with temp. rise
low blood pressure	high blood pressure
no change in pupils	dilated or constricted pupils
no change in urine	increased urine
abdominal cramps	twitching or relaxed
may be unconscious	unconscious, convulsions

First Aid:

heat exhaustion prostration	sunstroke or heatstroke
• bed rest, stimulants.	• cold bath/spray, no stimulants.
• usually not fatal, but may be, caused by circulatory failure.	• often fatal or may be subject to recurrence.

Herbal agents: if the person is not yet unconscious, administer sh**rubs** or vinegar to replace lost minerals, but these are better as preventatives.

heliotrope – see **valerian**.

hellebore, white — (*Veratrum viride*). Lily family. *Dangerous herb.* Large-ribbed leaves, white blossoms on spike, growing in low damp places. Can be mistaken (by those who have only book descriptions!) for skunk cabbage in early spring. Included here only to warn of danger. It is a drastic alkaloid, still used in some heart preparations, but not for the unskilled.

hemlock — (*Abies canadensis*) A large forest tree growing in damp, shady locations. Needles short and dark, arranged in two ranks on twigs. Small cones persist all winter. No relation to the poison hemlock below.

Parts used: twigs and needles.
Properties and use: astringent, stimulant; contains tannin. Used for mouthwash, hemorrhages, ulcers, diarrhea, colds. Too drying for internal use in most cases. Also used in tanning leather and as a dye.
Preparation: hot infusion (1 teaspoon of twigs to 1 cup of boiling water); fomentation for sprains and rheumatism.
Dose: ½ cup, 2-3 times daily.

hemlock, poison — (*Cicuta maculata*). A small plant of the *Umbelliferae* family. Feathery leaves and parsley-like flowers. It resembles sweet cicely, parsley, carrot, and caraway, and is sometimes mistaken for these with fatal results. *This and other poisonous members of this family are sufficient reasons for not seeking those plants in the wild but raising them in the garden from reputable seed.*

hemorrhages — See under **astringents** and hemostatics in Lesson 3. *Herbal agents:* for uterine hemorrhaging—**trillium** (bethroot), **shepherd's-purse**, lady's mantle; for alimentary canal—**alder, herb Robert, meadowsweet, shagbark hickory**.

hemorrhoids — Called piles in many older books. *Herbal agents:* Make an ointment (or suppositories) of fresh leaves of **plantain** and **burdock**, incorporated into fresh lard or oil; **mullein** and **white water lily** are also useful. **Witch hazel** and other astringent washes—such as **solomon's seal**—may be used.

herb Robert — (*Geranium Robertianum*). Geranium family. Small pink flowers, reddish stems, cut leaf. Common in shady places. Sometimes blooms until snow.

Part used: whole herb.
Properties and use: antiseptic, astringent; use in skin sores, eruptions, and chilblains (in decoction or ointment). Also for hemorrhages (internally, infusion).
Preparation: decoction, ointment, infusion.
Dose: standard infusion—1 teaspoon per cup; 1 cup per day.

hiccoughs — Hiccoughs seem to be caused by a faulty carbon dioxide mixture in the blood; can be life-threatening in elderly people. They can sometimes be cured by holding the breath, breathing into a brown paper bag, or drinking a glassful of water without stopping. A spoonful of sugar sipped slowly sometimes helps because of its high carbon content. Use **nervines** and **antispasmodics.**

hickory, shagbark — (*Carya alba*). Nut family. Compound leaves with five to seven leaflets. The bark hangs off the tree in long, vertical shreds. The nut, in a four-sectioned husk, is edible.

Part used: middle bark of the trunk.
Properties and use: stimulant, astringent, hepatic. Affects gall duct and cysts. Used for ague, coughs, jaundice, uterine or pulmonary hemorrhages.
Preparation: strong decoction (or in syrup for coughs).
Dose: 1 tablespoon, 5 to 6 times daily.

high blood pressure — *Herbal agents:* **garlic** (continued over long period of time), **hawthorn, basswood** blossoms. See **blood pressure, high.**

hives — May be from allergies. Use **alteratives**; **calendula** lotion, externally.

hollyhock — (*Althea rosea*). Mallow family. Hardy biennial, grown around the house. Can be used as a substitute for **marsh mallow** that grows only near the coast.

Parts used: root, flowers, buds, leaves. Use root of first-year plant, other parts of second-year plant.
Properties and use: antiseptic, demulcent; contains mucilage, iron, lime, soda, phosphorus. Use for irritated conditions of mucous membranes, especially bronchitis, pharyngitis, dysentery, diarrhea, diphtheria. Best combined with appropriate specific agents for these various conditions.
In lactation, infusion of flowers or leaves helps milk production.

honey — (*Mel*). Product of the honey bee. Can be found wild or from domestic hives. One of the most valuable natural products we have, for both food and medicine, it contains many minerals and enzymes needed by the body. (*Caution: Recent information indicates honey should be heat-treated for internal use with infants under 18 months.*) Honey is said to contain a potent bacteriostatic agent, apparently as good as penicillin for some purposes, but without the dangerous side-effects. Use as a vehicle for other medicines, especially in coughs or colds. Spread on diaper rash, burns, ulcers, or on skin after external cancer surgery.

horehound — (*Marrubium vulgare*). Labiatiae family. A cultivated plant, sometimes found escaped. Has white fuzz all over plant, with small, pale lilac flowers.

Part used: whole herb.
Properties and use: tonic to respiratory organs; stimulant; demulcent; decreases mucous discharges, expectorant, for coughs and colds.
Preparation: boil 1 ounce of dried or fresh herb in 1 pint of honey; strain and bottle. Or boil down to lozenges. Or extract juice from fresh green plant, with juicer, and combine with honey. Use 1 tablespoon of the juice to 1 pint of honey, as it is very strong and bitter.
Dose: ad lib.

horsetail — (*Equisetum*, any species). A fern ally; flowerless plant growing in waste places. Stems jointed. The large, unbranched variety makes excellent pot scrubbers when bundled, because of the great amount of silica.

Part used: whole herb .
Properties and use: diuretic, vulnerary; for broken bones, the silica is a useful substitute for calcium; also used for internal bleeding and ulcers.
Preparation: decoction, 1 teaspoon to ½ cup of water.
Dose: 1 tablespoon doses every 3-4 hours. *Caution: dangerous when used in excess.*

huckleberries — (*Vaccinium*, any species). The berries are edible, fresh and dried.

Part used: berries.
Properties and use: astringent; the dried berries are used for dropsy (edema), gravel, diarrhea, hemorrhage.

Preparation: infusion, 1 teaspoon dried berries to 1 cup of water.

Dose: take 1-2 cups per day, cold; hot infusion of berries for hemorrhage.

hydrophobia — See **rabies**.

hyperemia — Too much blood, or blood too thick, which causes circulatory disturbances, numbness, etc. This ailment is not readily recognized by orthodox physicians, although in the old days it was the reason for much bloodletting, sometimes carried too far. Sometimes caused by too much farinaceous food and dairy products; sometimes an inherent beefiness in make-up.

Treatment: acid fruit juices ad lib; Epsom salts laxative; reduce milk and cheese in diet, also reduce wheat products; **short fast**, repeated monthly for a time; reduce weight. *Herbal agent:* **yarrow**.

hyperventilation — Too much oxygen. Occurs in nervous and excitable persons who may be breathing quickly without realizing it. May resemble heart attack, with difficulty of concentration, numbness, perspiration. *Remedy:* breathe into a paper bag, in and out for five minutes during attack. This causes rebreathing of carbon dioxide, giving a more normal mixture to the blood.

hypoglycemia — See under **diabetes**.

hysteria — See **nervines**.

Self-review Questions for "H"

1. The agents listed in this section are hawthorn, herb Robert, hemlock tree, shagbark hickory, hollyhock, horehound, horsetail, and huckleberry. List the properties and parts used for each.

2. Which agents can be made up by using the expressed raw juice in a syrup or honey? What are the advantages of this method?

3. What is one of the unique properties of honey relevant for medicinal purposes?

4. What agent is *specific* for most kinds of heart disease and why?

5. What three references were made to dangerous plants? What cautions would occur to you if a friend offered you some "wild caraway seed"?

6. Vocabulary to define:

curative
dilated
endocarditis
farinaceous
fomentation
hyperemia
myocarditis
palliative
palpitation
thrombosis
vertigo

(Answers on page 210.)

joe pye weed

LESSON 12: "I" — "J" — "K" — "L"

increase weight — A balanced diet is needed, with more emphasis on protein and carbohydrates, and on eating light and more frequent meals if the stomach gets upset easily. *Herbal agent:* alfalfa tea, that contains most vitamins and minerals, helps to assimilate foods.

indigestion — See **aromatics and carminatives**. *Herbal agents:* especially **peppermint** and **chamomile**.

influenza —Also called grippe or flu. An acute infectious disease characterized by chills and fever, with pains in the joints.

Herbal agents: **boneset** is *specific.* This is very bitter, and only brown sugar seems to render it palatable. Start with standard infusion but only small, frequent doses—a 1/4 cup every 1/2 hour—to see how it goes. Too much will act as an emetic. Boneset is usually combined with **yarrow** and **peppermint** in proportions of 2 parts yarrow, 1 part boneset, 1/2 part peppermint. Always use hot. It should produce sweating.

Treatment: bed rest as long as fever lasts; **short fast**; fluids, including fruit juices and **shrubs**; vitamin C in massive doses: 2,000 mg first dose, then 1,000 mg every hour for four doses, then every three to four hours thereafter. (For children under 12, halve these doses.)

insects and parasites — (external only) *Herbal agents:*

- for nits and head lice—larkspur seed (cultivated as a garden ornamental)
- for mosquitoes and gnats—**pennyroyal**, especially the oil, combined with pine tar or other base (Pennyroyal oil can be bought from some drug stores or herbal supply houses. *Do not use internally.*)
- for houseflies—tansy; hang bundles of fresh tansy in a room or spread over open meat, food, etc.
- for moths—red cedar, **costmary, pennyroyal**; use dried herb in sachets in drawers or closets; renew often.

For internal parasites, see **anthelmintics**. Also **garlic**.

insomnia — See **nervines**. May be a symptom in overstimulation, nervous exhaustion, overwork, fatigue, asthma, anemia, endocrine malfunctions, various vitamin or mineral deficiencies, low blood pressure or high blood pressure, low blood sugar (especially if the person awakes in early morning and can't get back to sleep: try a glass of milk and a cracker).

Much insomnia that does not respond to nervines may be due not to mental stress but to physical malfunctions and may sometimes respond to circulatory stimulants (**yarrow**) or a brisk walk before bedtime or even to **emetics**.

Most persons know if they are awake because they're worried about something or worrying because they're awake. The former do not usually seek medical help, but if they do, should be encouraged to seek psychological or spiritual counseling.

Irish moss — (*Chrondus crispus*). A seaweed common on Atlantic shore; bleached by sun to creamy white.

Part used: whole herb.
Properties and use: demulcent, nutritive. Use for chronic coughs, bronchitis, irritations of bladder and kidneys, and for convalescence.
Preparation: blanc mange—1 tablespoon of Irish moss steeped in cold water for ten minutes; then boil in 3 pints of water or milk for 15 minutes. Strain, season to taste with sugar or honey, lemon juice or nutmeg. Allow to cool and set.
Dose: ad lib.

"J"

jaundice — A yellowed condition of the skin (and sometimes of whites of the eyes, sweat, and even milk) that indicates a disorder or disease of the liver and bile duct. *Herbal agents:* (sometimes referred to in old herbals as cholagogues) toadflax, **jewelweed**, chicory, **celandine, barberry** root and bark, **turtlehead (balmony)**, **St. Johnswort**, **hickory**, **ash**, **dandelion**. See under each entry. (Note that many of these have yellow flowers.)
There is also an infectious jaundice (hepatitis), sometimes locally epidemic. Use **alteratives**, and a building or convalescent **diet**.

jewelweed — (*Impatiens*, any species). *Balsaminaceae* family. Also called touch-me-not because ripe seed pods shatter at the slightest touch. Some species are cultivated as garden flowers. Very common in damp woods; succulent plant; flowers have spurs, some pale yellow, some spotted with madder.

Parts used: juice, whole herb.
Properties and use: caustic, styptic. Fresh juice applied immediately upon exposure to poison ivy; also externally for ringworm, eczema, warts, and corns.
Preparation: juice or infusion.
Dose: externally only, as needed.

Joe-Pye weed — (*Eupatoreum purpureum*). Composite family. Named after an Indian medicine man who used it extensively in colonial days. Also called gravel root and queen of the meadow. The leaves occur in whorls of five around the stem. Flowers are crushed-raspberry color, formed much like the flowers of boneset (that belongs to the same botanical genus). Both plants are usually in bloom together in damp places in late August, along with the blue candelabra of blue vervain.

Part used: root.

Properties and use: diuretic, stimulant to urinary system, mild tonic. *Specific* for urinary stone and gravel. Root is also *specific* for disorders and diseases of the urinary system—in males, spermatorrhea, prostate troubles, painful and scalding urination, urethral irritation, aching back, pelvic weakness; in women, may be used for the latter three or four conditions as well as amenorrhea. Do not use in pregnancy.

Preparation: standard decoction.

Dose: 1 tablespoon every 3 hours.

joints — pains in. *Herbal agents:* **boneset**, when due to influenza; **chickweed** for swollen finger joints. See **rheumatism** and **arthritis.**

Juneberry — See **shadbush.**

juniper — (*Juniperis communis*). A low evergreen sprawling shrub, common in dry pastures. Tends to go bare in center; prickly needles; blue berries that taste very piney or resinous. Dried berries are used as a flavoring in soups, stews, sauerkraut, and gin.

Part used: berries.

Properties and use: stimulating diuretic, emmenagogue (*do not use during pregnancy*). Juniper berries are said to help increase hydrochloric acid in stomach. Use for renal dropsy, cystic catarrh, renal congestions, typhoid fever. Not good in irritated conditions of the urinary tract. (For those cases, use Joe-Pye weed, combined with demulcents such as corn silk.) In gross excess can be irritating.

Preparation: 1 teaspoon dried crushed berries to 1 cup of water; infusion.

Dose: ½ cup, 3-4 times daily; or chew 1 or 2 dried berries daily.

"K"

kidneys, diseases of — Also see **stones** and **urinary** disorders, as well as **diuretics.** Unfavorable symptoms in kidney diseases are: temperature above 102° or below 97°; hard, quick pulse; difficult breathing, headache, vomiting, twitching, rigors, drowsiness, delirium or insomnia, decrease in quantity of urine, increasing dropsy (edema).

General treatment: Observe amount and character of the urine; amount and character of sweat; mental condition, especially drowsiness, delirium, or insomnia. Warmth is essential; acute cases should be nursed between blankets, warm clothing, hot water bottles, etc. A chill can be fatal.

Diet: In acute cases, milk is the staple, plus barley water, toast water, and bland drinks. Eggs are not allowed. This traditional diet is now under attack, and there seems to be much confusion on the subject. Nutritionists are finding better results along other lines, and it would be best to consult the latest findings on this subject.

Herbal agents: diuretics, especially **Joe-Pye weed, wild carrot, corn silk, trailing arbutus**, bearberry, **beech** leaves. See each.

"L"

lactation — *Herbal agents:* To increase milk supply use demulcents, especially **hollyhock, marsh mallow,** and all thistles (cook tender parts as greens; also drink water they are cooked in, or peel and eat stalks). Keep diet high in liquids, especially milk, yogurt, buttermilk, and hollyhock or mallow tea. To prepare for lactation, see **breasts**.

lady's bedstraw — (*Gallium verum*). Madder family. Common, weakly spreading plant with tiny leaves in whorls and clusters of creamy white flowers.

Part used: flowers, whole herb.
Properties and use: flowers are antispasmodic; herb is diuretic, astringent. Use for gravel, stone, and urinary diseases.
Preparation: infusion.
Dose: ½ cup, 3-4 times daily—cold for urinary ailments, warm as antispasmodic.

lady's-slipper — (*Cypripedium*, any species). Orchid family, found in boggy places. Not too common; protected by most states. When collected in moderate amounts without depleting the source, medicinal use does not threaten extinction as much as draining and bulldozing the natural habitat. It is possible to get plants from a botanical house to avoid the endangered species problem.

Part used: root.
Properties and use: pure, relaxing nervine, antispasmodic. Use for delirium of typhoid; restlessness and insomnia, especially in students, ministers, and office workers under mental strain; in hysteria, chorea, nervous headache, insanity from nervous irritation. In childbirth, relieves rigid cervix. Not to be used in cold,

slow cases. For postpartum hemorrhage, combine with **trillium (bethroot)** or **viburnum**. Forms an ingredient in many herbal nervines.

Preparation: decoction—5 tablespoons of ground dried root in 2 cups of water.

Dose: take 1 tablespoon per hour until preparation is gone. *Caution: do not overdose.*

laryngitis — An affliction of the larynx connected with an upper respiratory infection. *Herbal agents:* the *specific* is **garlic** syrup, made by grinding up 1 whole garlic bulb in 1 pint of honey and taking teaspoonful doses, if stomach permits, so frequently as to use the whole preparation in 24 hours. Also, **hollyhock**, **everlasting**, and **astringents**.

lemon balm — (*Melissa officinalis*). *Labiatiae* family. Semihardy perennial (mulch in winter) to be cultivated in the garden. Also called bee balm because bees like it, and it is often planted near hives.

Part used: whole herb.

Properties and use: contains iron, camphor, and a volatile oil; antispasmodic, carminative, diaphoretic. Used for colds, fever, headaches.

Preparation: infusion—2 teaspoons to 1 cup of water; give warm, sweetened with honey. This is an excellent substitute for hot lemonade in colds.

Dose: 1 cup every 3-4 hours and at bedtime.

leucorrhea — A white discharge from the vagina. *Herbal agents:* **white water lily** root (internally, and externally as suppository or douche); also **sumac** bark, **Solomon's seal**, **pine** bark, **self-heal**, **trillium (bethroot)**, **yarrow**, bur marigold. For more serious fungal and parasitic vaginal infections, some have had good results with a douche of a strong decoction of reindeer moss. See **lichens**.

leukemia — Cancer of the blood; increase of white blood cells. *Herbal agent:* Experiments seem to indicate that periwinkle (*Vinca major*), a hardy plant raised in gardens, is *specific*. But the whole plant must be used over a long period of time. Some herbalists tend to think that one factor of leukemia, especially in children, is indiscriminate use of X-rays, especially of the bones. Adele Davis says that many cases of leukemia occur in children whose mothers have been X-rayed before childbirth.

lichens — Nonflowering plants that are actually a combination, in symbiotic relationship, of a fungus and an alga. Lichens grow on rocks, trees, and poor acid soils, and are "pioneer plants" that prepare the soil for other plants. Lichens may be used as starvation foods (especially rock tripe and reindeer moss) but should be boiled or roasted first, as they all contain much acid that they use in dissolving their rock bed to make soil for themselves. Certain lichens, especially lung lichen, can be used for yeast in a kind of sourdough starter. Others are used as dyes that demand no mordant. Lichens of the *usnea* genus contain antibiotics similar to penicillin, for external use. Infusion of reindeer moss is useful as a douche in fungal infections of the vaginal canal.

lily-of-the-valley — (*Convallaria majalis*). Lily family. Found both wild and cultivated. Small, white bells above a pair of dark green, oval leaves. Strongly perfumed.

Part used: whole herb.

Properties and use: cardiac agent, similar to digitalis but safer because it is noncumulative and nonpoisonous; causes retardation of heart action. Used for tobacco heart, pericarditis, mitral insufficiency, asthmatic breathing from feeble heart, valvular heart disease. Quantity of urine is much decreased and edema is promptly absorbed.

Preparation: infusion—1 tablespoon of herb in 2 cups of boiling water.

Dose: 1 tablespoon, 4 times daily. Or 5-20 drops of extract, from reputable supplier, in water. Also in homeopathic preparation.

linden — See **basswood**.

liver, diseases of — See **jaundice**. *Hepatic herbal agents:* toadflax (butter-and-eggs), liverwort (hepatica), **dandelion**, chicory, **turtlehead** (balmony), **barberry, docks**.

lockjaw — See **tetanus**.

lumbago — An affliction of the lower back (lumbar region). Urinary agents sometimes help, especially **juniper** berries. Otherwise, as for **arthritis**.

lungs — See also **asthma, bronchitis, pneumonia**. *Herbal agents:* balm of Gilead buds (balsam poplar), **lungwort, Solomon's seal** (especially for bleeding from the lungs), liverwort, hyssop, **hollyhock**, chicory, balsam fir.

lungwort — (*Sticta pulmonaria*). A lichen, in rosettes up to one foot across, pitted like lung tissue, found on limestone rocks and on deciduous trees in colder regions.

Part used: whole herb.
Properties and use: pectoral, for coughs, lung complaints, asthma.
Preparation: infusion (or combine in a syrup).
Dose: wineglassful, ad lib.

Note: This lichen combines a yeast with an alga. To use as a yeast substitute, soak 1 rosette (complete lichen) in 2 cups of warm water to which 1/4 cup of flour and a pinch of sugar have been added. Store in a warm place for 36 hours, or until it is somewhat bubbly and a yeasty aroma is noticed. Strain out the lichen; to batter add another 1/2 cup of flour, enough additional warm (not hot) water to equal 2 cups total batter, and let bubble overnight. Then add 2 cups of warm water and 2 cups of flour, leaving overnight again. In the morning, store a 1/2 cup of the batter in the refrigerator to use as starter for next time. Make bread according to sourdough recipes with the rest.

lycopodium — (Club moss). A running ground pine. The variety *L. clavatum* is the one most often used and one of the most common. The spores are carried on raised yellow clubs and contain a fine yellow dust that is antiseptic. It is used for excoriated surfaces, diaper rash, prickly heat, and chafing. The powder is also useful as a tinder in starting fires from flint and steel, and was used in early days of photography for flash pictures.

Self-review Questions for "I" through "L"

1. The herbal agents listed in this section were Irish moss, jewelweed, Joe-Pye weed, juniper, lady's bedstraw, lady's-slipper, lemon balm, lily-of-the-valley, lungwort, and lycopodium. List the properties and parts used for each.

2. Which agent in this section is useful in disorders of the lungs?

3. Which agent in this lesson should be used with caution?

4. Which herb is said to be safer than a common heart medication, and why?

5. Which herb in this lesson is found cultivated more often than wild?

6. What is a lichen?

7. What plants called by names including the word "moss" are not mosses at all? What are they?

8. Which *specifics* were mentioned in this lesson for what conditions?

9. Vocabulary to define:

digitalis
douche
excoriated
madder
mitral
mordant
pericarditis
rigors

(Answers on page 211.)

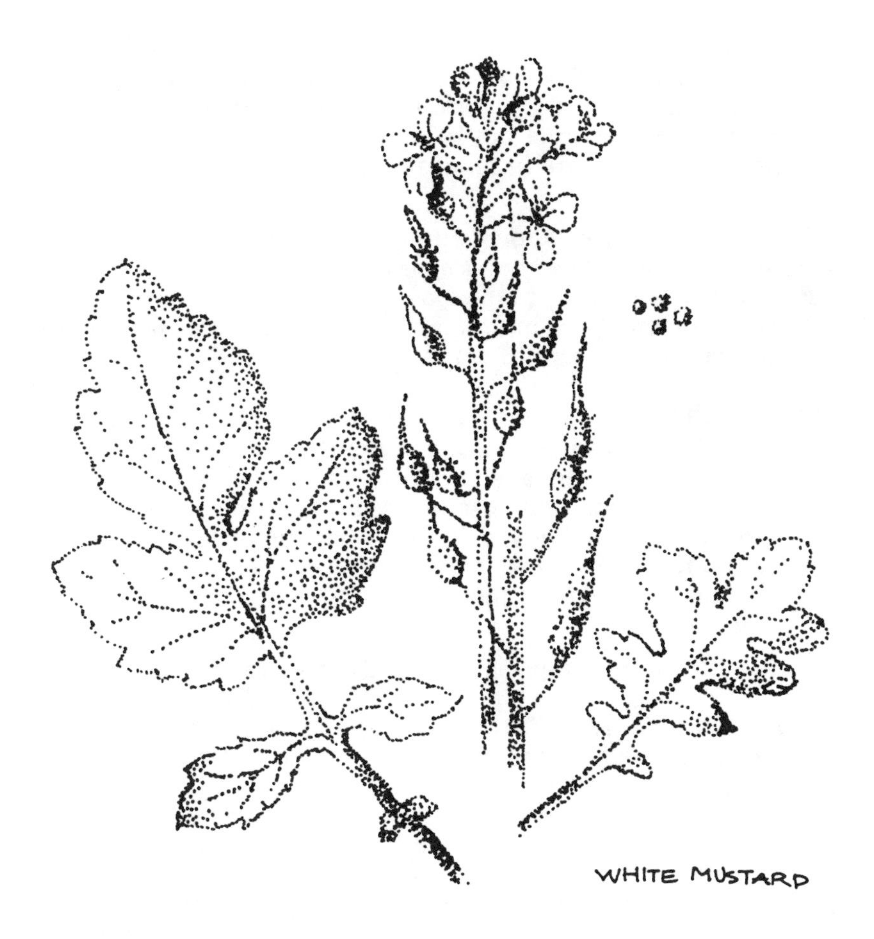

LESSON 13: "M"

malaria — A disease transmitted by certain mosquitoes, usually in tropical countries. Experimentally, sunflowers planted near the house in miasmic places have rid the environment of these mosquitoes.

Herbal agents: for centuries the remedy has been quinine, also a tropical product. Some **antiperiodics** can be used for local quinine substitutes that are safer and have not the side-effects of quinine. These are **aspen** bark, **alder** bark, black willow bark and catkins, cherry bark, **apple** bark, and **sunflower** leaves.

male fern —(*Aspidium felix-mas*). Fronds 1-5 feet high, arranged like a shuttlecock. Rootstalks are dug in autumn when fronds wither, and then dried. Use within the year, as they lose strength. Lady fern is a substitute but is milder and much more common. Male fern is rather rare in some areas.

Part used: root.

Properties and use: anthelmintic; this is still the *specific* for tapeworm in the *U.S. Pharmacopoeia.*

Preparation and dose: 1 tablespoon of powdered root in honeyed water on an empty stomach. Follow with a cathartic. Repeat another day if necessary. *Caution: do not exceed dosage.*

marsh mallow —(*Althea officinalis*). Mallow family. A native of Europe, this has been naturalized in the U.S. in salt marshes from Massachusetts to Virginia, and at scattered sites inland. There are several related species that can be used more or less interchangeably: the cultivated hollyhock, the common mallow (a garden weed), and the rose mallow, cultivated or escaped in waste places. The true marsh mallow is the best to use, if obtainable. It can be grown in gardens.

Part used: the root especially, but also the leaves, flowers, and buds.

Properties and use: The root is demulcent, emollient, and somewhat nutrient. It contains starch, much mucilage, pectin, oil, sugar, asparagine. Used especially in irritations and inflammations of the urinary and respiratory systems. The powdered or crushed fresh roots make a good poultice to remove inflammations and infections of wounds, burns, boils, etc. A mild infusion makes a good eyewash. It also enriches milk of nursing mothers and promotes its flow. Use in coughs, bronchitis, asthma, laryngitis, and urinary infections.

Preparation: in decoction—1 teaspoon of root to 1 cup of water; or cut up root (2 tablespoons) and let it stand in 1 cup of cold water for half an hour (it becomes mucilaginous on standing). For leaves, flowers, and buds, use 2 tablespoons to 1 cup of water as infusion; steep 5 minutes.

Dose: 1-2 cups a day, in small frequent doses.

Note: This is the source of our marshmallow confections. Originally the roots would be boiled up with sugar or honey, then allowed to set and gel. The pieces were cut up into lozenges and rolled in slippery elm powder or confectioners' sugar. The marshmallows sold these days are usually a mixture of flour, gelatin, and egg white with sugar, and have no marsh mallow in them (nor any nutritional virtues, either!).

meadowsweet — (*Spirea ulmaria*). Rose family. A shrubby plant with woody stems and spikes of small, pink apple-blossom-like flowers. Common on dry hillsides and roadsides in northern areas, but in damper situations than the steeplebush that it resembles.

Part used: whole herb.
Properties and use: antacid, astringent, tonic. Contains almost all vitamins and trace minerals. An excellent diet supplement. Used for diarrhea, tonic for anemia, convalescence; a major preparation for stomach ulcers. It can also be used at any time as a dietary supplement, especially for calcium, magnesium, and iron.
Preparation: as a tea, sweetened with honey; for a tonic, make a strong decoction and add equal parts of wine. Or use meadowsweet beer, below.
Dose: ad lib.

Meadowsweet beer is very tonic; it contains iron and all the various vitamins and minerals of the several plants. Take 1 cup each of the following dried herbs: meadowsweet, raspberry leaves, agrimony, and nettles. Boil these in 2 gallons of water for 15 minutes. Strain. Add 2 pounds of sugar or honey. Let stand until nearly cool, then bottle and cap securely with root beer capper. This recipe usually does not need yeast, especially if some fresh plants (nettles) are included and if it is being made in warm weather. However, if needed, add 1/4 of a teaspoon of dried yeast dissolved in 1/2 cup of warm (not hot) water; stir well before bottling. This amount makes 18-20 of the 12-ounce soda bottles. Let stand in a warm place for 24 hours; then store in a cool place. Ready to use in one week. Watch out when opening after some time.

measles, German —Symptoms: swelling and tenderness of lymph glands, slight fever, and malaise. Incubation 7-12 days. Rash on face and neck, spreading to limbs and trunk, usually lasting three days. Usually mild, but women in the first three months of pregnancy should avoid contact, as it sometimes results in congenital deformations. One attack protects for life, and infants seem to be immune up to one year of age. Possible ear complications occur but are rare.

Herbal agents: **calendula** flowers combined with **raspberry** leaves and/or **yarrow**. Soothing lotion or powder, such as **chickweed**, **calendula**, **slippery elm**, may be applied to the rash.

measles, red — Epidemics usually come in January and June. Symptoms: acute onset, sore throat, fever. Rash appears on the fourth day, behind ears, on the face, and extends downward. Small red spots run together to form patches, fading the seventh day. Complications: involvement of eyes or chest. Also, the affected person will become highly susceptible to other infections—tuberculosis, pneumonia, ear infections and others—as the rash begins to fade. The development of new symptoms of fever, malaise, or pain after the rash begins to fade, should alert to the possibility of complications.

Treatment: strict confinement to bed until rash clears up. Darken room if the eyes are weak; treat for chest symptoms if these appear. Protect the patient from cold or dampness for at least two weeks after an attack. Use lotions or powder on the rash, as above. Liquid diet or very soft foods, with herbal preparations as above.

melilot — (*Melilotus alba* and *officinalis*). White and yellow sweet clover; legume family. Lines roadsides in midsummer. Tall, clover-leafed plant with very sweet-smelling blossoms.

Part used: whole herb. *Danger: when drying melilot, care must be taken that it does not mold.* Moldy plants develop *dicoumarin* that can cause fatal hemorrhaging. This is the substance used in rat poison.

Properties and use: aromatic, emollient, carminative. It also has an antithrombotic agent and is a *specific* for embolisms or to prevent them if threatened and likely.

Preparation: infusion.

Dose: 1 cupful every 4 hours; continue 1 cup daily even after symptoms have subsided, until normal health is restored.

menopause — Menopause most often occurs in a woman's fifth decade of life. Childbearing functions and menstruation cease, a natural and expected change. Some women barely notice menopause. For others, there may be distressing symptoms caused by the imperfect shifting of endocrine secretions, metabolic balance, and eliminative processes, symptoms that have physical causes and are not "all in the head." Changes in blood pressure and cholesterol are common at this time. There may be a variety of physical and nervous complaints: headaches, dizziness, feelings of suffocation, palpitations, constipation, variable appetite, weakness, fear of impending evil (undefined), irritability, hysteria, "bad" feeling in the head, ringing in the ears, specks or sparks before the eyes, unsteady gait, wandering neuralgias or arthralgias, flushes, and sweats.

Part of the distress in menopause arises because the menstrual blood in women serves a secondary function, that of ridding the body of impurities. When this flow ceases, the general circulatory system is burdened, as well as the kidneys, bowels, and skin; all have an extra elimination job to do. This is the reason for many of the circulatory symptoms in the menopause (hot flashes, itching and tingling, dizziness and insomnia). It is also the reason why women after menopause are more subject to cancer, heart disease, and especially arthritis; uneliminated toxins accumulate in the body. This is the time—especially if the woman is at all overweight—for a good series of cleansing fasts. It is also important to reduce the diet (to account for a decrease in the body's changing needs) and to include more fresh air, calm exercise (walking is best, even two miles daily or more, but regularly), gardening, plus more attention to bathing and elimination.

Although the disorders of menopause are not in the mind, they can prey upon the mind, and this is why it is essential for a woman to have plenty of varied and healthful mental occupations, especially if this is a time of life when her family is grown up and needs her less. Yet, too many women take on a ceaseless round of volunteer and community activities or seek job advancement that puts too much of a strain on the nervous system when it is already preoccupied with the changes taking place. Menopause is a good time for the mild, outdoor occupations listed above, for more attention to prayer and meditation, as the woman often passes through a kind of crisis of identity similar to adolescence: Where do I go from here? It is indeed a "change of life" in more ways than one, and properly handled can be an open door to a new life.

It is almost certain that in many menopausal women, the symptoms that show up are the result of a lifetime of improper diet, and at least of a present improper diet. The major item needing attention will be calcium. At the cessation of the menses, with the diminution of endocrine secretions such as estrogen, calcium is not so well assimilated as before. By this time of life, women tend to take in less calcium, iron, and other minerals, as well as less B-vitamins. Serious deficiencies may result.

Diet: A program of diet supplementation should include added calcium and magnesium in the form of tablets, bone meal or added dairy products—milk, yogurt, buttermilk, or cheese. Vitamins D and C are needed to assimilate the calcium. (**Motherwort** contains high amounts of calcium chloride.) At the same time, vitamin E helps to control flushing and night sweats. The homeopathic *12 Tissue Salts* are recommended for menopause: three pills, four times daily.

Herbal agents: The herbal *specific* for most of these disorders is **motherwort**. However, this agent can greatly increase menstrual flow, so women who have not yet ceased menses must be warned of this and may have to weigh the relative advantages and disadvantages. **Motherwort** is especially recommended for the skipping heartbeats often occurring as a result of endocrine imbalance.

menstruation — disorders of:

• amenorrhea, absence of or obstructed menses. *Herbal agents:* See **emmenagogues**, especially **pennyroyal** and **peppermint** (under **mints**), and **catnip**. *Not to be used in pregnancy.*

• dysmenorrhea, painful menstruation with cramps, nausea, etc. *Herbal agents:* same as above, combined with **raspberry**. Standard infusion, hot, a cupful every half hour at the start of distress, or the day before if time is known. Stay warm, avoid extrastrenuous exercise, but get more exercise between periods.

• menorrhagia, profuse menstruation, especially at the menopause. *Herbal agents:* See **astringents**, especially **raspberry** leaves, **viburnum** (crampbark), lady's mantle, **Solomon's seal**, loosestrife, **trillium**, and **white water lily** root. Also increase calcium intake.

mesenteritis — Inflammation of the tissue that holds the intestines in place. *Herbal agents:* **Strawberry** leaves and **agrimony**.

migraine and nervous headache — Good results in migraine have been had with supplements of magnesium and vitamin B-6. Old-time herbal theory insisted that an excess of carbohydrates is sometimes responsible. I know of one person subject to migraine headaches who was instantly relieved by emetics. On the other hand, there is some indication migraines may be connected with low-blood-sugar attacks. There is strong evidence of food sensitivities or allergies, as well. More research needs to be done along these lines.

Suggested regimen:

- thorough cleansing of system (purgatives, laxatives).
- short fast (then limit carbohydrates, especially refined foods).
- daily dry friction rub in the morning with rough towel or loofah, or cold sponge bath; nightly warm bath.
- daily walk of two miles, or outdoor work in the garden.

Herbal agents: See **nervines. Betony** is *specific.* Also try inhaling **vinegar** fumes. Of use are **skullcap, valerian**, preparations containing silica (**horsetail**), **chamomile**, and **dogwood** bark.

milkweed — (*Asclepias syriaca*). Milkweed family. Common roadside plant with opposite, smooth oval leaves, and a milky juice. *Caution: Other plants of related families are dangerous.* Heavy head of rose-purple flowers, very sweet, followed by pods of downy seeds. One of our most useful plants. The floss is used as kapok in life preservers/jackets and for pillows; it also can be spun. The young shoots or tips, flower buds while green, and young pods can all be boiled and eaten for greens. (Best to throw off first water.)

Parts used: root, flowers.

Properties and use: diuretic, emetic, purgative (in larger doses). Cold infusions soothing to genito-urinary tract; gallstones; relieves aching back (kidneys). Hot infusion of flowers is used for nasal catarrh, cough, fever, asthma. Flowers, gathered when dewy, boiled down for syrup and strained; ad lib for coughs.

Preparation: infusion for root—1 teaspoon of powdered root in 1 cup of boiling water. *Can be dangerous, especially to children.*

Dose: ½ cup, cold, 3 times daily, for gallstones, edema.

mineral content — of some common plants (and foods), with emphasis on those in this course:

• calcium—lambs' quarters, amaranth (both called pigweed), chives, cleavers, borage, arrowroot, dandelion root and greens, meadowsweet, nettles, plantain, sorrel, shepherd's-purse, motherwort, silverweed, Irish moss, kelp, yellow dock, turnip greens, watercress, milk, egg shells, and canned salmon (bones)

• fluoride—garlic, watercress.

• iodine—seaweeds, Irish moss, garlic, calendula blossoms, asparagus, cabbage, sarsaparilla.

• iron—burdock (root, stems, and leaves), meadowsweet, mullein, parsley, silverweed, nettle, strawberry leaves, yellow dock, watercress, yeast, molasses, liver, peas, and beans.

• magnesium—seaweeds, dandelion leaves, black willow bark, kale, meadowsweet, yellow dock, silverweed, parsley, mullein, peppermint, watercress, wintergreen, nuts, corn, rice, wheat, dried beans, dried fruits.

• phosphorous—sweet flag, caraway seeds, sunflower seeds, chickweed, garlic, Irish moss, apple, borage, sorrel, calendula flowers, watercress, yeast, wheat germ, sardines, rye flour, liver, nuts, dried peas, and beans.

• potassium—birch bark, borage, sweet flag, chamomile, comfrey, dandelion, nettle, oak bark, parsley, yarrow, apples, elderberries, nearly all vegetables, especially potatoes.

• silicon—horsetail, skins of fruit and of vegetables, and seeds.

• sodium—(combines with chlorine for salt) black willow, cleavers, meadowsweet, nettles, okra, shepherd's-purse.

• sulphur—coltsfoot, garlic, meadowsweet, mullein, shepherd's-purse, silverweed, nettle, okra, watercress.

• manganese—celery seed, skunk cabbage, peppermint, cress, fruits, and seeds.

mints — Labiatiae family. This particular group of labiates are notable for their very aromatic, volatile oils that make them popular in culinary uses as well as medicinally. Infuse all mints in a covered vessel; don't boil, as the volatile oils go off in the steam.

• **peppermint** (*Mentha piperita*). Leaves are stalked, smooth; stems turn reddish, especially in older plants. Grows best in damp places, near streams. Distinct peppery taste.

Part used: whole herb.
Properties and use: contains menthol, an antiseptic; antispasmodic, aromatic, nervine, carminative, emmenagogue. Use for stomach upsets, especially with gas; sudden attacks of wind with dizziness and headache (especially in children); colic; vomiting; milder forms of chills.
Preparation: infusion, 1 teaspoon to 1 cup of water.
Dose: ½ cup, ad lib.

• **spearmint** (*Mentha spicata*). Leaves have no stalks and are more hairy or downy. Most use is culinary.

Part used: whole herb.
Properties and use: similar to peppermint but more diuretic and less emmenagogue. Can be used in small amounts for nausea of pregnancy, combined with **raspberry** leaves.
Preparation: infusion.
Dose: as above.

• **pennyroyal** (*Hedeoma pulegiodes* — formerly *Mentha pulegium* in old books). A very small, very odoriferous mint, common to dry pastures and ledges, but difficult to find unless crushed. Leaves have short stalks, lilac flowers in whorls at axils of leaves, not in terminal spikes as in the others above. The standard pennyroyal is imported (check seed houses), but the American variety, found wild, can be substituted in all cases.

Part used: whole herb.
Properties and use: contains oil of pulegium, that drives away insects. Also an emmenagogue (*do not use in pregnancy*). Good for menstrual cramps in girls. Also good for breaking up a cold, for

tardy eruptive diseases (to bring out rash), heatstroke, colic, and feverishness in infants.

Preparation: for internal use, infusion, tepid or cool; best preparation for repelling mosquitoes and black flies in the northern woods consists of oil of pennyroyal incorporated into a pine tar base for a body varnish (oil may be obtained in a drug store or herbal supply house). *Do not use oil internally.*

Dose: for infusion, as above.

• **wild mint** (*Mentha arvensis*). Very common in wet low locations. Probably can be used for all of the above mints but is stronger. Large doses may be emetic.

miscarriage —When miscarriage threatens, put the person to bed, elevate the foot of the bed if possible, provide a bedpan, and continue total bed care until all flow has ceased. Limit visitors, keeping the woman quiet and free from excitement. Do not overfeed, and keep bowels open by use of prunes, figs and herb teas (that do not contain senna or other strong cathartics).

Herbal agents: **black haw** (Viburnum prunifolium) is *specific.* Use 1 teaspoon to 1 cup of boiling water. If flow increases, give 3 or 4 times daily; otherwise, ½ cup, twice a day. Continue to take 1 cup a day for a week or two after flow ceases. For women who habitually miscarry, start on black haw as soon as pregnant, ½ cup twice daily, and continue through the sixth month. Then cease taking it; if taken through the ninth month, difficulty going into labor may result as it is a uterine sedative. *Do not use excessive doses of black haw, as excess can cause over-sedation.* If this occurs, even on normal dose, stop treatment for a day, then resume on lower strength or dosage until tolerated level is reached.

Raspberry leaves should also be taken throughout pregnancy and should be continued and increased if miscarriage threatens (cramps, bearing down pains, or show of blood). Can be combined with the black haw, if desired.

If black haw is unavailable, use crampbark (highbush cranberry) or any other viburnum locally available. (See under **viburnum**.) Use the bark of the branches, gathered in winter. Also, **squawvine** (partridgeberry) can be used.

If miscarriage actually occurs, use **trillium** (bethroot) to reduce after-bleeding—1 tablespoon to 2 cups of boiling water, steep and stir. Use 1 wineglassful every 15 minutes until pint is gone. Be sure to get powdered sediment evenly stirred up in the dose each time, as this is valuable. Do not make up another pint until 6-8 hours later. If hemorrhage is out of control or not abating, be sure to call a doctor. *Do not* use trillium for threatened miscarriage, as it contracts the uterus too much.

mononucleosis — (Not found by that name in old herb books, but it may be comparable to what they called glandular fever.) An infectious disease that often affects young people in schools, nurses' training homes, etc., when there is general fatigue; sometimes appears in epidemic proportions. Not common after age 35. Symptoms: swollen lymph glands and usually some fever; flu-like symptoms, headache, and chills. Great fatigue is characteristic of the disease (or perhaps a contributing cause), and sometimes hangs on for months. The spleen is sometimes involved—enlarged and painful. Additional complications can include jaundice, heart involvement, and meningitis. Modern medicine has no specific for this disease but suggests rest and a building diet.

Herbal agents: an astringent gargle in the early stage of a sore throat. Periwinkle (*Vinca major*) is used when there is an increase of mononuclear blood cells. Spleenwort, a family of ferns, is used if the spleen is involved. For the general symptoms—alteratives, especially **lady's bedstraw**, **yellow dock**, **burdock**, and **red clover** blossoms give good results; antiperiodics (**yarrow** or grippe mix) to bring down the fever if high.

Additional treatment: Bed rest during acute stage. Fluids, especially fruit and vegetable juices. Vitamin C in massive doses (up to 1,000 mg every 2-4 hours for 24 hours, even by injection) have produced amazing results and can do no harm. Do not allow the person to return to school or normal activities until all fatigue is past. This is a good time for a change of air or scene.

moth repellant — *Herbal agents:* red cedar chips or wood in chests; **costmary**, wormwood, **everlasting**, **melilot**, or tansy—all or in any combination, dried, and made into sachet balls to keep in closets and drawers. Renew frequently. Keeping clothing out in the open or in a closet where they will be constantly disturbed is frequently a good solution.

motherwort — (*Leonurus cardiaca*). *Labiatiae* family but with no minty flavor. A tall, attractive plant in waste places, sometimes mistakenly called nettles because the calyx containing the seeds is very prickly. Basal leaves are palmate; stem leaves are toothed and oblong.

Part used: whole herb. This herb does not store well; it loses strength rapidly. Get a fresh source each year.

Properties and use: cardiac tonic, antispasmodic, nervine, emmenagogue. A *specific* for palpitations of the heart caused by endocrine or functional nervous disorders in men or women. Can be taken routinely as a mild tea, especially in the elderly, as a mild cardiac tonic. *Not to be used in pregnancy or in women subject to heavy flow at menstrual periods, as it tends to induce uterine bleeding.* It is the agent of choice for the various nervous disorders of the menopause, keeping in mind the caution just mentioned. Also used in fevers attended by delirium, or in anemic or chlorotic nervousness and restlessness.

Preparation: infusion; this is one agent that makes up nicely as a syrup, using the expressed juice (put through a juicer) added to liquid honey in proportions of 3 tablespoons of green, fresh juice to 1 cup of honey. *Caution: this is strong.*

Dose: 1 teaspoon of syrup in ½ glass of water, 3 times daily until symptoms subside. For elderly, use half strength.

mouthwash — See **astringents**. The standard herbal mouthwash is goldenseal, but this is rare and expensive. Instead use: **goldthread**, **silverweed**, **cinquefoil**, **strawberry** leaves.

mullein — (*Verbascum thapsus*). Figwort family. Very common plant of dry pastures and roadsides. Flannel-like leaves form a rosette on the ground in early summer, followed by a tall woody stalk bearing yellow blossoms.

Part used: leaves.

Properties and use: anodyne, astringent, alterative; use for diarrhea in adults. Also for swollen glands, whooping cough, asthma, hay fever.

Preparation: 1 leaf or 1 teaspoon of crushed leaves simmered or even boiled in 1 pint of milk (boiled milk is binding to bowels); let steep 15-20 minutes.

Dose: ½ cup every 15-20 minutes until gone. If necessary, make another batch, and take a dose every hour. Do not make a third batch for a while, as there may be a delayed reaction to the first doses. If a couple of days on mullein does not stop diarrhea, switch to an astringent of the rose family: **blackberry**, **meadowsweet**, steeplebush, or **cinquefoil**.

Externally—boiled in vinegar—use mullein for sprains, bruises, soreness of chest, swollen joints, rheumatism. (Use 1 tablespoon of powdered leaves to 2 cups of vinegar.) Expressed juice of the green leaves, mixed with lard, suet, butter, or cream, makes a salve for hemorrhoids (piles). Oil, for earaches, can be extracted from the blossoms. See **St. Johnswort**.

mumps — An infectious disease, usually of children, sometimes in epidemics. Symptoms: pain in glands of jaw, with swelling and fever. Fever may go up to 108° in adults, with serious results. Complications may include the subsequent infection of sex glands, possibly resulting in sterility, or acute affliction of the pancreas.

Herbal agents: warm poultices of **mullein** leaves to the glands. Infusion of **raspberry**, **calendula**, **yarrow**, and **everlasting**. Drink juices only, or follow **short fast** regimen until fever is gone.

For complications: in the brain—**skullcap**; in the pancreas—periwinkle; in the sex glands—pulsatilla (not in our course, but available in homeopathic preparations).

mustard — (*Sinapsis alba* and *nigra*). *Cruciferae* family. Many plants are called mustard in this family, but the specific varieties mentioned are those used medicinally. The greens of these and other mustard species can be boiled and eaten. There are no dangerous members of this family.

Part used: The seeds, ground into powder, are used as the familiar condiment in cooking, but also in the following ways.
Properties and use: antiscorbutic, stimulant; powerful local irritant (ginger is less drastic and usually as effective) for causing blisters in diseases such as arthritis; in a foot bath, to aid circulation after a chill; internally as an emetic in poisoning cases.
Dose: for emetic, 1 teaspoon or less in a glass of warm water.

Self-review Questions for "M"

(Note: This is one of the most important lessons in the course. You may wish to reread various portions carefully.)

1. The herbal agents in this lesson were male fern, meadowsweet, melilot, milkweed, mints, motherwort, mullein, and mustard. List the properties and parts used for each.

2. Name five *specifics* mentioned in this lesson and the conditions for which they are used.

3. What two plants were mentioned as milder and safer substitutes for two of the plants in this lesson?

4. What were the three ferns named in this lesson? (You may want to check a botany book or encyclopedia to find the major difference between ferns and the other plants we usually use.)

5. Which two conditions in this lesson require strict bed rest as part of the care?

6. List at least five remedies (both herbal and nonherbal) for difficulties of menopause.

7. What condition in this lesson has no specific treatment by modern medicine but does have herbal remedies?

8. What herb(s) in this lesson appeared most frequently on the mineral list?

9. What herbs might serve as a replacement for table salt?

10. Vocabulary to define:

arthralgia
axil
calyx
chlorosis
congenital
flush
miasmic
neuralgia
palmate

(Answers on page 212.)

Additional suggested project: Using an encyclopedia or other good source book, list on a separate sheet each of the minerals given, tell what it does for the body, and the minimum daily requirement.

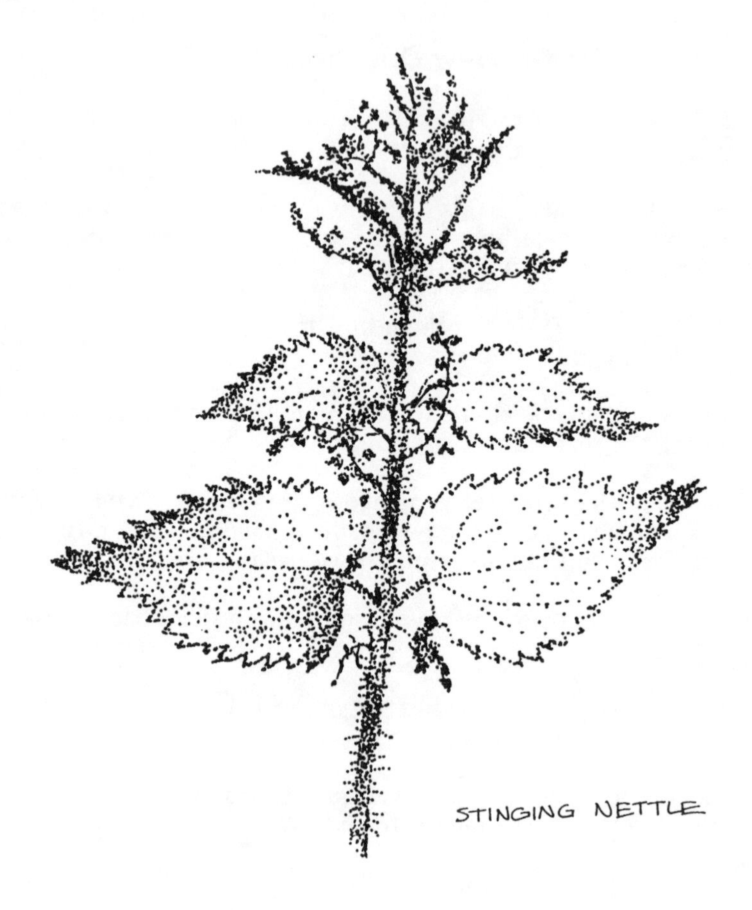

LESSON 14: "N" — "O" — "P" — "Q"

narcotics — Substances that deaden or kill nervous tissue; sometimes habit-forming and personality-destroying. Antidotes: vomiting (use emetics) and caffeine (including cola drinks). Mild herbal "narcotics" are not habit-forming, have no side-effects, and do not kill nerve cells. Avoid overdose that may produce symptoms of oversedation.

We do not include any herbs which are actually narcotic in this course. Use **nervines**.

nasal membranes — For stuffy dry nose, hay fever, and nasal polyps, effective *herbal agents:* decoction of **lungwort**; spray or bathe nose. Also **yarrow** internally.

nasturtiums — (*Tropaeolum majus*). *Cruciferae* family. Cultivated annual.

Parts used: flowers, leaves, and seeds.
Properties and use: antiscorbutic; contains many vitamins and minerals.
Preparation: used mostly in salads; seeds may be pickled in vinegar and used as capers.

nausea — *Herbal agents:* **peppermint, spearmint, wild mint,** cloves, **sage, raspberry.**

For nausea and vomiting due to intestinal virus: let it proceed until the stomach is emptied. Then, to prevent low blood sugar symptoms and useless retching, use the following: 1 teaspoon of peppermint leaves (dried); 1/8 teaspoon of ground cloves; 1 teaspoon of sugar. Grind these together in a mortar and pestle until very fine. Put into a cup and add very hot water. Let the patient sip slowly, warm, as much as can be tolerated.

Nausea in pregnancy: use mints, preferably **spearmint**, in trace only, for flavor; combine with **raspberry** leaves, **red osier** bark, or **poplar** bark.

nervines — These herbs tend to build up nervous tissue. (Also use B-vitamins and minerals such as calcium, magnesium, and potassium.) Common useful nervines include **catnip**, sweet **chamomile, skullcap, valerian, yarrow, motherwort**, blue **vervain, lady slipper**, and **oats**. See Lesson 3.

nervous headache — See **migraine.** *Herbal agents:* See **oats, lady slipper, betony, rosemary, speedwell.**

nervous irritation — *Herbal agents:* **oats, lady slipper.**

nettles — (*Urtica dioica*). Nettle family. A common weed that has stinging hairs on glands underside the leaf; may cause a serious eruption on susceptible individuals. Antidote: as soon as being stung, apply crushed, juicy green leaves of any type (except poison ivy and nettles!). In spite of this drawback, nettles are among the most useful plants we have. Nettles contain iron, other minerals, and many vitamins. Nettle greens in spring make an excellent potherb; the stinging properties disappear in hot water. Dried leaves added to tea make a nutritious supplement. The fibers, retted like flax, are spun and woven into cloth.

Part used: whole herb.
Properties and use: antiscorbutic, tonic, and antiseptic; arrests hemorrhages from any source, especially stomach.
Preparation: infusion, 3 tablespoons to 1 cup of water.
Dose: wineglassful, 3 times daily; more often—every hour—for hemorrhaging.

neuralgia — *Herbal agents:* **valerian** is *specific*, especially for facial neuralgia. Also **lady slipper, chamomile** (both internally and in hot packs), **betony**. See each entry.

neuritis — See **arthritis.** *Herbal agents:* **St. Johnswort** externally (in oil). Infusion of **red clover, burdock, skullcap, yellow dock**. Use B-vitamins.

nightmares — *Herbal agents:* **catnip, chamomile**. Especially suitable for children.

nipples, sore — *Herbal agents:* **elder** flowers, **St. Johnswort** oil.

To prepare for nursing, use a **white oak** or **hemlock** bark wash during the ninth month of pregnancy, followed by a rub of **castor oil**. Do not use while nursing.

nosebleed — *Herbal agents:* **yarrow** (make a strong infusion) or lemon juice. (Spray it up the nose or use a dropper.) Apply pressure to the back of the neck and pinch the bridge of the nose. Ice packs are also good. A plug of dry **sphagnum moss** would also be useful.

"O"

oaks — (*Quercus*, any species). Common trees. Leaves have lobes or points. Acorn fruit.

• **white oak group** — This group includes white oak, chestnut oak, and post oak. Leaves have rounded lobes; acorns commonly in pairs and annual. Acorns are edible when tannin is leached out; can be used as grits or flour.

Part used: inner bark.
Properties and use: astringent, tonic; decoction externally for sores, bruises, spongy gums; suppositories for fallen womb, rectal

prolapse; gargle for sore throat; wash for sweaty and tender feet, and nipples toward end of pregnancy; a deodorant (but do not use too constantly, as it tends to contract tissue).

Preparation: decoction as douche or enema—1 teaspoon ground, dried bark boiled 10 minutes in 1 quart of water; strain well; cool to lukewarm. Or make into suppositories for vaginal or rectal prolapse.

• **black oak group** — Includes black oak and northern red oak. Leaves have sharp pointed tips at the end of lobes. Acorns are biennial, very bitter and inedible.

Part used: inner bark.

Properties and use: similar to above, but because of greatly increased tannin content, should not be used internally. Escharotic for external cancer.

Preparation (as escharotic): make a potash from black oak bark; apply until cancer is gone. Then apply **honey** to heal.

oats — (*Avena sativa*). Common cultivated grain. Little known for its medicinal properties.

Part used: fresh, unmilled grain, or uncooked cracked or Scotch cut oats.

Properties and use: soothing, demulcent, stimulating, nervine, tonic; restores wasted nerve tissue and is not habit-forming; can be stopped at any time. Used for irritability of nerves, nervous prostration, chronic sick headache, chorea, depression, excesses of narcotics or alcohol. *Specific* for general nervous exhaustion (and when combined with gastric ulcers) especially in mental and professional workers. Also in uterine disorders with hysteria.

Preparation: To make a fluid extract—soak 4 ounces (½ cup) of bruised or cut oats in 1 pint of brandy for 1 week. Shake daily. Press out and filter.

Dose: between 10-15 drops, 3 or 4 times a day in water. Work up to 20 drops per dose. Give dose in hot water during the day and in cold water, to extend the effect, at the night. (One preparation called *Passavena*—oats with passion flower—is sold by homeopathic suppliers.) Combines well with **skullcap**. Overdose: produces heavy pain of oversedation at the base of the brain. Antidote: caffeine. Discontinue a day or two and resume with smaller doses.

obesity — When caused by glandular dysfunction, especially at menopause, *herbal agents:* seaweeds (kelp), **yarrow**, **prickly ash**. Also see **alteratives**, and **diet**. A **short fast** once a month for a time may be effective. For long-term weight control, try to establish a good natural foods diet. See **diuretics**.

oils — Can be cold-pressed from many seeds: **sunflower** seeds, **corn**, and flaxseed (linseed oil comes from flaxseed, but not all brands are refined for internal use); **beechnuts** yield an oil that will keep for two years without spoiling (see entry). Some flowers, such as **mullein**, also secrete an oil that can be extracted in small quantities by packing flowers into a jar and setting the jar in a sunny window. Use these oils for cooking (except linseed and mullein), also for soaps and herbal lotions. See **St. Johnswort**.

"P"

palpitations of the heart — When caused by endocrine, other functional or nervous derangement: *herbal agents:* use **motherwort**. Otherwise, **hawthorn**.

papilloma — A benign tumor, of the eyes or anywhere on the body. *Herbal agents:* Rub castor oil into the area well, both morning and night, and if possible during the day. Be sure the oil is as fresh as can be obtained. Takes a long time to be effective.

pennyroyal — See **mints**.

peppermint — See **mints**.

peritonitis — An acute infection of the inner abdominal region, sometimes resulting from a perforated appendix. Very serious. If medical help cannot be obtained, *herbal agents* to use: **agrimony**, with **calendula** added for antiseptic.

pertussis — See **whooping cough**.

pharyngitis — See **throat**.

piles — See **hemorrhoids**.

pimples — *Herbal agents:* **agrimony**, **yellow dock**, and **burdock** seeds. Also see **alteratives**.

pine, white — (*Pinus strobus*). A common evergreen forest tree; needles in groups of five in each sheath.

Parts used: fresh inner bark, needles.

Properties and use: expectorant, diuretic, demulcent; used for coughs, colds, and chest diseases. Usually combined with wild **cherry** and **balsam poplar** in a cough syrup.

Preparation: pine-cherry cough syrup (must be made in winter when there are no leaves on cherry twigs) — Use 2 cups of fresh, green pine needles (chopped) and 1/2 cup of chopped twigs and buds of wild cherry or chokecherry. (Consult a botanical handbook for winter identification of twigs.) Add 1 quart of water and boil until the liquid is reduced to 1/2 cup. Strain and add 1 pint of liquid honey. Meanwhile, soak overnight 1 tablespoon of the sticky end-buds of the balsam poplar (or, if not available, cottonwood buds) in 2 ounces of brandy. Strain out the next day and add to the above mixture, stirring well.

Dose: ad lib.

plantain — (*Plantago major*). Plantain family. A common little wayside plant with oval, ribbed leaves and a green flower spike.

Part used: root, leaves, whole herb.

Properties and use: roots and leaves are mild alterative, antiseptic, and vulnerary; influence glandular system, urinary tract. Use externally for scrofula, some eczema, sprains, erysipelas, ophthalmia, neuralgia, hemorrhoids (in ointment, also by mouth when combined with horehound). Leaves are also germicidal and antihemorrhagic (put a pulped fresh leaf on a cut). Use locally: for cuts, insect and spider bites; for earache (in poultice or strong decoction dropped into ear); for tender gums in children; for pain of dental caries (use strong decoction drops in cavity until repaired).

Preparation: infusion, for internal use or wash.

Dose: externally, as needed; internally, 1-2 cups daily.

pleurisy — A lung disease involving inflammation of the membranes that cover the lungs and line the inside of the chest.

Symptoms: sharp and stinging pain in chest, especially when taking a deep breath; low fever.

Herbal agents: **pleurisy root** (below), **yarrow**, **boneset**. A diaphoretic mixture and laxative are in order.

Treatment: Bed rest, **short fast** until fever subsides; later a building, nutritious diet. A sedative may be needed if the pain is great. Poultices, an ice bag, or blistering plaster (see under **arthritis**, **mustard** or **ginger**) may be applied to the affected side. After recovery, breathing exercises are given that may include blowing bubbles or a wind instrument. Tonics and a change of air are desirable.

pleurisy root — (*Asclepias tuberosa*). Milkweed family. Also called butterfly weed, as it attracts monarch butterflies. Orange flowers, sap slightly milky. May be raised in the garden.

Part used: root, dried (do not use fresh root or leaves).
Properties and use: relaxant, expectorant, and diaphoretic (hot infusion); influences skin and serous membrane surfaces. Used for bronchitis, peritonitis, pleurisy, pneumonia, acute catarrh, membranous croup (but not for diphtheria), eruptive diseases. Safe for children.
Preparation: decoction, 1 teaspoon of dried root to 1 cup of water.
Dose: 1-2 cups a day.

pneumonia — Inflammation of the lungs, with congestion; sometimes a sequel of viral diseases. Symptoms: dry, hacking cough; sputum may be colored with blood, or dark; high fever and chills.

Herbal agents: **pleurisy root**, **yarrow**, **veronica**. *Treatment:* complete bed rest, propped up only to allow easy breathing, if necessary. Nourishing liquids (such as eggnog or slippery elm drink) every two hours. Sleep very necessary—do not wake to feed. A fever over 104° should be brought down by tepid sponging and sucking ice. Cold packs may relieve head symptoms. Steady rise of pulse rate, and cyanotic fingernails, mean the heart is failing, and stimulants such as digitalis, **lily of the valley**, or caffeine are needed. Linseed or **mustard** poultices or ice packs can be applied. Any exertion must be avoided, until after the crisis that occurs between the fifth and tenth day. After this, an increased light, solid diet and more activity are allowed, with caution. **Tonics** during convalescence. Massive doses of vitamin C (5,000 to 15,000 mg daily, as tolerated) and increased vitamin A are indicated and may lessen the severity of the disease.

poison ivy — (*Rhus toxicodendron*). Rhus family. A low vine-like plant having three leaves with pointed ends, small whitish flowers, and drooping white berries. The juice raises blisters on susceptible persons and can even be transmitted by smoke from burning poison ivy leaves, or by dogs who have rubbed against it.

Herbal agents: scour area with strong yellow laundry soap (Fels Naphtha) or juice of **elder** leaves or **jewelweed**. If rash develops, use the soap rubbed on until it cakes. The blisters, if broken, will infect nearby areas, so the idea is to dry them up without spreading the oily juice.

poisons, antidotes for — *Universal antidote:* equal parts of strong tea, charcoal, and milk of magnesia or egg white. Use 1 teaspoon in water. (This does not induce vomiting but absorbs and neutralizes the poisons.)

- for narcotic overdose—caffeine.
- for quinine overdose—ragweed.
- for mountain laurel poisoning—charcoal.
- poison hemlock—wormwood.
- lead poisoning—**gill-over-the-ground**.
- strychnine poisoning—passion flower.
- poisons in general—**oats** (avena).

poisonous and dangerous plants — See Appendix VI.

polypody — (*Polypodium vulgare*). A common fern found on rocky ledges; simply pinnate (no spurs); spores on tops of fronds.

Part used: root.
Properties and use: soothing demulcent, expectorant, laxative. Use for coughs, colds.
Preparation: infusion.
Dose: wineglassful, 3 times daily.

polyps — For nasal polyps, *herbal agents:* **lungwort**, **castor oil** (rubbed in).

poplar, balsam — (*Populus balsamifera*). A common tree in northern areas of the United States and Canada.

Part used: buds, in early spring.
Properties and use: expectorant; resinous buds are *specific* for lung disorders. See under **white pine**, this section, for use in cough syrup.

poplar, white — (*Populus tremuloides*). Also called aspen. Bark smooth, yellowish-gray. Leaves heart-shaped, set on long stems that quiver in the breeze. Common in upper and northern climates; often appears in cut-over land with birches.

Part used: bark.
Properties and use: universal tonic, antiperiodic, quinine substitute (without side effects). Used as a female tonic for leucorrhea and menorrhagia. Tonic to urinary system.
Preparation: decoction.
Dose: cold wineglassful, 3-4 times daily.

poultice — See page 33. Use emollient or demulcent agents underneath these; the skin absorbs the active ingredient quickly. Most often used for pneumonia, pleurisy, sprains, bruises, and rheumatism.

pregnancy — *Herbal agents:* **raspberry** leaves are to be used throughout pregnancy and lactation. **Squawvine** (partridgeberry) can also be used throughout, especially for women who have had reproductive disorders (such as irregular menses, miscarriage) in the past.

• threatened miscarriage—use crampbark (**viburnum**), especially **black haw** (see under miscarriage).
• for nausea in pregnancy—**raspberry** leaves, **poplar** bark, **viburnum**; a little spearmint for flavor only.
• for labor—**raspberry** leaves.
• after delivery—**trillium** (bethroot), to anticipate flooding and facilitate passage of placenta.

Avoid in pregnancy, especially for women susceptible to miscarriage, all agents labelled emmenagogues, especially the mint (Labiatiae) family.

prickly ash — (*Xanthoxylum americanum*). A shrub with compound leaves and sharp thorns. Common in cut-over land or old pastures. Leaves and berries have a strong lemon-oil smell. Dried berries can be used (sparingly) as pepper.

Parts used: bark, berries—dried.
Properties and use: tonic, alterative, diaphoretic. Used mostly for rheumatism and neuralgia. Dust dry powdered bark on old sores or ulcers. Fresh berries can be used to blister the skin. See under **arthritis.**
Preparation: decoction, 1 teaspoon of dried bark or berries in 1 cup of water.
Dose: wineglassful, 2-3 times daily.

prostate gland, enlarged or inflamed — *Treatment:* warm water enemas nightly for five nights. Daily friction bath. Twice weekly, hot pine bath. Hot and cold fomentations for ten minutes, three times daily. Fresh fruit diet for one week, then standard therapeutic diet. Zinc deficiency is indicated; use zinc supplements, 10 mg daily. *Herbal agents:* **calendula** is *specific.* Also use **Joe-Pye weed, corn silk, betony,** black willow.

proud flesh — Excessive granulation tissue in wounds that are slow in healing. *Herbal agents:* **raspberry** leaves, combined with **slippery elm** and **calendula**, externally as a poultice; internally, infusion of **raspberry** or **calendula**.

pruritus — Itching around anus and vagina; common at menopause. *Treatment:* lower carbohydrates in diet. Cold sitz bath 3-5 minutes daily. *Herbal agents:* **yellow dock** and **burdock** in infusion, internally and externally (add to sitz bath).

psoriasis — A persistent skin disease characterized by superficial patches of thickened, scaly skin, usually starting at elbows and knees. The disease is characterized by unaccountable remissions followed by another outbreak. It is stubborn to cure, and modern medicine has little or no treatment for it. It seems to attack persons of conscientious temperament (similarly to migraine), and although disfiguring, it is not dangerous or fatal. Some indication exists that it is linked with faulty fat assimilation, and good results are being had by use of lecithin (4-8 tablespoons a day), plus vitamins A and B-6. Spas in Israel are treating psoriasis with mud packs from the Dead Sea, with some success.

Herbal agents: **alder** bark (taken over a long period of time), **yellow dock**, and other alteratives. Experiment with several as there is considerable individual variation in response. A natural diet, short fasts, attention to elimination, fresh air, exercise, and sufficient rest are important. This temperament type tends to take on too many community responsibilities and should be encouraged to substitute gardening or bird watching!

"Q"

Queen Anne's lace — See **wild carrot**.

quinine substitutes — Without side-effects: **poplar** (aspen), black willow, **prickly ash**, **chokecherry**. See **antiperiodics**.

quinsy — A special kind of sore throat—formerly much spoken of, but not so much these days—that includes an abscess of the tonsils, usually one side. Very high fever. Occasionally the abscess opens and drains; otherwise it may be lanced by a doctor. *Herbal agents:* use **everlasting**, cranesbill, **chamomile**, sage—in vinegar for gargle. Internally, use **calendula** for the infection.

Self-review Questions for "N" through "Q"

1. The herbal agents covered in this lesson are nasturtiums, nettles, oaks, oats, white pine, plantain, pleurisy root, polypody, two kinds of poplar, and prickly ash. List the properties and parts used of each.

2. Which agents in this lesson may be used as food as well as in medicinal situations?

3. List the *specifics* mentioned, and for what conditions they are used.

4. What family of herbs should be used sparingly in pregnancy? What other herbal caution is relevant to pregnancy?

5. Which agents in this lesson are quinine substitutes?

6. Vocabulary to define:

antidote
cyanotic
escharotic
menorrhagia
neuritis
ophthalmia
pinnate
potash
potherb
prolapsed
serous
sputum

(Answers on page 213.)

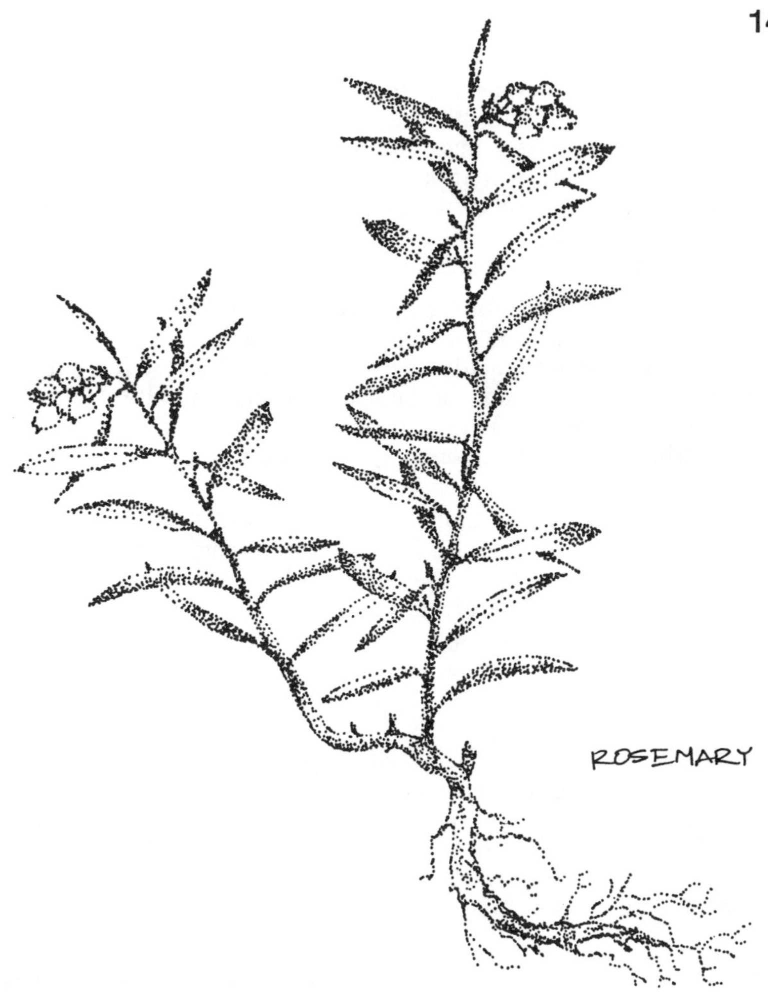

LESSON 15: "R"

rabies — (*Hydrophobia*). Caused by the bite of an animal that has the disease, especially dogs, skunks, cats, horses, cows—almost any mammal. Bats are especially susceptible.

If bitten by a tame animal that is not acting normally, or by a wild animal that is acting unusually tame, try to catch and kill the animal without injuring brain tissue; take it to a laboratory for analysis. If the animal is infected, treatment is in order and should not be neglected. The disease is carried by saliva, generally, and is dangerous only if carried to the nervous system. Rabies is almost always fatal once symptoms develop. The victim may bite those attending; death is very painful.

Nearly 20,000 persons are treated each year for exposure to rabies. The latest form of treatment is not painful, involving a series of six arm injections. There was one U.S. death caused by rabies in 1987, and in that case, treatment was not sought.

Do not take any chances with this disease. Animals that are kept around the house as pets should have immunization; any suspected wild animal should be killed.

Herbal agents: Only one herb, **skullcap**, is said to be *specific* for this disease, but little is known about dosage or administration. It can be administered rectally or hypodermically if the patient is not able to swallow. It could also be used prophylactically if one fears exposure to rabies, or at least it could do no harm. Massive doses of vitamin C—even intravenously—may help.

radiation sickness — Can be caused by X-rays or other nuclear exposure, from industrial accident or war. One of the by-products of nuclear fallout, strontium-90, is readily taken up by the body to replace calcium. Therefore, one of the best defenses against it would be to maintain a high intake of calcium. Also vitamin E.

Herbal agents: for nausea, as well as for radiation burns, **aloe** is the best agent.

raspberry — (*Rubus idaeus*). Red raspberry, wild or cultivated, is the one referred to in this course unless otherwise specified. It can be distinguished from other similar species by the bristly stems (not true thorns, as roses have) and chalky white deposit on the underside of the leaves. Berries are pleasant and nutritive, one of the preferred ingredients for making **shrubs**.

Part used: leaves.

Properties and use: astringent, tonic; said to collect morbid matter from the mucous membranes. Traditionally used throughout pregnancy and lactation; also used for uterine hemorrhage, menorrhagia, hematemesis (vomiting of blood), nausea, and in all children's diseases, especially the eruptive diseases.

Preparation: standard decoction.

Dose: 1 to 2 cups a day; be sure to stir up and use the chalky deposit in the liquid, as this contains calcium and other agents.

rectum — Rectal pain may be caused by:

- hemorrhoids, with itching or loss of clear blood.
- catarrh or inflammation of the bowels, with lumps of stringy passage.
- dysentery, with burning, colic-like pains, bloody stools, pus.

Herbal agents: **bittersweet, chickweed** ointment.

red osier — See **dogwood.**

rheumatism — A general constitutional disease caused by accumulation of toxins in the body. Sometimes a focus of infection (e.g., the teeth) can be found and treated; sometimes the cause is more elusive and may be in the diet, faulty elimination, etc. See also **arthritis.**

• **muscular rheumatism**—cramp-like pain (especially when affected muscles are brought into motion), aching, and stiffness. Large swellings may be found in the muscles, with a thickening of fibrous tissue around the muscles.

Treatment: sun, fresh air, natural diet, and a daily massage. Bee venom treatment may be helpful. (See under **arthritis.**) For massage: from the spot of discomfort, feel around in a radius of 18 inches for a nerve with nodules on it. This is the real source of the referred pain. Concentrate on that spot, rubbing ever more heavily in a clockwise direction, always toward the heart. Use corn starch or slippery elm powder on hands. After three minutes of the rub, knead the sore spot as heavily as permitted, kneading fingers into the flesh, trying to lift the nodule off the bone, for five minutes. Finish with light rubbing. Repeat the same process over the sore muscles. After the massage, rub in a lotion or oil containing capsicum, oil of wintergreen and **thyme**, or **prickly ash** berries.

• **rheumatoid arthritis**—symptoms referred to joints more than to muscles. *Treatment:* build up bones and teeth with organic salts, **meadowsweet, nettles,** bone meal and vitamins A, D, and C. Walk two miles daily, if possible. Treat with massage as above. Keep bowels open. Once a week have an Epsom salts bath (or use wood ashes in the water), followed by a rough rubdown, massage, and tattoo-slapping routine. A diet of raw fruits and salads, if tolerated, sometimes does more good than a complete fast. Do not force liquids.

ringing in the ears — (tinnitus). May be a symptom of:

- diseases of the ear, middle ear, or Eustachian tubes.
- anemia, especially when at night.
- low or high blood pressure.
- high fever.
- obstruction by wax.
- overuse of quinine or aspirin.
- iodine-potassium deficiency.

Herbal agents: **violets, valerian, thyme, gill-over-the-ground.**

ringworm — A fungus disease of the skin, very contagious. *Herbal agents:* **bloodroot** and **jewelweed**, externally only.

root beer — When made from natural products, as follows, this is a good alterative tonic:

2 tablespoons each of black birch twig, yellow dock root, wintergreen herb
1 tablespoon each of sliced wild ginger root, wild cherry bark
2 quarts molasses or honey (or 2 pounds of raw sugar)
4 gallons of water

Boil roots and herbs together in the water for 45 minutes. Add sweetening. Cool to lukewarm; add 1 cake of yeast (or 1 package of dry yeast) dissolved in water. Let stand 24 hours before bottling. Cap with a bottle capper or tie down corks. Let sit for two weeks before using. Store in cool place. This beer develops a slight alcoholic content but not enough to make it objectionable for young children.

rose — (*Rosa*, any species). Rose family. The wild rose is best. If using cultivated roses, make sure they have not been sprayed with any poisons. Rose hips are an excellent source of vitamin C. Dry, grind, and steep them in tea without boiling; or add to salads, fruit cups, etc.

Parts used: petals, leaves, hips.
Properties and use: petals are used as a heart tonic; leaves (dried) are astringent, tonic, stimulant.
Preparation: infusion (one of the most acceptable substitutes for commercial teas for those who like a tea with body to it).
Dose: ad lib, but not to the point of overstimulating.

rosemary — (*Rosmarinus officinalis*). *Labiatiae* family. A cultivated herb that in northern parts should be brought into the house during winter; elsewhere, as in England, it is hardy and develops into a shrubby, small tree. Culinary use often combines this with lamb.

Part used: whole herb.
Properties and use: antispasmodic, emmenagogue. Used for headaches, migraine, dizziness; strong infusion for eye wash and hair rinse for dandruff.

Preparation: infusion, 1 teaspoon to ½ cup of water.
Dose: up to 1 cup per day. *Caution: can be dangerous in excess.*

rupture — (or hernia). *Herbal agents:* **daisy**—infusion, decoction, or daisy wine; taken over a long period of time. Also **comfrey**.

Self-review Questions for "R"

1. The herbal agents listed in this section are raspberry, rose, and rosemary. List the properties and parts used for each.

2. What agent (and what additional course of action) is most useful in radiation sickness?

3. What therapies may be helpful in the treatment of rheumatism?

4. What disease in this lesson might prove fatal without immediate medical treatment?

5. What is the remedy for ringworm?

6. What herb is helpful in treating dandruff?

7. Vocabulary to define:

capsicum	rose hips
hematemesis	tinnitus

(Answers on page 214.)

LESSON 16: "S"

sage — (*Salvia officinalis*). *Labiatiae* family. Also a culinary herb.

Part used: leaves.
Properties and use: antispasmodic, astringent, diaphoretic in hot infusion. Used in night sweats in tuberculosis; for drying up milk when weaning a baby; soothing to nerves, for trembling depression, vertigo; also for diarrhea and gastritis. Used for gargle (with vinegar); cleansing to mucous membranes.
Preparation: hot infusion, 1 teaspoon of leaves in ½ cup of water.
Dose: tablespoon doses, up to 1 cup per day. *Caution: do not exceed dosage.*

St. Vitus' dance — See **chorea.**

St. Johnswort — (*Hypericum perforatum*). Called common St. Johnswort. St. Johnswort family. Shrubby plant with light yellow flowers blooming around St. John the Baptist's Day, June 24th. Leaves have oil glands, making visible pinpoint dots when the leaf is held up to the light.

Part used: flower heads.

Properties and use: analgesic, antispasmodic, astringent, nervine, vulnerary. Used for intermittent fevers, swelling of breasts and tumors. St. Johnswort is especially recommended, both internally and externally, for wounds such as toes or digits crushed in an accident, with great trauma and pain attending. It is also indicated internally for neuritis, neuralgia, and certain excitable nervous states, but *is contraindicated in depressive states.* This agent is one that needs to be used with some caution, as it can induce depression if used to excess.

Preparation: because of the oily content of this plant, it does not yield its properties readily to water. It is best infused in light wine (1 teaspoonful to 1 cup) or oil. Oil of St. Johnswort is a beautiful red color. Pick the flowers as they bloom, putting them into a jar. Cover with vegetable oil and close the jar. Place the jar in a sunny window for about two weeks. Use the oil for external rubs.

Dose: for wine infusion, wineglassful, 1-3 times daily.

sarsaparilla — See **wild sarsaparilla.**

scabs and blotches — *Herbal agent:* **spearmint** wash (especially for children).

scarlet fever — One of the eruptive diseases not so common now as formerly. Symptoms: sudden onset, chills and fever, pains in limbs and back; throat red, "strawberry tongue." A rash appears on the second day in the neck and chest area—red, diffuse with small dots; after increasing for two days, it will be gone in a week. Possible kidney complications.

Treatment: avoid chills. Pitcher plant (found in bogs) is *specific.* **Raspberry** leaves, **calendula** flowers, **short fast**, fruit and vegetable juices, vitamins A and C. **Slippery elm** powder for rash.

sciatica — Inflammation of the sciatic nerve. Classed with **arthritis** and **rheumatism**, with similar causes. See each. *Herbal agents:* **Elderberries** seem to be *specific* and are best used in a **shrub**. Also

chokecherry bark (hot infusion made fresh every six hours) and **gill-over-the-ground**; high doses of vitamin C.

scurvy — A disease caused by a deficiency of vitamin C. While cases of full-blown scurvy are rarely seen now, the following symptoms may begin when the diet is insufficient. (Stress, alcohol, and smoking all make extra demands for vitamin C.) *Symptoms:* gradual onset, skin pale and sallow; gums swollen and bleed easily; teeth become loose; purpuric spots develop on the skin. Firm swelling in the calves, caused by hemorrhages in the muscles may occur; death may follow from complication such as heart failure or hemorrhages.

Treatment: responds well to vitamin C and foods with a high C concentration—parsley, green peppers, tomatoes, black currents, winter cress, **mustards** (various species), watercress, blue **violets**, **nettles** as greens.

Herbal agents: **antiscorbutics—elderberries, rose** hips, **gill-over-the-ground**, highbush **cranberries**, **spearmint**, **boneset**, **strawberry** (fruit and leaves).

self-heal — (*Prunella vulgaris*). *Labiatiae* family. Also called heal-all. Purplish flower head; low plant. Common in pastures and dooryards.

Part used: whole herb.
Properties and use: astringent, vulnerary. Used as gargle for sore throat; internal bleeding, leucorrhea, and for wounds in general.
Preparation: standard infusion.
Dose: ½ cup, 3 times a day.

shadbush — (*Amelanchier*, any species). Also called Juneberry. Rose family. Small tree that blooms before most others in the spring (at the time of the shad run). Flowers are whitish pink with five strap-like petals appearing before the leaves. Ten-seeded, small, apple-like fruit are borne in June or early July.

Part used: fruit.
Properties and use: antiscorbutic. Fruits, high in vitamins and minerals, can be dried and incorporated into pemmican as an emergency ration. Usually too dry and seedy to be tasty unless you are hungry, but occasionally a tree with better fruit can be found. Can be used as a substitute for rose hips, especially in an area where roses are less common.
Dose: ad lib.

shepherd's-purse — (*Capsella bursa-pastoris*). Mustard family. Rosette of toothed leaves at the base; flower spike with tiny, white four-petalled flowers; seeds in a heart-shaped capsule, like an old-time coin purse.

Part used: whole herb.

Properties and use: stimulant, astringent, antihemorrhagic, antiscorbutic. This plant is *specific* for uterine fibroid tumors. In innumerable cases, persistent taking of shepherd's-purse resulted in the tumors disappearing completely. Also used for renal catarrh, scalding urine, enuresis, and for uterine hemorrhaging.

Preparation: concentrated decoction—2 tablespoons leaves or whole herb to 12 ounces of water. Boil down to 1 cup.

Dose: wineglassful, 3 times daily. This agent has a rather unpleasant taste that can be masked by adding it to ginger syrup. (Or use standard infusion. Take by mouthfuls, up to 1 cup per day.)

short fast — See **diet**.

shrubs — Cooling drinks made with fruit, vinegar, and honey or sugar. Shrubs are one of the most versatile preparations using natural materials—they are especially cooling in hot weather, replacing minerals lost in perspiration. In cold weather, served hot, they can be equally invigorating. In all seasons they provide a drink rich in vitamins, minerals, and refreshment, better than the so-called "soft drinks" or sodas. They are also excellent for use in fevers, sipped from a glass with cracked ice.

Recipe: fill an earthen crock, or glass or enamelware vessel with as much as you have of raspberries, elderberries, chokecherries, or any other strong-flavored fruit (experiment a bit). Add enough cider vinegar to cover the fruit. Let stand ten days to two weeks, or until the flavor and color of the fruit have come out into the vinegar. (A towel over the crock will keep fruit flies away.) Strain and press out fruit. Discard fruit (or use for chutney). Measure the remaining liquid and add an equal amount of honey, preferably, or raw sugar. (If sugar is used, the mixture must be heated just enough to dissolve it.) Pour into sterile bottles and cap. It does not need to be processed to preserve it, as the vinegar and honey take care of that.

Use about 1/4 cup of the concentrated syrup to each glass of ice water or mug of hot water. It may be used a little stronger as a gargle or undiluted as a cough syrup.

Bottles of shrub, properly made, will keep for years, will not freeze in winter until about -30°, nor spoil in the heat of summer. If it becomes ropy with time, it can be strained out for use as before.

The most elegant shrub is that made with red raspberries; the most medicinal are those made with elderberries and chokecherries. Or try rhubarb (diced), strawberries (especially wild ones too small to hull), blueberries, blackberries, or wild grapes.

silverweed — (*Potentilla aserina*). Rose family. Long, compound silvery leaves, growing profusely in sandy or rocky beaches. Contains many minerals.

Part used: whole herb.
Properties and use: astringent. Use as a mouthwash for sore throat, canker sores, and dental extractions.
Preparation: infusion or decoction.
Dose: wineglassful, ad lib, for mouthwash.

skin diseases — See **alteratives**. Also the following *specifics:*

- scaly skin—**bittersweet**.
- acne—**yellow dock, burdock** seeds.
- moist, cutaneous eruptions of infants—pansy and **spearmint**.

skullcap — (*Scutellaria latifolia*). Labiatiae family. Common around cold, rocky lakes and streams. (Does not grow in England and commands a high price among herbalists there.) Small lilac flowers at axils of leaves are followed by a small capsule with the shape of a skullcap, hence the name. Sometimes called mad dog skullcap because of its reputation in the treatment of rabies in former days. Still one of our most versatile and useful nervines.

Part used: whole herb.
Properties and use: nervine, antispasmodic, tonic to nervous tissue. Used for hysteria, convulsions, nervous prostration, chorea, epilepsy, puerperal convulsions, delirium tremens, drug withdrawal symptoms. Combines well with other nervines. No reported contra-indications or side effects.
Preparation: standard infusion.
Dose: ½ teacupful, 3-4 times a day.

slippery elm — See **elm**.

Solomon's seal — (*Polygonatum multiflorum*). Lily family. A common plant of the woods, with large, deeply ribbed leaves and bell-like flowers drooping from the underside of the stem;

followed by a blue berry. Root has a scar where each year's stem went up, the scar resembling the signet of a ring, hence the name. There is also a false Solomon's seal; see below.

Part used: root.
Properties and use: astringent, demulcent, tonic. Used for leucorrhea, bleeding from the lungs. Poultice of the powdered root for external use—for bruises, hemorrhoids, inflammation, tumors.
Preparation: standard infusion.
Dose: 1/2 cup, 3 times a day.

spatterdock — See **water lily, yellow.**

spearmint — See **mints.**

speedwell — See **veronica.**

sphagnum moss — (*Sphagnum cymbifolium*). Grows in cold, northern bogs or in upper elevations. Accumulates as peat, sometimes many feet in thickness. When dried, it is highly absorbent and, due to iodine content, very antiseptic.

Part used: whole herb.
Properties and use: antiseptic. Use as a dressing on an open wound and bind with a bark bandage. Absorbent in use for babies' diapers and women's sanitary pads. A long dissertation on the preparation and uses of sphagnum is found in Grieve's *A Modern Herbal.*

spikenard, Amer. — (*Aralia racemosa*). Ginseng family. Tall, branching woodland herb, 3-5 feet tall, with round blackish stem, compound leaves, 15-21 leaflets; greenish-white flowers in fives on terminal spikes; fruit a brownish-red berry in clusters at the end of branches.

Part used: roots.
Properties and use: alterative, glandular agent. Large roots are spicy and aromatic.
Preparation: See **root beer**. Or 1-2 teaspoons powdered dried root to 1 cup of water.
Dose: 1-2 cups daily.

spikenard, false — (*Smilacina racemosa*). Also called false Solomon's seal. Lily family. No plant is false, each being true to its own nature. Small woodland plant with deeply-ribbed leaves like those of Solomon's seal, but flowers and fruit (a cluster of red berries) are borne at the end of the stem instead of dangling along it. Not so large as spikenard, above, and with single instead of compound leaves. This plant is listed here to distinguish it from the two given above, as it is somewhat like them both. Its properties are not known, but it is not recorded anywhere as dangerous.

sprains — *Herbal agents:* **mullein** in vinegar; oil of **St. Johnswort**; fomentation of **chamomile** or **comfrey**.

spruce — (*Picea*, any species). The white spruce is most common in many areas, often in company with balsam. The black spruce is usually found in bogs. There is also a red spruce, quite common. All are coniferous trees with short needles that surround the twig. Roots are used for cordage.

Part used: green twigs.
Properties and use: antiscorbutic, used for spruce beer or spruce tea. Put in vaporizer for bronchitis.

squawvine — (*Mitchella repens*). Also called partridgeberry. Bedstraw family. A small creeping vine with round leaves (white stripe) and paired red berries. Found in pine woods.

Part used: whole herb.
Properties and use: astringent, parturient, male and female tonic to genito-urinary system—our best general tonic for this purpose. Used for uterine cramps, leucorrhea, dysmenorrhea, fallen womb, and in pregnancy. This is the agent of choice in cases where there is a long-standing menstrual irregularity or difficulty in conceiving. Taking squawvine as a simple tea for a month or two usually straightens things out, and they do not tend to recur. Also used for male prostate troubles and spermatic disorders.
Preparation: infusion.
Dose: ½ cup, 3-4 times a day.

stimulants — These herbs temporarily quicken body functions. Common stimulants include **ginger**, **mustard**, **prickly ash**, **vervain**, and **yarrow**. See Lesson 3.

stomach symptoms —

• gastritis—pain is gnawing and burning in the pit of the stomach after eating. Heartburn with gas present, and tenderness in epigastric region. Vomiting at times, without relief from pain. *Treatment:* restrict tea, coffee, spices, alcohol. Start a mild diet. *Herbal agents:* use **aperients**, **peppermint**, **chamomile**, **goldenseal**, **agrimony**, **raspberry**, **aloe**.

• dyspepsia—pain as above, but less severe; no fever, no tenderness. Vomiting relieves. *Treatment:* as above. Yogurt or buttermilk is good. Citrus fruits may create gas; use fruits such as apples, pears, grapes, and berries. *Herbal agents:* use bitter herbs in small amounts: **boneset**, **yarrow**, **chamomile**.

• gastric ulcer—pain below breast bone, often radiating backward toward the shoulder; area very sensitive to pressure; pain almost always occurs after eating. Vomiting of sour fluid, sometimes blood. See under **ulcers**.

• neuralgia or cramps of stomach—sudden attack of severe gripping pain in the stomach, extending to back and lasting until expulsion of gas and a watery fluid. *Herbal agents:* use **peppermint** ground to a powder with cloves and sugar in a strong infusion. Take small teaspoonful doses frequently. Also **chamomile**.

stones and gravel — in urinary system (kidneys and bladder): rare where apple cider or vinegar are a staple item of diet. *Herbal agents:* **lady's bedstraw**, **Joe-Pye weed**.

strawberry, wild — (*Fragaria virginiana*). Rose family. Common, low plant of pastures and fields. Toothed leaves in threes, white five-petalled flowers. Red edible berry and leaves are high in vitamin C content. The pounded root is good for gum massage and for a toothbrush. (There is also a wood strawberry, differing slightly from the common one but used interchangeably.)

Part used: leaves—in infant diarrhea; stalks and dried hulls taken from the berries—in tea.
Properties and use: mild astringent to mucous membranes; *specific* for mesenteric glands; antiscorbutic.
Preparation: infusion.
Dose: ½ cup, 3-4 times a day. For infants, strain and put into nursing bottle. Do not sweeten and do not give any other food for 12 hours.

stroke — May result in partial paralysis. *Treatment:* bed rest, with head raised, absolute quiet, moved little. Ice bag to head and hot water bottle to feet. Liquid diet during acute stage, then light diet. No stimulants. Keep at rest six weeks. Light massage of afflicted parts when possible. Keep limbs in proper position to prevent deformity during paralysis. *Herbal agent:* see under **hawthorn**.

styptics — Very drying agents, for external use only; hemostatic for small cuts or sores. *Herbal agents:* cranesbill, **tormentil** root.

sumac — (*Rhus typhina, glabra*, and *aromatica*). Staghorn, smooth and fragrant sumac, respectively. The first two are tall shrubs common in dry pastures and roadsides with fern-like compound leaves. The fragrant sumac is a low shrub with three-part leaves. Fruit forms in a pyramid of small, red, velvety berries that persist in fall and winter. *Poison sumac is found in swamps and bears white berries.*

Part used: berries; cones may be collected in fall and stored in a cool, dry place all winter.
Properties and use: astringent, tonic, diuretic; contain citric and malic acids, and vitamin C. Used as wash or in decoction for fevers and colds; in small amounts for diarrhea, dysentery.
Preparation: decoction. (Or as a lemonade substitute and refreshing drink: macerate in cold water; strain fine hairs out; sweeten as desired.)
Dose: for diarrhea, wineglassful, 3-4 times daily.

Root bark of sweet sumac (*Rhus glabra*) can be used for a beverage in diabetes, as an unsweetened "lemonade." Also for **enuresis**.

sunburn — *Herbal agents:* **vinegar**, applied right after exposure, will prevent blistering and peeling; also **aloe** gel.

sunflower — (*Helianthus annuus*). Composite family. Sometimes grown as an ornamental in gardens. Large Russian sunflower cultivated by farmers is used as a forage plant, for wild bird and poultry food, and for oil.

Part used: seeds.
Properties and use: nutritious, mucilaginous, vermifuge; "prevents smallpox," according to old herbals, and *specific* for malaria. Roasted and ground, the seeds can be used as a coffee substitute.

sunstroke — See **heatstroke**.

suppositories — A useful way to administer certain medications, especially to children or comatose patients. Medication is readily absorbed by the mucus lining of the rectum or vaginal tract. See directions on page 34.

sweating — A symptom in anemia, obesity, heart or kidney disorders, menopause, general weakness, fevers, AIDS. Yellowish sweat denotes disease of liver or gall bladder. *Herbal agents:*

external wash (mild decoction) of **oak** or **hemlock** bark, **sumac** bark or root; **sage**, in infusion, controls sweating.

swelling — A symptom in anemia, obesity, heart or kidney disorders: a slight swelling in the ankles, disappearing overnight, may be from anemia; extensive swelling, up to knees or hips, indicates heart or kidney disorder. See **edema**.

Self-review Questions for "S"

1. The herbal agents in this lesson are sage, St. Johnswort, self-heal, shadbush, shepherd's-purse, silverweed, skullcap, Solomon's seal, sphagnum moss, spikenard, spruce, squawvine, strawberry, sunflower, and sumac. List the properties and parts used for each.

2. What *specific* is mentioned in this section and for what condition is it used?

3. What plant in this lesson is our best general tonic for the genito-urinary tract?

4. What plant in this lesson is one of the finest nervines ever discovered?

5. What disease mentioned here is rarely heard of today but has beginning symptoms that are quite common? What is the cause?

6. What two agents were mentioned for enuresis?

7. Vocabulary to define:

analgesic
chutney
cutaneous
delirium tremens
digits
epigastric
mesenteric
pemmican
puerperal
purpuric
sallow
sciatic nerve
styptic
trauma

(Answers on page 214.)

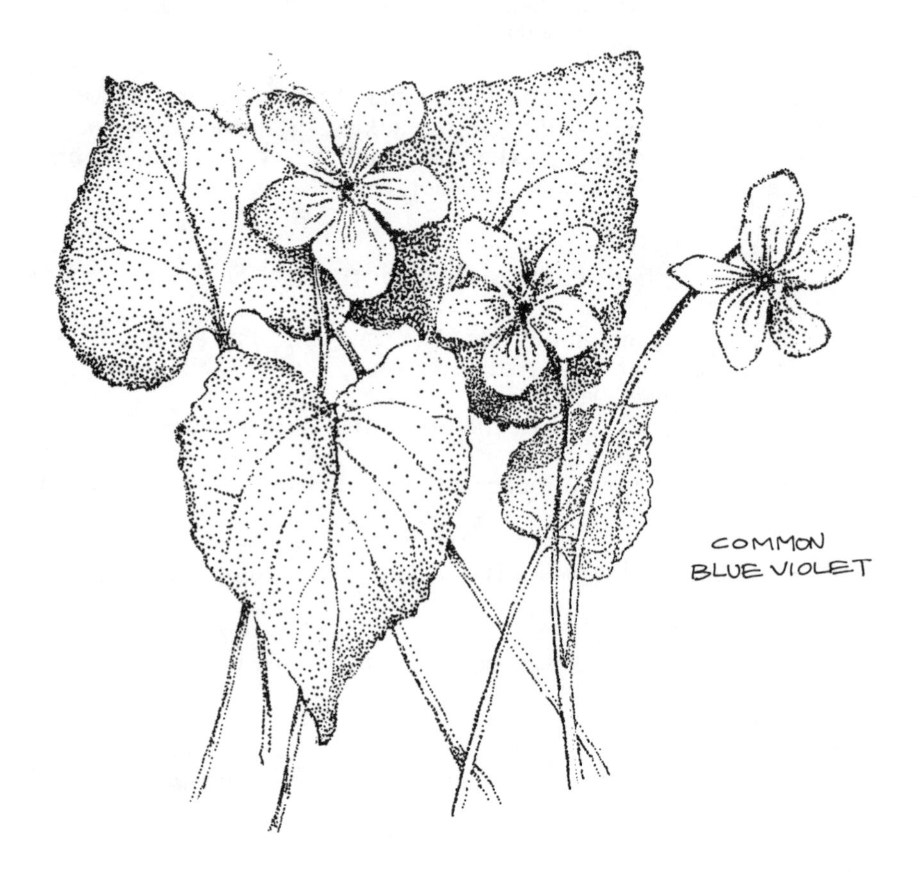

LESSON 17: "T" — "U" — "V"

teeth — Fresh **apple** juice has a reputation for preventing cavities. Strawberry roots, alfalfa roots, or any sweet-tasting twigs such as maple, yellow birch, or dogwood may be used as a toothbrush: crush or pound the end of the twigs to make the brush. When caries develop, drop **plantain** juice into the cavity, then pack with bone meal, until the dentist can be reached. Internal use of bone meal has helped strengthen loose teeth when under stress from bite or pressure. For toothache, *herbal agents:* chamomile in poultices. **Valerian** is *specific* for facial neuralgia.

testes — enlarged. *Herbal agents:* **spikenard** and **squawvine.**

tetanus — (lockjaw). A disease usually resulting from a deep puncture infection. Results in muscular spasm so that the person cannot open the jaw. Whole body has spasms that become very violent. At the end, the respiratory muscles may be affected, resulting in death by asphyxia.

Treatment: serums to prevent tetanus are available and should be renewed periodically, especially among those whose work exposes them to deep wounds or when a dangerous wound has been received. Once the disease develops, the outlook is grim. Herbal treatments that might be tried consist of more dangerous herbs not in the content of this course. However, a report by Adelle Davis states that some doctors have had marvelous results in treating tetanus and other severe and formerly fatal infections with massive doses of vitamin C; 2,000-4,000 mg were administered by injection every 2-4 hours around the clock. See under **vitamin C**.

throat, sore —

- tonsillitis—*Herbal agents:* **astringents**, especially **sage**; also **hollyhock** flowers, fleabane, and **gargles**.
- pharyngitis—*Herbal agents:* **chickweed** infusion or strong decoction to paint the pharynx. See also **astringents**.

thyme — (*Thymus vulgaris*). *Labiatiae* family. Used much in cooking, as in stuffing, meat loaf, etc. Does best in gravelly or rocky soil.

Part used: whole herb.
Properties and use: antiseptic (contains a volatile oil, thymol, that is an ingredient in many antiseptic preparations); diaphoretic, emmenagogue. Used for colds, colic, headaches.
Preparation: hot infusion, 1 tablespoon to 1 pint of boiling water.
Dose: tablespoonful, 3-4 times daily. *Caution: do not exceed recommended dosage.*

tobacco heart — Irregularities found in heavy smokers. *Herbal agent:* **lily-of-the-valley**. See also **cardiac agents** and **heart**.

tonics — For convalescence from fevers, *herbal agents:* wild **cherry** bark, **yarrow**, tansy (*caution*), angelica, **boneset**, **chamomile**, **meadowsweet**. See Lesson 3.

tonsillitis — See **throat**.

tormentil — (*Potentilla tormentilla*). Rose family. One of the cinquefoils, but it is also called septfoil because it has seven fingers, not five.

Part used: whole herb and root.
Properties and use: one of our strongest astringents; tonic. Use for diarrhea, nausea, tonics, gargle.
Preparation: infusion or decoction, 1 tablespoonful to 1 cup of water.
Dose: wineglassful, 3-4 times daily.

trailing arbutus — (*Epigaea repens*). Heath family. A small creeping plant, one of the earliest spring flowers in the East, with fragrant, pinkish-white blossoms. This is one of the most famous urinary agents in herbal medicine, but it is becoming rare and is on the list of protected plants. Therefore, it would be well to seek a source of plants from a garden supply house to nurture carefully, although it is sensitive to abrupt environmental disturbances and is difficult to cultivate. You also may be able to buy the dried herb from a reputable herb company.

Part used: whole herb.
Properties and use: astringent, diuretic. Influences urinary tract and is used for disorders of the bladder, kidney, urethra, etc. It is excellent when there is pus or blood in the urine. It can be combined with other such agents, e.g., **Joe-Pye weed**.
Preparation: standard infusion.
Dose: wineglassful, ad lib.

trillium — (*Trillium erectum* and *grandiflorum*). The purple and white trillium, respectively. Lily family. Also called bethroot, which is a corruption of "birthroot." Early spring flower with three leaves. (Painted trillium is not used.)

Part used: root. The roots should be dug after the plant has set its fruit (that happens by August) but before the whole plant has withered back so that it is hard to find. (Beware of jack-in-the-pulpit that grows in similar locations and is difficult to distinguish from trillium when young. The turnip-shaped root of the jack-in-the-pulpit is violently acrid, burning, and purgative.) The trillium root looks like a walnut.
Properties and use: soothing, stimulating, astringent, tonic, especially influencing the generative system. Its *specific* use is in childbirth (just after delivery to prevent flooding) and where ergot is used. If given too soon in childbirth (before delivery), it can delay the course of labor. When given afterwards, it helps contract the uterus and expel the afterbirth. Other uses: gastric, respiratory,

or rectal hemorrhaging; uterine or heavy menstrual bleeding; leucorrhea, weak vagina, and prolapsed uterus; diarrhea.

Preparation: roots should be washed, cut or sliced, and dried in the oven until brittle enough to snap. Can be powdered and stored in air-tight jars until needed. Use 1 tablespoon of powdered root (or 1 whole sliced root) to a cup of boiling water.

Dose: wineglassful doses, every 15 minutes, until the one-cup preparation is gone. If it is necessary to make another batch, give doses at greater intervals.

tuberculosis — an infectious disease caused by the tubercule bacillus that usually affects the lungs. *Treatment:* diet should be very well balanced, fortified with vitamins and minerals. Rest and fresh air are also recommended. *Herbal agents:* **elecampane** is *specific* and contains a substance that kills the bacteria.

turtlehead — (*Chelone glabra*). Also called balmony. Figwort family. The pinkish-white flowers look like a turtle's head. Opposite, lance-shaped leaves. Grows 1-3 feet high in moist places in northern areas and upper altitudes.

Part used: whole herb.

Properties and use: stimulating tonic, anthelmintic, antibilious. Uses: mild cathartic in chronic constipation, dyspepsia, jaundice. A safe and certain remedy for worms in children. A good liver stimulant and tonic in convalescence.

Preparation: infusion.

Dose: 1 wineglassful (cold), ad lib for tonic and dyspepsia. For worms: 1 dose at night, followed by another on an empty stomach in the morning. Fast all day, followed with a laxative at night.

"U"

ulcers, external — *Herbal agents:* **prickly ash** bark, cranesbill.

ulcers, gastric — *Symptoms:* pain below breast bone; area very sensitive to pressure, with pain often radiating back towards shoulder blade. Occurs almost always after eating. Vomiting of sour fluid, sometimes blood. Stools may be tarry, indicating bleeding in the gastric system.

Herbal agents: **meadowsweet** is *specific* to control stomach acid; continue indefinitely. To heal over the floor of the ulcer: **calendula** and **comfrey** herb. To close over the ulcer when there is no longer any pain, use cranesbill; it is astringent but not drying, and reduces risk of hemorrhage. Do not use this before floor of ulcer is healed or it will open up again. Also **comfrey** root.

If the ulcer perforates the stomach wall, there will be severe abdominal pain, with facial features pinched; shock is likely, and the abdomen will be distended. Seek medical help. Flat bed rest will be required (bolster under knees). *Herbal agent:* **agrimony**. Feed **slippery elm** gruel, milk, eggs; add iron (supplements, or in the form of iron-rich **tonics**), no **aperients**. Enemas may assist elimination.

urethritis — *Herbal agents:* **beech** leaves. See **diuretics**.

urinary disorders — See **diuretics**, especially **Joe-Pye weed**; also, **beech** leaves, **lady's bedstraw**, **trailing arbutus**, **wild carrot**.

uterine tumors — (fibroid). *Herbal agent:* **shepherd's-purse** is *specific.*

"V"

vaccinium — The group to which **blueberries**, bilberries, **huckleberries**, and **cranberries** belong. Heath family. Most are edible. They cross readily with each other. Most are astringent, nutritive. Cranberry juice contains a substance that is *specific* for recurrent types of kidney infections.

valerian — (*Valeriana officinalis*). Also called garden heliotrope. Valerian family. Found in old gardens and escaped to roadside. Strong, pungent odor; pinkish flowers.

Part used: root.
Properties and use: antispasmodic; strong nervine without narcotic effect. Used for irritability, hysteria, insomnia, neuralgia of face. In France, Valerian is used commonly with bromides. Root has a strong, unpleasant taste that can be masked with ginger, peppermint, or other aromatics.
Preparation: fresh root, chopped; 1 teaspoonful in 1 pint of boiling water.
Dose: Take cold, 1 cup per day or at bedtime. *Caution: do not use over extended periods—not more than two to three weeks at a time.*

varicose veins — *Herbal agents:* witch hazel compresses; internally—**calendula**, **daisy**, **yarrow**.

veratrum viride — (false or white hellebore, or Indian poke). Lily family. *Dangerous herb.* Leaves may be mistaken for skunk cabbage in early spring.

vermifuges — These herbs expel intestinal worms. See **anthelmintics** and Lesson 3.

veronica — (*Veronica officinalis*). Commonly called speedwell. Figwort family. A small trailing plant with lilac flowers borne in spikes at the axils; leaves hairy and toothed.

Part used: whole herb.
Properties and use: alterative, expectorant, diuretic, emmenagogue. Used as a laxative tea; hot infusion also soothes nervous system. Also for coughs, colds, pneumonia. With **burdock**, for skin diseases.
Preparation: infusion; 2 teaspoons in 1/2 cup of water.
Dose: 1 mouthful at a time, up to 1 1/2 cups per day.

vertigo — Common in elderly. *Herbal agent:* **daisy**.

vervain, blue — (*Verbena hastata*). Vervain family. This is the native American variety, with dark blue spikes; grows in damp places with boneset and Joe-Pye weed; flowers at the same time.

Part used: whole herb.
Properties and use: antispasmodic, nervine; emetic in large doses. Given in small frequent doses for overwork, insomnia, anxiety, nervous headache.
Preparation: infusion; 2 teaspoons to 1 pint of boiling water.
Dose: wineglassful, warm, 3-4 times a day and at bedtime. Cold infusion is tonic.

viburnum — A family of common wayside shrubs, none dangerous. The most useful medicinally is **black haw** (*viburnum prunifolium*). Check under **miscarriage** for use.

An acceptable substitute is the **highbush cranberry** (*Viburnum opulus*). Also called guelder rose or **crampbark**. Leaves three-lobed like a maple, but smaller. Flowers in flat-topped cluster, like most viburnums, but the outside florets are larger than the inner ones. Fruits are scarlet, and may be used as cranberries.

Part used: inner bark.
Properties and use: Astringent, antispasmodic. Used for cramps of all sorts, but especially at menses and in pregnancy. Prevents miscarriage. Also used for menorrhagia.

Preparation: decoction. May be combined with **squawvine**.
Dose: 1 tablespoonful to wineglassful, ad lib.

vinegar — (*Acetum*). Made from pure apple cider (although vinegars are sometimes made from wine and other juices). Do not use distilled vinegar.

Properties and use: astringent; contains potassium, acetic acid, various minerals. Antiseptic to typhoids and food poisoning organisms. An ingredient in many preparations: use for fevers and heat exhaustion, to allay thirst (make up as a **shrub**); as a gargle for sore throats; for sprains and swellings, in warm poultice; pat on sunburn to prevent blistering; for delirium tremens, 1 wineglassful. For head colds, add 1/4 cup of vinegar to 1 quart of water and bring to a simmer; inhale steam, or add to a small humidifier.

violet — (*Viola papilionacea*). Common blue violet, but any violet may be used.

Part used: fresh leaves (high in vitamin A).
Properties and use: laxative, anodyne. (Has been used successfully in cancer of the larynx. See Mrs. Grieve's *A Modern Herbal*.
Preparation: pour 1 pint of boiling water over handful of fresh leaves. Steep 12 hours.
Dose: wineglassful every 4 hours. (Externally, place leaf pulp dressing over wound, wrapped with oiled silk. Renew frequently.)

Part used: flowers.
Properties and use: laxative for children.
Preparation: pour 1 cup of boiling water over 1 cup of fresh violet flowers; steep overnight. Strain and add 1 pound of sugar or honey. Heat until sugar is dissolved but do not boil. Keep in a covered jar.
Dose: 1/2 to 1 teaspoon at bedtime.

vitamins — in common herbs:

• vitamin A (carotene)—especially in alfalfa, **dandelion**, lamb's quarters, paprika, watercress, parsley, **docks, nettles**.

• vitamin B (in general)—seaweeds, wheat germ, alfalfa, **nettles, sunflower** seeds, most nuts, members of the **mustard** family.

• vitamin C—**rose** hips, **strawberry** leaves and fruit, blue **violet** leaves and flowers, **elderberries**, parsley, **gill-over-the-ground, spearmint, boneset**, garlic, most berries, most greens.

(For life-threatening or major illness, vitamin C may be administered intravenously by your physician: 350-700 milligrams of ascorbic acid crystals per kilogram of body weight, dissolved in a 5 percent dextrose solution, using 18 milliliters per gram of vitamin C.)

- vitamin D (as sterols)—water cress, wheat germ.
- vitamin E—most oils, seeds, and grains; also **dandelion** greens, asparagus, **nettles**.
- vitamin K—alfalfa, **blueberry** leaves, **burdock** seeds, parsley, watercress.
- vitamin P (rutin)—buckwheat, paprika.

vulneraries — Aid in healing wounds. Common herbal vulneraries: **calendula**, **plantain**, **chickweed**. For internal use: **daisy** and **comfrey**. See Lesson 3.

Self-review Questions for "T" — "U" — "V"

1. The agents listed in this lesson are thyme, tormentil, trailing arbutus, trillium, turtlehead, vaccinium, valerian, veronica, vervain, viburnum, vinegar, violet. List the properties and parts used for each.

2. Which of these are for urinary or kidney troubles?

3. Which agent in this lesson is one of the most important herbs we have for childbirth?

4. Which other agent is also used in pregnancy?

5. Which agent is a safe and certain remedy for worms in children?

6. Which two of these herbs are among the most-used nervines?

7. Which herb is mentioned most often in the vitamin listing?

8. Which *specifics* were mentioned in this lesson?

9. Vocabulary to define:

distended
generative
larynx
pharynx
urethra

(Answers on page 215.)

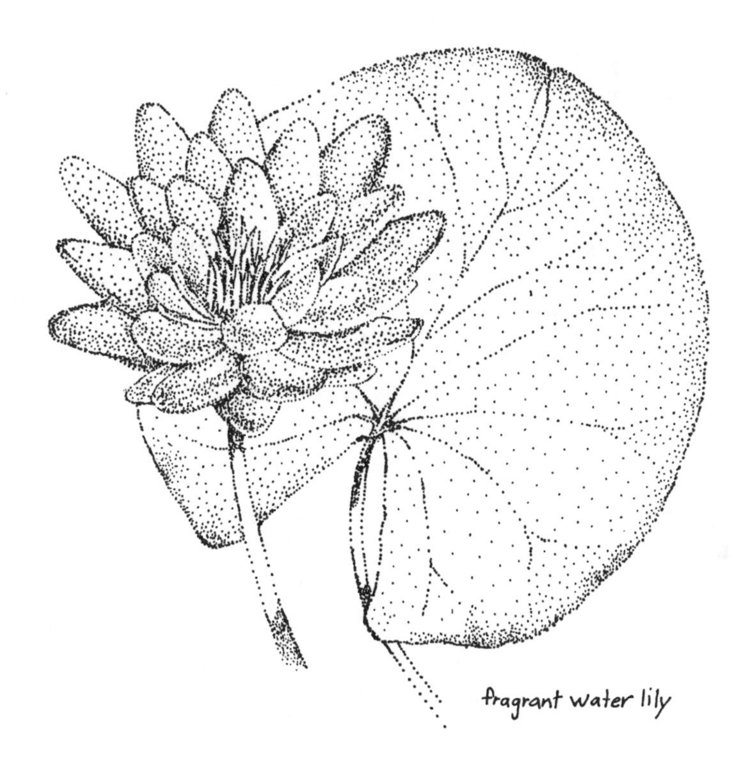

LESSON 18: "W" — "X" — "Y" — "Z"

warts — *Herbal agents:* **castor** oil, rubbed in thoroughly night and morning, for a period of weeks or months, is the most successful treatment. Also **jewelweed** and **bloodroot**.

water lily, white — (*Nymphaea odorata*). The familiar water lily of quiet ponds and lakes.

Part used: root.

Properties and use: demulcent, astringent. Affects particularly the female system; *specific* for prolapsed uterus (in **suppositories**). Also for leucorrhea, ophthalmia, diarrhea. Externally as a wash for sores, or as a gargle or mouthwash. Powder may be used for chafing, diaper rash, etc.

Preparation: decoction.

Dose: wineglassful, 3-4 times daily.

water lily, yellow—(*Nuphar variegatum*). Also called spatterdock. This has somewhat the same properties as the above but is less astringent and more generally used for food. The root may be roasted as a starchy vegetable or dried and pounded into flour. The fall seeds are edible, parched as grain.

weight reduction — See **obesity** and **diuretics**.

whooping cough — An infectious disease, usually of childhood, characterized by a whoop before inspiration. In severe cases the person has difficulty drawing breath. Occurrence of this disease has been drastically reduced by immunization. *Herbal agents:* **red clover** flowers are *specific*. Also, sundew, evening primrose, and blue cohosh.

wild carrot — (*Daucus carota*). Also called Queen Anne's lace. Umbelliferae family. (*Caution: be sure of correct identification, especially if collecting in damp areas where poison hemlock and other poisonous members of this family might be found.*) Another name is bird's nest, because after flowering, the umbels curl inward in the shape of a bird's nest. When in full flower, most of the umbels have a purple flower in the center of the cluster. This helps in identification. Wild carrot is the ancestor of the garden carrot, and occasionally a wild carrot root can be found that is orangy and sweetish; usually the root is white and bitter.

Part used: seeds, although dried leaves may be used. The Indians used the mature seeds of wild carrot (when brown) as a seasoning and salt substitute. The seeds can also be sprouted.

Properties and use: aromatic, mild diuretic, anthelmintic, and carminative. Contains large amounts of potassium. Use for all urinary disorders, including kidney and bladder stones.

Preparation: 1 tablespoon of dried seeds to 1 cup of water; infuse or simmer gently for 15 minutes.

Dose: ½ cup, 3 times daily. One teaspoon of wild carrot seeds, in a decoction, can be used after a heavy meal as a carminative to settle the stomach.

Cultivated carrots are high in vitamin A and are effective in some forms of eye disease and night blindness. Take raw carrot juice or make carrot soup, mashing the carrots in their own liquid. This is also excellent for infant diarrhea. (Don't add salt, butter, or sugar.) For worms (especially round worms in children), take the juice of two or three carrots a day (use a juicer or grate finely in a blender). Grated fresh carrots can also be used as a poultice for sores and wounds.

wild sarsaparilla — (*Aralia nudicaulis*). Ginseng family. A woodland plant with three-part compound leaves; leafless flower stem rises from root; spherical greenish flower head. Not in the same family as the commercial sarsaparilla.

Part used: root.
Properties and use: alterative, somewhat diuretic; may be used in hot infusion for head colds, congestion of lungs, stomach or other mucous membranes.
Preparation: hot infusion, as tea. (Two tablespoonsful of wild sarsaparilla root can be added to root beer formula. See page 152.)
Dose: 2-3 tablespoons, 3 or 4 times a day.

wild strawberry — See **strawberry**.

witch hazel — (*Hamamelis virginiana*). A common shrub or small tree, growing along stream banks. The species is unusual in that the yellow blossoms appear in the fall instead of the spring.

Parts used: twigs, bark, and leaves.
Properties and use: astringent, tonic, sedative. Used to check internal hemorrhaging, for leucorrhea, dysentery, and diarrhea, nasal catarrh (use in atomizer), rectal prolapse and hemorrhoids, eye wash, mouth wash, scaly skin, varicose veins.
Preparation: decoction—1 teaspoon of bark or leaves in 1 cup of water. (*Note—the commercial preparation of witch hazel bought in drug stores contains rubbing alcohol and cannot be used internally.*) Can also be made into an ointment.
Dose: 1 tablespoon doses, up to 1 cupful a day.

worms — See **anthelmintics**.

wounds — See **antiseptics, hemostatics, vulneraries. Sphagnum moss** is an antiseptic dressing. **Calendula** lotion or ointment externally, and infusion internally. Also **daisy**.

"X"

xerophthalmia — Dryness of the eyeball, caused by vitamin A deficiency. See under **vitamins** and **wild carrot**.

"Y"

yarrow — (*Achillea millfolia*). Composite family. Common weed with feathery leaves; flowers in broad-topped clusters, white with grayish centers.

Parts used: leaves and tops.

Properties and use: mild tonic, astringent, diaphoretic, stimulant. Use in early stages of a cold and fevers. For painful and profuse menses, leucorrhea, enuresis, pneumonia, nephritis, acute Bright's disease (because it influences the pituitary). Infusion snuffed up the nose for hay fever. As a wash for varicose veins.

Preparation: infusion, warm, or cold as a tonic; 1 tablespoon to 1 cup of water. (Usually combined with boneset and peppermint for flu.)

Dose: wineglassful, 3-4 times daily.

yellow dock — See **dock**.

"Z"

zea mays — See **corn silk**.

Self-review Questions for "W" — "X" — "Y" — "Z"

1. The herbal agents listed in this lesson are white water lily, wild carrot, wild sarsaparilla, witch hazel, and yarrow. List the properties and parts used for each.

2. Which *specifics* were mentioned in this lesson?

3. Under **worms** it says, "See **anthelmintics**." Which ones are safe for children?

4. Vocabulary to define:

umbels

(Answers on page 216.)

Part Three

Appendices

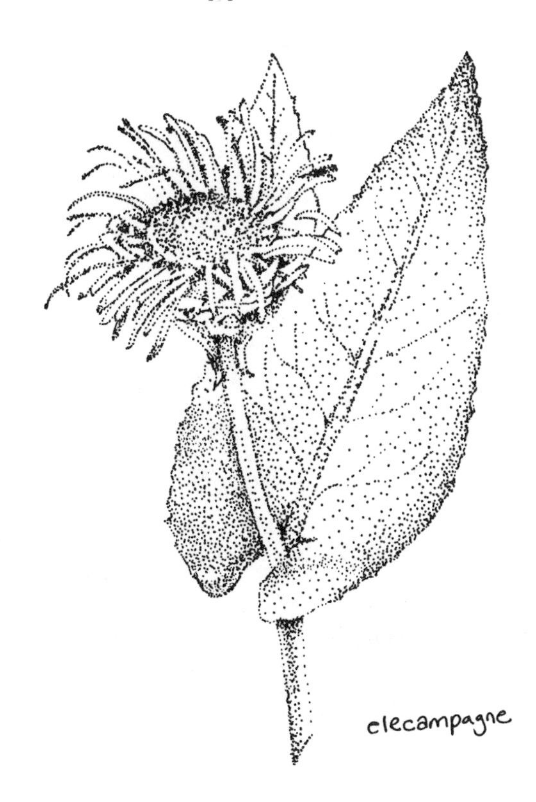

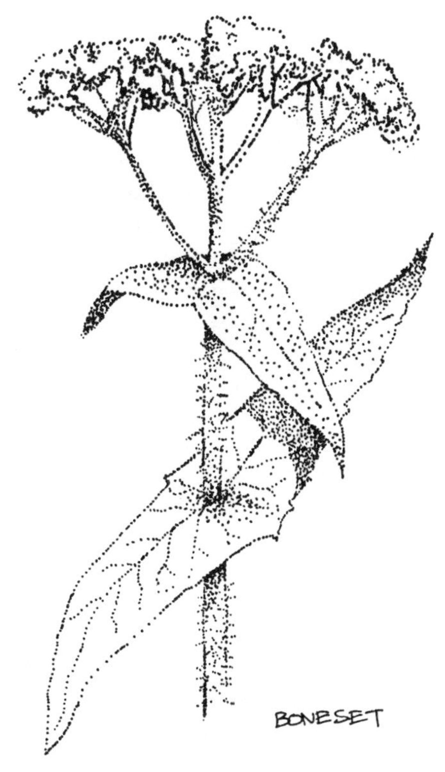

Appendices

I

The Ten Most Useful Herbs For Beginners

Boneset — for flu.
Calendula — for general antibiotic, children's diseases, healing.
Chamomile — for children's colic, nervous stomach in children and adults.
Catnip — for nervous children.
Daisy — for internal healing.
Mullein — for adults' diarrhea.
Peppermint — for stomach, fevers, flavor.
Raspberry leaves — diseases of women and children.
Slippery elm — nutritive gruel when no other can be tolerated; demulcent, poultices.
Yarrow — for colds, circulation, stimulant, fevers.

II

Common Herbs to Collect Wild

This longer list covers herbs that are not only plentiful but among the most useful of the herbs mentioned in this book.

- **Alder bark**
- **Boneset**
- **Burdock seeds**
- **Daisy**
- **Elderberries**
- **Elecampane**
- **Joe-Pye weed**
- **Meadowsweet**
- **Motherwort**
- **Mullein**
- **Prickly ash**
- **Red clover blossoms**
- **Slippery elm bark**
- **Squawvine**
- **Trillium**
- **White poplar bark**
- **Wild mint**
- **Wild strawberry plants**
- **Yarrow**
- **Yellow dock**

III

Herbs To Grow Near The House

These are herbs that are sometimes hard to find in the wild, or are not hardy, and seed must be saved. Most of them are easily obtained from nurseries that specialize in herbs, and are easily grown.

Barberry — Makes a pleasant hedge. Found wild in some areas, but often available in nurseries.

Bee balm — Semihardy; mulch well in winter. Plant near bee hives. Plants easily divided.

Calendula — Old-fashioned, prolific annual. Save seeds each year or purchase in garden stores.

Catnip — Hardy. Transplant from wild. Put it where you won't mind if it spreads.

Chamomile — Hardy. Thrives in gravelly soil, even in driveways. Once used to make paths in herb gardens.

Costmary — Hardy. Get plants or grow indoors from seed. Rather rare in the wild.

Garlic — Easily grown. Plant single cloves from larger bulb. Save dried bulbs from previous year or use commercial product.

Hawthorn — Try to find the English variety. Small tree.

Hollyhocks — Hardy biennial, often available from another's garden. Or buy started plants.

Horehound — Hardy over the winter, once established. Buy plants or raise indoors from seed.

Nasturtiums — Annuals; save or purchase seeds. Plant in vegetable garden, near vine crops, to discourage pests.

Parsley — A diuretic, high in potassium, easily grown from seed each year. Or pot inside for winter use.

Pennyroyal — Hardy when established. Needs damp location.

Peppermint — Hardy. Plant in wet places, if possible. Plants easily divided for transplanting.

Red raspberry — Buy plants from nursery or garden store. Canes pruned annually provide leaves for medicine and tea.

Rosemary — Not hardy in the far north. Bring indoors in winter. Available in plant or seed.

Sage — A good culinary as well as tonic herb. From plant or seed. Start anew every few years.

Spearmint — Hardy. Rank spreader once it gets started.

Tansy — Old-fashioned tonic and insect repellant, often found in colonial gardens. Plants easily divided.

Thyme — Many varieties. Hardy. From plant or seed.

Valerian — Garden heliotrope. Hardy and attractive. From plant or seed.

Viburnum — Especially highbush cranberry. Transplant from wild or order from nursery. Also attracts songbirds.

IV

Botanical Supply Houses

These may be of help for herbs and preparations you cannot find or make yourself. Write for their catalogs.

- Boericke and Tafel, 1011 Arch Street, Philadelphia, PA 19107. The original and well-established supplier of homeopathic preparations of all kinds. Most of these are botanical in origin and simple to administer. Also investigate their calendula products such as calendula ointment. It doesn't sting, and children will accept it readily for scrapes and bruises.

- Herb Pharm, P.O. Box 116, Williams, OR 97544. This is the best source for special herbal tinctures and extracts such as *echinacea* (see under AIDS) as well as some very good compound formulas. This company is run by a practicing herbalist.

- Indiana Botanic Gardens, P.O. Box 5, Hammond, IN 46325. This is one of the oldest and most reputable botanical supply houses. Their regular catalog is now heavily weighted with natural cosmetics and vitamin supplements, as their customers demand mostly these. But look carefully and you can find their plain herbs and various compounds.

- Penn Herb Company, 603 North 2nd Street, Philadelphia, PA 19123. This catalog gives a list of plain herbs as well as their special herbal formulas, with indications for their use. This company also handles homeopathic preparations, some natural foods, and an extensive selection of herbal fluid extracts (in small bottles with dropper).

All of these companies carry additional useful items such as juicers, books, tea infusion spoons, and other health care products.

Also check out your local natural food stores for herbal products packaged by these and other established companies. However, *do not buy* herbs that they have on display in large glass jars without any indication as to what company supplied them. Some are brought in by local herb gatherers who may not have their identification correct, and who may not have dried them carefully. (See the *caution* under **melilot**.)

V

How to Make an Herbarium

The purpose of an herbarium is to preserve specimens of plants in a dried form so as to identify them and show them to others. You will need:

- **a press** — for pressing the fresh plants until they are dried. The best type for this is a folded newspaper of tabloid size (12" by 18"), held under a weight until the herb is dry. Some magazines work well, too, but they are not as absorbent for the more succulent plants, and may impart their own color if the page is heavily printed. Sheets of corrugated cardboard can be used to maintain a rigid shape, as well as to serve as a separation between the newspaper-clad specimens.

- **a scrapbook** — for mounting the specimens once they are dried. Other choices might be a photo-type album, manila folders, a three-ring binder, or a large card file.

- **paste or tape** for mounting and labels. File cards may be useful.

In the field:

- For trees, shrubs, and woody vines, clip off a sufficient length of twig to show several leaves. Also include flowers or fruit. Take enough specimens for ample identification (including some to send to a professional botanist, if you have any question). In picking specimens, be careful not to break down a tree, and do not take more than a twig or two if it is the only tree of this sort around.

- For herbaceous plants, try to get the whole plant, including some of the root (brush the dirt off). Get a typical plant, neither the smallest nor the largest. Be sure to get several complete flowers or fruits/seeds. If fruits are too bulky or juicy to press, keep them in a separate plastic bag. Do not collect an herb if it is the only one of its species you can see anywhere around. Be aware of legally protected species that should not be picked. Do not collect in state or national parks and forests.

• Immediately spread the specimens out, one to a page of your newspaper, magazine or folder. Show all aspects to advantage; gently flatten the flowers with a finger before final pressing, if need be, so that all parts will be displayed. Be sure the leaves don't overlap. If the stem is too long for the page, bend it into a

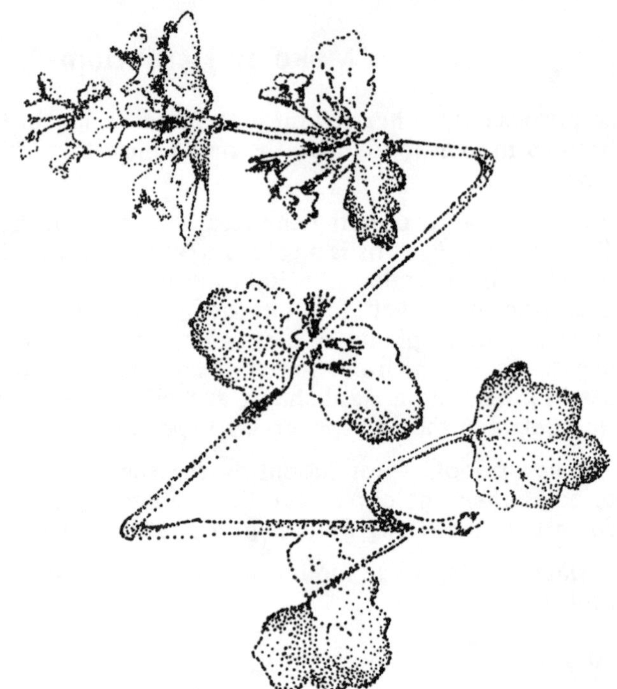

"Z" shape, but try to get it all. For very tall specimens, collect upper parts and basal leaves, if they are different from the upper leaves. **Be sure to label:** where and when collected, type of habitat where found (marsh, pine woods, field, etc.), and name of plant if known. Strap or tie the press securely, so it will stay flat.

On getting home:

• Put corrugated cardboard sheets or cut-up cardboard boxes between each two or three newsprint folders and press under a heavy weight on a smooth surface. This instruction is important for aerating the collection while drying. Every few days, check to see that plants are drying in a good position. If there appears to be any dampness, change to fresh dry newsprint, arranging plants nicely each time. Be sure to include the file card or slip with identification for each.

• When the plants are thoroughly dry (brittle), fasten them with paste or tape into your scrapbook or filing system. Be sure to include all identification and additional description. Give each one a number. You may organize these alphabetically, by geographic location, by use, or by plant families. A master list or index cards can be helpful in keeping track, once your collection becomes more than just a few.

Do's and Don'ts

1. Don't let your plants wilt before pressing!

2. Don't forget to change your driers, or your plants may mold.

3. Don't put specimens of different things on the same page, unless you deliberately want to compare or contrast: for example, two kinds of chamomile.

4. Do show several surfaces of the leaf of each specimen, and several flowers from different angles, without crowding.

5. Don't assume you can remember the date and location for your specimens without recording each on the spot.

6. Don't expect to get a botanist to give you a positive identification if you don't get sufficiently complete specimens.

7. If you expect to ask a professional botanist to help you identify your specimens, or some of them, have the courtesy to write or phone first before dumping your collection on the botanist's doorstep. If you want your collection back, include return postage or give directions for "express collect." Be sure to include your name and address.

8. Don't be a "snipper"—one who collects only bits and pieces of plants — even if *you* know what they are. Such a specimen is not useful to others.

9. Do collect a plant when you see it. Don't count on finding it another day!

VI

Poisonous Plants

No attempt is made here to cover all the possible poisonous plants that might cause serious or fatal reactions in humans or animals. I have not touched on the poisonous fungi, mushrooms, and toadstools. I will consider only those plants related to plants in the course (or that resemble them in appearance or name), commonly met wild plants, and common houseplants or garden ornamentals that are dangerous.

In many cases, the humans most at risk are children who are sometimes attracted by bright berries or unusual leaves. Next at risk are back-to-nature enthusiasts who go out after wild food plants with only a vague description or inaccurate picture in a book for guidance. In all these cases, do not depend just upon book details, ours or anyone else's. Try to go out into the field with an experienced botanist or herbalist. Many cities offer courses in foraging for wild foods, and these should be taken if possible.

The plants in this appendix are arranged in order of families, since the chemical constituents responsible for poisonous reactions are the same in a whole group of related plants. By learning the warnings for some, you can be more prudent about unknown members of that family.

Some of the poisonous plants that may be very dangerous or fatal to children may be less harmful to adults, considering the proportion of poison to body weight. In other cases, however, the poison is so concentrated or so composed that even a little can be fatal to anyone.

Various plants are dangerous mainly to livestock feeding on them, and, in some instances, can pass the poison on in milk or meat.

Molds, fungi, and algae

Aside from mushrooms and toadstools, there are other fungi that can be dangerous. Mostly they grow on grains and have sometimes found their way into flour. Ergot, which is used in the treatment of migraine and in childbirth, can be fatal. In former times, when grains were not inspected and cleaned as they are today, there were more cases of ergot poisoning.

Algae can sometimes be dangerous to swimmers, especially the blue-green algae that forms a skin like paint on the surface of some ponds. The gas and blooms of this alga cause a botulism that can be fatal. Another alga that creates a red tide on seacoasts can cause reactions when it—or fish that have eaten it—is ingested by humans.

Some molds, such as penicillin, are beneficial to man; others, such as *candida albans*, can cause dangerous reactions and should be avoided.

Ferns and other non-flowering plants

Some ferns, such as bracken, have been found to be poisonous to horses and cattle. In addition, some common ferns—maidenhair, royal, and bladder ferns—are said to be poisonous because they contain HCN (hydrocyanic acid).

Horsetail (*Equisetum*) has long been considered poisonous to livestock. It is possible, that in excess, this herb could be harmful to humans, but when used in moderation and with caution, this herb can be useful.

Trees and shrubs

• Yew. An ornamental evergreen shrub, sometimes also found wild in northern U.S. The wood was used for bows. Leaves, twigs, and seeds are poisonous. The red, fleshy part of the berry is said to be edible, but avoid the seed.

• Juniper and red cedar. The foliage is poisonous to goats and has produced abortions in animals. The oil of cedar, used in household cleaners, is dangerous.

• Locust. Native to the northern U.S. and Canada but planted as an ornamental in many places. It has finely-divided leaves and pea-like blossoms, with seeds developing in long pods like beans. The leaves, twigs, and seeds can be poisonous to children.

• Apple. This most useful tree nevertheless contains high amounts of HCN in its seeds. The tale is told of a man who so loved apple seeds that he collected a half-cupful, ate them all at once and died. The four or five seeds in one apple should not cause trouble.

• Cherries. Wild red cherries, chokecherries, wild black cherries —all contain large amounts of cyanide in their seeds and leaves, especially in leaves that are partially wilted. Sometimes browsed by cattle in pastures. All their fruits are wholesome and edible, and cherry bark is used in cough medicines. Plums are related, and their seeds and leaves are similarly dangerous.

• Apricots, peaches, and almonds. The sweet almonds of commerce are harmless, but the bitter almonds have HCN, as do apricot and peach seeds. The drug laetrile, sometimes promoted as a cure for cancer, is made from the apricot seed, but uncontrolled eating of these seeds is dangerous.

• Castor oil plant. A shrub or tall annual, sometimes cultivated in homes or gardens. The oil, that is pressed out of the seeds, is harmless and used in medicine. But the foliage, beans, and pressed seed cake (after the oil is removed) are all very toxic. One to three seeds can be fatal to a child, two to eight for an adult.

• Box. Cultivated in the eastern states for hedges. The leaves and wood are highly poisonous. *Note:* this is not the same as box elder trees.

• Privet. Also cultivated as a hedge. Its berries and leaves are very toxic, and children have died from eating them.

• Horse chestnuts and buckeyes. Related trees, sometimes grown as ornaments, others native in the western and southern areas of the country. The nuts, that sometimes resemble edible chestnuts, are poisonous.

• Laurels, rhododendrons, and azaleas. Common ornamental shrubs, native to many parts of the country. All of them are noted for their poisonous attributes, not only to livestock that may feed on them, but even the honey made from their flowers has sometimes been toxic.

• Elderberry. The berries of the common, purple-fruited elderberry are harmless when fully ripe, but the leaves and twigs can be irritating or dangerous. The red-berried elder, on the other hand, which has red berries in cones, is poisonous in all parts.

• Honeysuckle. The fruits are generally dangerous, especially from the large Japanese or bush honeysuckle, an ornamental with enticing red berries.

• Poison ivy and poison sumac. Poisonous to touch; may cause severe skin reactions. The poison sumac with droopy white berries is found only in northern bogs, whereas all other sumacs with red berries are harmless or beneficial. Poison ivy grows almost everywhere in the U.S. and can be dangerous not only to touch, but from indirect contact such as smoke, if it is burned, or from the fur of a pet. Some people are more susceptible than others, or more susceptible at different stages of life or health.

Vines

• Virginia creeper. A climbing woody vine similar to grape, but the leaves have five distinct leaflets, like the palm of a hand. It turns brilliant scarlet early in the fall. The danger is in the berries, that are blue-black and can be mistaken for grapes when the leaves of both vines have fallen. They are very toxic.

• Moonseed. Another vine that can be mistaken for grapes. Its berries are very poisonous, even fatal.

Plant families

• Lily family. Camas, very common in the west. The root is fatal to livestock and humans. Hellebore (*Veratrum*) is common in swamps, north and east. A coarsely ribbed plant that comes up folded in the spring and is often mistaken for skunk cabbage. *If eaten, death may result.*

• Daffodils and narcissus. Bulbs are poisonous.

• Iris and blue flag. The roots are poisonous and might be eaten if mistaken for some other swamp-growing roots. However, these may be used medicinally, according to instructions.

• Mistletoe. A parasitic plant growing on trees in some areas, and used as a Christmas ornamental. Leaves and berries are poisonous.

• Buttercup family. A large family (*Ranunculaeceae*), with mostly dangerous or poisonous members. The following are the best-known and most dangerous, both to cattle and humans: larkspur, delphinium, lupine, red and white baneberry (that attract children), monkshood (aconite), common field buttercups, anemones, clematis, crowfoot, and meadow rue. In general, the buttercup family contains irritating alkaloids that blister the mouth, tongue, and digestive tract, and, in highly concentrated species, can lead to death.

• Spurge family. Many, with white markings on leaves, are used as low, ornamentals. The plants can cause skin reactions and may be poisonous.

• Parsley family (*Umbelliferae*). See discussion in Lesson 1. This family contains some of the most poisonous plants known to man. Always be very sure of your species if collecting any of these in the wild. The most poisonous are: poison hemlock, water hemlock, or cowbane (various kinds).

• Nightshade family (*Solonaceae*). The most common members, potato and tomato, are poisonous in their green parts. Even potatoes that turn greenish on exposure to light can poison poultry. Heating destroys the active principle. Other dangerous species: bittersweet (*Solanum*), jimson weed (*Datura*), tobacco, deadly nightshade (belladonna), and henbane.

• Composite family. Most members of this family are quite safe. Only a few need noting: white snakeroot (resembles boneset); coneflower (black-eyed-Susan, poisonous to sheep); common tansy (can be fatal, especially the oil); wormwood (absinthe, contains a strong narcotic poison); arnica (Rocky Mountains).

Useful Texts

• *Poisonous Plants of the U.S. and Canada* by John M. Kingsbury. Englewood Cliffs, NJ: Prentice-Hall, Inc., 1964.

• *Plants That Poison* by Ervin M. Schmutz and Lucretia B. Hamilton. Flagstaff, AZ: Northland Press, 1979.

• *A Manual of Poisonous Plants* by L.H. Pammel. Cedar Rapids, IA: The Torch Press, 1910.

VII

Trees and Plants in this Course

Trees & Shrubs	Parts Used	Uses
alder, spotted	bark	alterative, tonic, astringent
apple	juice	antiseptic, nutritive, antiperiodic
ash, white	inner bark	tonic, hepatic
barberry	bark berries	tonic, hepatic astringent
basswood	flowers	tonic, antispasmodic
beech	leaves	diuretic, nuts edible
birch, black	leaves inner bark, twigs	alterative, tonic, diuretic antiseptic
birch, yellow	leaves inner bark, twigs	alterative, tonic antiseptic
butternut	inner bark	aperient, vermifuge
cherry	bark,twigs	demulcent
chokecherry	bark	antiperiodic
dogwood, red osier	bark flowers	astringent, antiperiodic tonic
elder	blossoms leaves berries	stimulant, sudorific, diaphoretic diuretic, purgative aperient

Trees & Shrubs	Parts Used	Uses
elm, slippery	inner bark	demulcent, emollient mucilaginous, nutritive
hawthorn, Eng.	berries	cardiac tonic
hemlock	bark	astringent, stimulant, antiscorbutic
hickory, shagbark	inner bark	astringent, stimulant, hepatic, nuts edible
juniper	berries	diuretic, emmenagogue
oaks	inner bark	astringent, tonic
pine, white	bark, twigs	antiscorbutic, demulcent, diuretic
poplar, balsam	buds	expectorant
poplar, white	bark	tonic, antiperiodic
prickly ash	bark, berries	tonic, alterative, diaphoretic
shadbush	berries	edible, antiscorbutic
spruce	twigs	antiscorbutic
sumac	berries	astringent, tonic, diuretic, antiscorbutic
viburnum	inner bark	astringent, antispasmodic
witch hazel	bark, twigs, leaves	astringent, tonic, sedative

Plants	Parts Used	Uses
agrimony	herb	astringent, hepatic, tonic, stimulant, aromatic
aloe	leaves	emollient, antiseptic
betony	herb	antispasmodic, tonic, nervine
bittersweet	root, bark, twigs	alterative
blackberries	root, leaves	astringent, tonic, berries edible
bloodroot	root	caustic, fungicide
blueberries	berries, root,bark	astringent, diuretic, febrifuge
boneset	herb	diaphoretic, tonic, antiperiodic
bugleweed	herb	sedative, nervine, cardiac
burdock	seeds, root, leaves	alterative, tonic, aperient
calendula	blossoms	antibiotic, vulnerary, antispasmodic
castor oil	oil from seeds	emollient, cathartic
catnip	herb	antispasmodic, carminative, nervine, aromatic, emmenagogue
celandine	herb	purgative, caustic, cholagogue
chamomile	herb	antispasmodic, carminative, nervine
chickweed	herb	antiseptic, vulnerary
cinquefoil	herb	astringent
cleavers	herb	diuretic, diaphoretic

Plants	Parts Used	Uses
clover, red	blossoms	alterative
clover, white	blossoms	specific: mumps
comfrey	leaves, roots	demulcent, vulnerary
corn silk	silk	diuretic, demulcent
costmary	herb	astringent
cranberry	berries	astringent, diuretic
daisy	herb, blossoms	tonic, vulnerary, diuretic, antispasmodic
dandelion	root, greens	aperient, hepatic, tonic, nutritive
dock, yellow	root	alterative
elecampane	root	demulcent, antibiotic
everlasting	herb	demulcent, astringent
garlic	root bulb	antiseptic, diuretic
geranium	leaves	astringent
gill-over-the-ground	herb	tonic, alterative, antiscorbutic
ginger, wild	root	carminative, stimulant, aromatic
herb Robert	herb	antiseptic, astringent
hollyhock	root, leaves, bud	demulcent, antiseptic
horehound	herb	expectorant, tonic, demulcent, stimulant
horsetail	herb	diuretic, vulnerary

Plants	Parts Used	Uses
huckleberry	berries	astringent, diuretic
Irish moss	herb	demulcent, nutritive
jewelweed	herb, juice	fungicide, caustic
Joe-Pye weed	root	diuretic, stimulant
lady's bedstraw	herb flowers	astringent, diuretic antispasmodic
lady's-slipper	root	antispasmodic, nervine
lemon balm	herb	antispasmodic, carminative, diaphoretic
lichens (various)	plant	antibiotic, nutritive
lily-of-the-valley	root	digitalis substitute, cardiac
lungwort	herb	pectoral
lycopodium	herb	antiseptic
male fern	root	anthelmintic
marsh mallow	herb root	demulcent, emollient nutrient
meadowsweet	herb	antacid, astringent, tonic
melilot, sweet	herb	antithrombotic, aromatic, emollient, carminative
milkweed	root	diuretic, emetic, purgative
mint, wild	herb	emmenagogue, diuretic, aromatic
motherwort	herb	cardiac tonic, emmenagogue, antispasmodic, nervine

Plants	Parts Used	Uses
mullein	leaves	astringent, alterative, sedative, anodyne, emetic
mustard	herb, seeds	antiscorbutic, emetic, stimulant
nasturtium	herb	antiscorbutic
nettles	herb	antiscorbutic, antiseptic, astringent, tonic
oats	seeds	nervine, tonic, demulcent
pennyroyal	herb	emmenagogue, insect repellent
peppermint	herb	antiseptic, nervine, antispasmodic, aromatic, carminative, emmenagogue
plantain	herb; root	antiseptic, vulnerary, hemostatic
pleurisy root	root	diaphoretic, expectorant
polypody	root	demulcent, laxative
raspberry, red	leaves	astringent, tonic
rose, wild	leaves, fruit	astringent, stimulant, antiscorbutic, tonic
rosemary	herb	emmenagogue, antispasmodic
sage	herb	astringent, antispasmodic, diaphoretic
St. Johnswort	herb	astringent, nervine, antispasmodic, analgesic, antiperiodic
self-heal	herb	astringent, vulnerary

Plants	Parts Used	Uses
skullcap	herb	antispasmodic, tonic, nervine
shepherd's-purse	herb	stimulant, astringent, hemostatic, antiscorbutic
silverweed	herb	astringent
Solomon's seal	root	astringent, demulcent,tonic
spearmint	herb	emmenagogue, carminative
sphagnum moss	herb	antiseptic
spikenard	root	alterative
strawberry, wild	herb, root	astringent, antiscorbutic
squawvine	herb	female tonic, astringent
sunflower	seeds	vermifuge
thyme	herb	antiseptic, astringent, emmenagogue
tormentil	herb, root	astringent, tonic
trailing arbutus	herb	astringent, diuretic
trillium	root	astringent, uterine
turtlehead	herb	aperient, anthelmintic, tonic, cathartic
valerian	root	antispasmodic, nervine
veronica	herb	alterative, expectorant, diuretic, emmenagogue
vervain, blue	herb	antispasmodic, nervine
viburnum, several	inner bark	astringent, antispasmodic

Plants	Parts Used	Uses
violet	herb, blossoms	laxative, anodyne
water lily, white	root	astringent, demulcent
water lily, yellow	root, seeds	edible
wild carrot	seeds, leaves	aromatic, diuretic, anthelmintic, carminative
wild sarsaparilla	root	alterative, diuretic
yarrow	herb	astringent, stimulant, diaphoretic, tonic

YARROW

Final Exam

1. List five major families of safe herbs to use. (Add examples of specific herbs you remember.)

2. List five families of dangerous herbs, with identifying characteristics.

3. What family of herbs is useful at other times but should not be used (except sparingly) during pregnancy?

4. Following are some of the major classes of herbal agents. Describe the effects of each class of agent. Then list at least five herb examples.

alteratives
antiseptics
astringents
demulcents
diuretics
nervines
stimulants
tonics

5. One unique class of agents is not listed above; it is useful in treating the diseases and complaints caused by a vitamin deficiency. List that class of agent, the vitamin deficiency, and at least five herbal remedies. (Do you remember one symptom of this deficiency that is frequent and easily diagnosed?)

6. Name what you would consider the ten most important herbs for your needs and give the general use of each.

7. Describe the procedure (and proportions) for the following herbal preparations:

standard infusion
concentrated infusion
decoction
herbal syrup
ointment
poultice
suppositories

8. Modern medical theory differs greatly from herbal theory. Discuss five conditions for which modern medicine has few answers and for which there may be herbal relief. Be sure to include the rationale for the herbal remedies.

9. Herbal remedies often work best when combined with other non-medical treatment. Name three such treatments.

10. For many conditions, herbalists have identified *specifics*—remedies that equal or surpass prescription medicine because of their efficacy and safety. (Some of these herbs have additional applications, as well.) Match the herb with the condition for which it is suited.

agrimony	acid stomach
aloe	acne
betony	bedwetting
black haw	burns
boneset	fibroid tumors
costmary	flu
hawthorn	headache
Joe-Pye weed	heart disease
meadowsweet	kidney stones, gravel
motherwort	menopause
raspberry leaves	morning sickness
shepherd's-purse	mumps
trillium	sinus, head cold
white clover blossoms	threatened miscarriage
yellow dock	uterine bleeding

11. I have listed some physical complaints and medical problems. You fill in the herbal remedy that might be helpful for each condition. (There may be more than one answer for each.)

angina	diarrhea
arthritis	epilepsy
athlete's foot	headaches
bedwetting	hemorrhoids
bleeding gums	insomnia
burns	menopause
colic	menstrual cramps
constipation	overweight
cough	pimples or acne
dandruff	ringing in the ears
diaper rash	ulcers
	warts

(Answers on page 217.)

Answers

Self-review Questions for Botanical Families

1. The trillium has three petals and three sepals. The veins of its leaves are parallel to each other. To which of the two major classes of plant families do you think it belongs—monocot or dicot? **Monocot.**

2. Which three large plant families of many species would you consider the safest for a beginner? **Rose, mustard, composite.**

3. Which three, similarly, are the most dangerous, medicinally? (Do not include the Rhus family here.) **Umbelliferae, solanaceae, crowfoot (buttercup).**

4. Although no one plant family can claim a monopoly of any of the various classes of herbal agents, to which one, according to this lesson, would you look for an appropriate astringent? **Rose.**

5. To which one would you look for a nerve tonic (nervine)? **Labiatiae (mint).**

6. In which family would you find an agent for the urinary system? **Heath family, which includes vaccinium species.**

7. If you heard someone talking about wanting some "bittersweet" and also some "thorn apple," what four different plants might be referred to? **Thorn apple (cratageus) is safe; thorn apple/jimson weed (solanaceae) is dangerous. Bittersweet (staff tree) is safe; bittersweet (solanaceae) is dangerous.**

8. What is the value of using Latin names for plants? **Latin names are unique to each species.**

9. Vocabulary words to define: **See glossary.**

Self-review Questions for Herbal Preparations

1. What determines when and how you will collect an herb? **Part used, plant maturation, preparation intended.**

2. Why are leafy herbs to be gathered when just coming into full flower? **Easiest to identify; reached full growth and strength.**

3. What time of year, generally speaking, would you collect the following for herbal use:

catnip herb — **Early summer.**
yellow dock root — **Fall.**
sunflower seeds — **Late summer.**
slippery elm bark — **Spring.**

4.What are two exceptions to the rule that herbs should be picked dry and stored dry? **When expressed juice or the fresh berries are to be used.**

5. What is the main difference between infusions and decoctions? **Infusions are never boiled, decoctions are.**

6. When would you need a concentrated infusion? **In a preparation with alcohol, syrup, or honey; for an ointment or poultice.**

7. Decoctions are used most often in preparing what parts of a plant? **Roots, bark, and seeds.**

8. Name four kinds of preservative agents that can be added to herbal preparations? **Alcohol, vinegar, oil, sugar, or honey.**

9. What is the advantage of using brandy instead of wine in some herbal preparations? **It has better keeping qualities.**

10. For what purpose might you choose a vinegar mix? **For gargles or shrubs.**

11. When would you use a poultice? **Sprains, arthritis, sore joints, or boils.**

12. Which preparation method is probably the best way to make use of herbs? Why? **Infusion; less of the herbal action is lost in a simple preparation.**

13. Vocabulary words to define: **See glossary.**

Self-review Questions for Agents

1. Name three classes of herbal agents that herbalists find very useful but that modern medicine uses rarely. **Alteratives, astringents, nervines.**

2. In what category of agents would you look for herbs for the following:

adolescent acne — **Alteratives.**
diarrhea — **Astringents.**
insomnia — **Nervines.**
sore throat — **Astringents.**
flatulence — **Carminatives.**
sprained ankle — **Vulneraries.**

3. List five or six herbs that are especially appropriate for children and the class or category each belongs to.

Blackberry — astringent.
Butternut — vermifuge.
Calendula — antibiotic.
Raspberry — astringent.
Strawberry — astringent.
Turtlehead — cathartic, anthelmintic.

4. What three classes of agents do you think would be especially helpful to the elderly? **Aperients, nervines, tonics.**

5. What cautions would you think of if someone asked you for:

a laxative — **Be sure the case is not appendicitis.**
a sedative — **Find the cause of tension; beware of dependency.**
a stimulant — **Beware of exhaustion, especially in heart patients.**

6. What class of agents should not be used in pregnancy? **Emmenagogues.**

7. What is the best herbal antibiotic? **Calendula.**

8. Give two reasons for avoiding the use of anodynes. **Many are dangerous; it is better to heal the cause of the pain.**

9. Vocabulary to define: **See glossary.**

Self-review Questions for "A"

1. Five herbs in this section were discussed in detail:

agrimony — **Herb: astringent, tonic, stimulant.**
alder — **Bark: alterative, astringent, tonic.**
aloe — **Leaves: emollient, antiseptic.**
apple — **Juice: antiseptic.**
ash — **Inner bark: tonic, hepatic.**

2. Why might abortifacients be dangerous? **Difficulty in controlling hemorrhaging; some are toxic.**

3. What is a safe and common substance that prevents dental caries? **Apple juice.**

4. What two agents included in this lesson are said to have an effect on the liver? **Ash, agrimony.**

5. What one agent (not listed in this section) was mentioned three times in association with heart disease? **Hawthorn.**

6. For what condition mentioned in this lesson is immediate surgery usually indicated? **Acute appendicitis.**

7. Under what situations would the same condition be treated herbally? **Chronic, low-grade, or in uncertain diagnosis.** With what? **Agrimony.**

8. What herb is recommended for bedwetting? **Agrimony.** In what preparation? **Cold infusion.**

9. What agents stimulate the immune system? **Echinacea, red clover.**

10. List five natural therapies, other than herbs, that were recommended for some of the conditions in this section. **Diet, fasting, massage, elimination, bee venom, chiropractic, osteopathic.**

11. Vocabulary to define: **See glossary.**

Self-review Questions for "B"

1. Thirteen agents were listed in this lesson:

barberry — **Bark, berries: tonic, astringent.**
basswood — **Flowers: tonic, antispasmodic.**
beech — **Leaves: diuretic.**
betony — **Herb: nervine, tonic.**
birch — **Leaves, inner bark: alterative, tonic, diuretic.**
bittersweet — **Root, bark, twigs: alterative.**
blackberry — **Root, leaves: astringent, tonic.**
bloodroot — **Root: caustic, fungicide.**
blueberry — **Berries, root, bark: astringent, diuretic.**
boneset — **Herb: diaphoretic, antiperiodic, tonic.**
bugleweed — **Herb: nervine.**
burdock — **Seeds, root, leaves: alterative, tonic, aperient.**
butternut — **Inner bark: aperient, vermifuge.**

2. Under bladder agents, it says to see diuretics. Which agents in this lesson were listed as diuretics? **Beech, birch, and blueberry.**

3. Which agent was mentioned as being a specific for headaches of undetermined origin? **Betony.** Where would you find it? **Garden flower.**

4. Several agents in this lesson were mentioned as being useful in skin diseases which are nervous in origin or caused by disorders of the blood. Which ones? **Bittersweet, burdock.**

5. Which agents in this lesson would be good for skin diseases resulting from external causes such as fungus? **Bloodroot.**

6. Which agents in this lesson should be used with caution? **Bloodroot, bugleweed.**

7. "The leaves of the trees shall be for the healing of the nations." (Revelations 22:2) The leaves of what trees were mentioned in this lesson for healing? **Beech, birch.**

8. Which plants mentioned in this lesson have useful berries? For what?

Barberry — astringent.
Blackberry — astringent, tonic.
Blueberries — diuretic, astringent.

9. Vocabulary to define: **See glossary.**

Self-review Questions for "C" (part one)

1. What would you advise friends who are told they have inoperable cancer? **Diet, fasting, herbs, and other natural therapies may offer an improved quality of life and health. What would you say of an herbalist who made up a compound of podophyllum, celandine, red clover, and dandelion, and advertised it as a "cancer cure?" No herbalist can guarantee a "cure." Otherwise, the formula is good.**

2. What herb in this lesson is better cultivated in the garden rather than being sought in the wild? **Calendula.**

3. Which herb mentioned in this lesson should not be used in pregnancy? **Catnip.** What one word in its description leads you to think so? **Emmenagogue.**

4. The herbal agents listed in this lesson were:

   calendula — **Antibiotic.**
   castor oil — **Emollient, cathartic.**
   catnip — **Nervine, emmenagogue, carminative.**
   celandine — **Caustic, purgative.**
   chamomile — **Nervine, carminative.**
   chickweed — **Antiseptic, vulnerary.**

5. Of the agents listed above, which is the most universally useful? **Calendula.**

6. Vocabulary to define: **See glossary.**

Self-review Questions for "C" (part two)

1. The herbs mentioned in this lesson were:

   chokecherry — **Bark: antiperiodic**
   cleavers — **Herb: diuretic, diaphoretic.**
   red clover — **Blossoms: alterative.**
   comfrey — **Leaves, roots: demulcent, vulnerary.**
   cornsilk — **Silk: diuretic, demulcent.**
   costmary — **Herb: astringent, demulcent.**
   cranberry **Berries: astringent, diuretic, antibacterial.**

2. What herbs in this lesson are mentioned as prophylactic? **Red clover, white clover.**

3. How many kinds of flowers are mentioned for herbal use in children's diseases? **Red clover, white clover, calendula, violets, lilacs, sweet chamomile.**

4. Which herbs appear most frequently in the treatment of children? **Raspberry leaves, calendula.**

5. Chokecherry is listed as an antiperiodic. Therefore, it can be used for what? **Fevers.** What caution do you need to remember? **The leaves and seeds are dangerous.**

6. What three herbal agents in this lesson are listed as diuretic or good for kidney diseases? **Cleavers, corn silk, and cranberry.**

7. Vocabulary to define: **See glossary.**

Self-review Questions for "D"

1. Herbal agents covered in this lesson are:

   daisy — **Herb, blossoms: tonic, vulnerary, diuretic.**
   dandelion — **Root, greens: aperient, hepatic, tonic.**
   yellow dock — **Root: alterative.**
   dogwood — **Bark, flowers: astringent, antiperiodic, tonic.**

2. Which of the above agents could be used for diarrhea or for dysentery? **Dogwood.**

3. Which herbal agent in this lesson is a specific for skin diseases? **Yellow dock.**

4. What herb or herbs in this lesson would you use in convalescence from an operation? **Daisy.**

5. What is the remedy for insulin shock? **Sugar or glucose.**

6. What is the remedy for diabetic coma? **Insulin.**

7. Which of the above symptoms could occur in a nondiabetic? **Symptoms similar to those of insulin shock occur in people with hypoglycemia.**

8. What are the extra dietary needs of teenage young women? **Iron.**

9. Vocabulary words to define: **See glossary.**

Self-review Questions for "E"

1. The herbal agents covered in this lesson were:

   elder — **Blossoms: stimulant; leaves: diuretic; berries: aperient, diuretic.**
   elecampane — **Root: demulcent, antibiotic.**
   elm — **Inner bark: demulcent, emollient, nutritive.**
   everlasting — **Herb: demulcent, astringent.**

2. What three plants are mentioned as specifics and for what conditions? **Sweet melilot for embolisms, elecampane for TB, and elderberry wine for sciatica.**

3. What remedy would you recommend to persons with poor hearing? **B vitamins.**

4. What remedy would you try if an invalid had trouble keeping down anything eaten? **Slippery elm gruel.**

5. What plant is mentioned in this lesson only as a warning that it is dangerous? **English ivy.**

6. How is erysipelas different from eczema? **Erysipelas is caused by an infection. Eczema is a constitutional, allergic-type response.**

7. In one entry you are directed to make a concentrated infusion. How does that procedure differ from the standard infusion? **Eight times the usual amount of herb, three-quarters the amount of water.**

8. Some older herbals call for "1 dr." of a dried herb. Consult a dictionary to see how much that would be. **One-eighth of an ounce.**

9. Vocabulary to define: **See glossary.**

Self-review Questions for "F" and "G"

1. The herbal agents covered in this lesson are:

   garlic — **Root (bulb): antiseptic, diuretic.**
   geraniums — **Leaves: astringent.**
   gill-over-the-ground — **Herb: tonic, alterative, antiscorbutic.**
   ginger — **Root: carminative, stimulant, aromatic.**

2. Vinegar appears as an important agent for which three conditions? **Food poisoning, gravel and kidney stones, and for gargles.**

3. What substance mentioned in this lesson is best used fresh? **Garlic.**

4. Identify one reason why fasting may be of importance when using herbal remedies. **It allows the herb to go to work without competing with additional matter.**

5. Which agents in this lesson were identified as specifics and for what conditions? **Colchicum for gout; Joe-Pye weed for kidney stones or gravel; boneset for flu.**

6. What remedy might you suggest for athlete's foot? **Bloodroot or jewelweed.**

7. Which agent listed in this lesson is probably most appropriate for bronchitis? **Garlic.**

8. Which agent in this lesson may speed the action of other agents? **Ginger.**

9. Vocabulary to define: **See glossary.**

Self-review Questions for "H"

1. The agents listed in this section are:

hawthorn — **Berries: cardiac tonic.**
herb Robert — **Herb: antiseptic, astringent.**
hemlock tree — **Bark: astringent, stimulant.**
shagbark hickory — **Inner bark: astringent, stimulant, hepatic.**
hollyhock — **Root, leaves, buds: demulcent, antiseptic.**
horehound — **Herb: expectorant, demulcent, tonic, stimulant.**
horsetails — **Herb: diuretic, vulnerary.**
huckleberry — **Berries: astringent, diuretic.**

2. Which agents can be made up by using the expressed raw juice in a syrup or honey? **Hawthorn and horehound.** What are the advantages of this method? **Contains all the properties in the fresh condition.**

3. What is one of the unique properties of honey relevant for medical purposes? **It is bacteriostatic.**

4. What agent is specific for most kinds of heart disease and why? **Hawthorn; it tends to normalize heart function and strengthen heart tissue.**

5. What three references were made to dangerous plants? **Hellebore, similar to skunk cabbage; poison hemlock is not related to the hemlock tree; hawthorn is sometimes called thorn apple, which should not be confused with a member of the nightshade family.** What cautions would occur to you if a friend offered you some "wild caraway seed?" **If misidentified, it could be poison hemlock.**

6. Vocabulary to define: **See glossary.**

Self-review Questions for "I" through "L"

1. The herbal agents listed in this section were:

Irish moss — **Herb: demulcent, nutritive.**
jewelweed — **Herb, juice: fungicide, hepatic, caustic.**
Joe-Pye weed — **Root: diuretic, stimulant.**
juniper — **Berries: diuretic, emmenagogue.**
lady's bedstraw — **Herb, astringent, diuretic; flowers, antispasmodic.**
lady's-slipper — **Root: antispasmodic, nervine.**
lemon balm — **Herb: antispasmodic, carminative, diaphoretic.**
lily-of-the-valley — **Root: cardiac, digitalis substitute.**
lungwort — **Herb: pectoral.**
lycopodium — **Herb: antiseptic.**

2. Which agent in this section is useful in disorders of the lungs? **Lungwort.**

3. Which agent in this lesson should be used with caution? **Lily-of-the-valley.**

4. Which herb is said to be safer than a common heart medication and why? **Lily-of-the-valley; no side effects, noncumulative.**

5. Which herb in this lesson is found cultivated more often than wild? **Lemon balm.**

6. What is a lichen? **Symbiotic relationship between a fungus and an alga.**

7. What plants called by names including the word "moss" are not mosses at all? What are they? **Irish moss is a seaweed; reindeer moss is a lichen.**

8. Which specifics were mentioned in this lesson for what conditions? **Boneset for influenza; Joe-Pye weed for urinary stone and gravel; garlic syrup for laryngitis.**

9. Vocabulary to define: **See glossary.**

Self-review Questions for "M"

1. The herbal agents in this lesson were:

male fern — **Root: anthelmintic.**
meadowsweet — **Herb: antacid, astringent, tonic.**
melilot — **Herb: antithrombotic, aromatic, emollient, carminative.**
milkweed — **Root: diuretic, emetic, purgative.**
mints — **Herb: emmenagogue, aromatic.**
motherwort — **Herb: nervine, emmenagogue, cardiac tonic, antispasmodic.**
mullein — **Leaves: astringent, alterative, sedative, anodyne, emetic.**
mustard — **Herb, seeds: antiscorbutic, stimulant.**

2. Name five specifics mentioned in this lesson and the conditions for which they are used. **Male fern for tapeworm; meadowsweet for acid stomach; melilot for embolism; motherwort for problems of menopause; betony for headache; black haw for threatened miscarriage.**

3. What two plants were mentioned as milder and safer substitutes for two of the plants in this lesson? **Lady fern for male fern; wild ginger for mustard.**

4. What were the three ferns named in this lesson? (You may want to check a botany book or encyclopedia to find the major difference between ferns and the other plants we usually use.) **Male fern, lady fern, and spleenwort.**

5. Which two conditions in this lesson require strict bed rest as part of the care? **Mononucleosis and threatened miscarriage.**

6. List at least five remedies (both herbal and nonherbal) for difficulties of menopause. **Exercise, elimination, diet, vitamin supplement, and motherwort.**

7. What condition in this lesson has no specific treatment by modern medicine but does have herbal remedies? **Mononucleosis.**

8. What herb(s) in this lesson appeared most frequently on the mineral list? **Meadowsweet.**

9. What herbs might serve as a replacement for table salt? **Cleavers, meadowsweet, and nettles are high in sodium, but any culinary herb serves a similar taste function.**

10. Vocabulary to define: **See glossary.**

Self-review Questions for "N" through "Q"

1. The herbal agents covered in this lesson are:

nasturtiums — **Herb: antiscorbutic.**
nettles — **Herb: antiscorbutic,tonic, antiseptic, astringent.**
oaks — **Inner bark: astringent, tonic.**
oats — **Seeds: nervine, tonic, demulcent.**
white pine — **Bark, twigs: antiscorbutic, demulcent, diuretic.**
plantain — **Herb, root: antiseptic, vulnerary, hemostatic.**
pleurisy root — **Root: diaphoretic, expectorant.**
polypody — **Root: demulcent, laxative.**
balsam poplar — **Buds: expectorant.**
white poplar — **Bark: tonic, antiperiodic.**
prickly ash — **Bark, berries: tonic, alterative, diaphoretic.**

2. Which agents in this lesson may be used as food as well as in medicinal situations? **Nasturtiums, nettles, oats, white oak acorns.**

3. List the specifics mentioned, and for what conditions they are used. **Valerian for facial neuralgia; balsam poplar buds for lung disorders; calendula for prostate problems.**

4. What family of herbs should be used sparingly in pregnancy? **Mints (Labiatiae).** What other herbal caution is relevant to pregnancy? **Avoid any herb that is an emmenagogue.**

5. Which agents in this lesson are quinine substitutes? **Prickly ash, white poplar.**

6. Vocabulary to define: **See glossary.**

Self-review Questions for "R"

1. The herbal agents listed in this section are:

raspberry — **Leaves: astringent, tonic.**
rose — **Leaves, fruit: astringent, antiscorbutic, tonic, stimulant.**
rosemary — **Herb: emmenagogue, antispasmodic.**

2. What agent (and what additional course of action) is most useful in radiation sickness? **Aloe, plus a high intake of vitamin E and calcium.**

3. What therapies may be helpful in the treatment of rheumatism? **Bee venom and diet.**

4. What disease in this lesson might prove fatal without immediate medical treatment? **Rabies.**

5. What is the remedy for ringworm? **Bloodroot or jewelweed.**

6. What herb is helpful in treating dandruff? **Rosemary.**

7. Vocabulary to define: **See glossary.**

Self-review Questions for "S"

1. The herbal agents in this lesson are:

sage — **Herb: astringent, antispasmodic, diaphoretic.**
St. Johnswort — **Herb: astringent, nervine, analgesic, antiperiodic.**
sarsaparilla — **Root: alterative, diuretic.**
self-heal — **Herb: astringent, vulnerary.**
shadbush — **Berries: antiscorbutic, edible.**

shepherd's-purse — **Herb: stimulant, astringent, hemostatic, antiscorbutic.**
silverweed — **Herb: astringent.**
skullcap — **Herb: antispasmodic, nervine, tonic.**
Solomon's seal — **Root: astringent, demulcent, tonic.**
sphagnum moss — **Herb: antiseptic.**
spikenard — **Root: alterative.**
spruce — **Twigs: antiscorbutic.**
squawvine — **Herb: astringent, female tonic.**
strawberry — **Herb, root: astringent, antiscorbutic.**
sunflower — **Seeds: vermifuge.**
sumac — **Berries: astringent, tonic, diuretic, antiscorbutic.**

2. What specific is mentioned in this section and for what condition is it used? **Shepherd's-purse for fibroid tumors.**

3. What plant in this lesson is our best general tonic for the genitourinary tract? **Squawvine.**

4. What plant in this lesson is one of the finest nervines ever discovered? **Skullcap.**

5. What disease mentioned here is rarely heard of today but has beginning symptoms which are quite common? **Scurvy; bleeding gums.** What is the cause? **Insufficient vitamin C.**

6. What two agents were mentioned for enuresis? **Shepherd's-purse and sumac.**

7. Vocabulary to define: **See glossary.**

Self-review Questions for "T" — "U" — "V"

1. The agents listed in this lesson are:

thyme — **Herb: antiseptic, astringent, emmenagogue.**
tormentil — **Herb, root: astringent, tonic.**
trailing arbutus — **Herb: astringent, diuretic.**
trillium — **Root: astringent, uterine.**
turtlehead — **Herb: aperient, anthelmintic, tonic, cathartic.**
vaccinium — **Berries: astringent, diuretic, nutritive.**
valerian — **Root: antispasmodic, nervine.**
veronica — **Herb: alterative, expectorant, diuretic, emmenagogue.**
vervain — **Herb: antispasmodic, nervine.**

viburnum — **Inner bark: antispasmodic, astringent.**
vinegar — **Astringent, antiseptic.**
violet — **Herb, blossoms: laxative, anodyne.**

2. Which of these are for urinary or kidney troubles? **Trailing arbutus and vaccinium family (blueberries and cranberries).**

3. Which agent in this lesson is one of the most important herbs we have for childbirth? **Trillium.**

4. Which other agent is also used in pregnancy? **Black haw or other viburnums.**

5. Which agent is a safe and certain remedy for worms in children? **Turtlehead.**

6. Which two of these herbs are among the most-used nervines? **Valerian and blue vervain.**

7. Which herb is mentioned most often in the vitamin listing? **Alfalfa.**

8. Which specifics were mentioned in this lesson? **Trillium for hemorrhaging in childbirth; elecampane for TB; meadowsweet for gastric ulcer; shepherd's-purse for uterine tumors; vaccinium family for kidney infections.**

9. Vocabulary to define: **See glossary.**

Self-review Questions for "W" — "X" — "Y" — "Z"

1. The herbal agents listed in this lesson are:

white water lily — **Root: astringent, demulcent.**
wild carrot — **Seeds, leaves: aromatic, diuretic, anthelmintic, carminative.**
witch hazel — **Bark, twigs, leaves: astringent, tonic, sedative.**
yarrow — **Herb: astringent, stimulant, diaphoretic, tonic.**

2. Which specifics were mentioned in this lesson? **White water lily for prolapsed uterus; red clover for whooping cough.**

3. Under worms it says, "See anthelmintics." Which ones are safe for children? **Butternut bark, turtlehead, pumpkin seeds.**

4. Vocabulary to define: **See glossary.**

Final Exam Answers

1. List five major families of safe herbs to use. (Add examples of specific herbs you remember.) **Rose, mustard, composite, goose-foot, violet.**

2. List five families of dangerous herbs, with identifying characteristics.

Umbelliferae (parsley) – ferny leaves with flower umbrellas; the wild carrot (Queen Anne's lace) is useful.
Solanaceae – learn individually, as this family also includes the potato and tomato.
Ranunculacea (buttercup) – flowers in fives; leaves like a crow's foot.
Rhus – includes poison ivy, poison oak, and poison sumac.
Heath – such as rhododendron and laurel; but some are useful, e.g., trailing arbutus and cranberries.
Dog-bane and milkweed – milky-juiced plants, with flowers in five parts; some useful, including milkweed and pleurisy root.
Figwort – Mullein is useful, but many others, including digitalis (foxglove), can be dangerous.

3. What family of herbs is useful at other times but should not be used (except sparingly) during pregnancy? **Mint (Labiatiae).**

4. Following are some of the major classes of herbal agents. Describe the effects of each class of agent. Then list at least five herb examples.

alteratives — **alter the condition of the blood; alder, black and yellow birch, prickly ash, bittersweet, burdock, red clover, yellow dock, gill-over-the-ground, mullein, sarsaparilla, spikenard, veronica.**
antiseptics — **kill bacteria; apple, black and yellow birch, aloe, chickweed, garlic, herb Robert, hollyhock, lycopodium, nettles, peppermint, plantain, sphagnum moss, thyme.**
astringents — **contract tissue; nearly one-third of the herbs in this book are astringent. Some of the more commonly used include barberry, sumac, viburnums, vacciniums, costmary, meadowsweet, mullein, nettles, red raspberry, trillium, yarrow.**

demulcents — **soothing to mucus membranes; cherry, elm, white pine, comfrey, costmary, elecampane, everlasting, hollyhock, horehound, Irish moss, marsh mallow, oats, polypody, Solomon's seal, white water lily.**

diuretics — **increase the flow of urine; beech, black birch, elder, juniper, white pine, sumac, blueberries, cleavers, corn silk, cranberries, daisy, garlic, horsetail, huckleberries, Joe-Pye weed, lady's bedstraw, milkweed, wild mint, sarsaparilla, trailing arbutus, veronica, wild carrot.**

nervines — **calm or strengthen the nervous system; betony, bugleweed, catnip, chamomile, lady's-slipper, motherwort, oats, peppermint, St. Johnswort, skullcap, valerian, blue vervain.**

stimulants — **speed up the action of body systems; elder, hemlock, shagbark hickory, agrimony, ginger, horehound, Joe-Pye weed, mustard, rose, shepherd's-purse, yarrow.**

tonics — **promote the general healing and well-being of the body as a whole, or of specific systems; nearly one-third of the herbs are tonics. Some of the more common ones include alder, barberry, black and yellow birch, hawthorn, prickly ash, agrimony, betony, boneset, burdock, daisy, dandelion, meadowsweet, motherwort, red raspberry, skullcap, squawvine, turtlehead, yarrow.**

5. One unique class of agents is not listed above; it is useful in treating the diseases and complaints caused by a vitamin deficiency. List that class of agent: **Antiscorbutics,** the vitamin deficiency: **Vitamin C,** and at least five herbal remedies: **Hemlock, white pine, shadbush, spruce, gill-over-the-ground, mustard, nasturtium, nettles, rose, shepherd's-purse, strawberry.** (Do you remember one symptom of this deficiency that is frequent and easily diagnosed: **Bleeding gums.)**

6. Name what you would consider the ten most important herbs for your needs and give the general use of each. **I'll leave that up to you.**

7. Describe the procedure (and proportions) for the following herbal preparations:

standard infusion — **Steep one-third of a cup of loose leaves or 1-2 tablespoons of coarsely ground roots and bark in two cups of boiling water for 15-20 minutes. Strain.**

concentrated infusion- **Use eight times the usual quantity of herb and three-quarters of the usual amount of water. Steep.**

decoction — **Similar to infusion, but may be boiled to release herbal properties.**

herbal syrup — **Use a concentrated infusion; add an equal amount of honey. Or add 3 tablespoons of raw juice to 1 cup of honey.**

ointment — **Boil herb in a vegetable oil, or for firmer ointment use lard, suet or tallow.**

poultice — **Steep one handful of herb in one pint of boiling water for 15 minutes. Add two or three tablespoons of oatmeal or other starchy material to thicken. Wrap quickly in a cloth and apply to treatment area.**

suppositories — **Use three ounces of cocoa butter, tallow, or suet, heated in a double boiler with two tablespoons of powdered herb. Pour into molds and refrigerate.**

8. Modern medical theory differs greatly from herbal theory. Discuss five conditions for which modern medicine has few answers and for which there may be herbal relief. Be sure to include the rationale for the herbal remedies.

Natural therapies have no side-effects as do some of the standard treatments. Natural therapies generally respect the body's own healing powers and work to strengthen them.

The present treatments for AIDS all have serious side-effects, with little permanent hope. Sufficient testing of herbal remedies has not yet been tried, but when combined with diet and nutritional supplements, herbal treatment may build up the body's ability to cope.

Arthritis is a chronic condition rarely alleviated by modern medicine. Herbalist theory suggests that the cause may be due to a build-up of metabolic waste. In addition to diuretics and aperients, alteratives might be helpful. Diet and counter-irritation should also be considered.

Some cancers are quickly taken care of by surgery. However, herbal and dietary attention may decrease the danger of recurrence. In the case of inoperable cancer, herbal remedies, vitamin supplement, and diet certainly offer the possibility of improved quality of life at a time when no other options exist.

Mononucleosis is traditionally treated with a long period of bed rest. By adding herbal remedies—alteratives—the convalescence may be shortened.

Modern diets, high in saturated fats, contribute to most cases of heart disease. Surgery is the usual response. Dietary changes, combined with herbal and other natural therapies, may offer a more permanent cure.

There are several other possibilities that you might have discussed here. But in all cases of illness and disease, natural remedies will offer alternatives to surgery and to medications with potentially toxic side-effects. Natural remedies are something over which you have control, something you can often do for yourself, with little cost.

9. Herbal remedies often work best when combined with other nonmedical treatment. Name three such treatments. **Diet, fasting, massage, bee venom, chiropractic, osteopathy, homeopathy.**

10. For many conditions, herbalists have identified specifics—remedies that equal or surpass prescription medicine because of their efficacy and safety. (Some of these herbs have additional applications, as well.) Match the herb with the condition for which it is suited.

agrimony — **bedwetting.**
aloe — **burns.**
betony — **headache.**
black haw — **threatened miscarriage.**
boneset — **flu.**
costmary — **sinus, head cold.**
hawthorn — **heart disease.**
Joe-Pye weed — **kidney stones, gravel.**
meadowsweet — **acid stomach.**
motherwort — **menopause difficulties.**
raspberry leaves — **morning sickness.**
shepherd's-purse — **fibroid tumors.**
trillium — **uterine bleeding.**
white clover blossoms — **mumps.**
yellow dock — **acne.**

11. I have listed some physical complaints and medical problems. You fill in the herbal remedy that might be helpful for each condition. (There may be more than one answer for each.)

angina — **Hawthorn.**
arthritis — **Prickly ash, yarrow, and agrimony, among others.**
athlete's foot — **Jewelweed, bloodroot.**
bedwetting — **Agrimony.**
bleeding gums — **Antiscorbutics such as rose hips, strawberry, sumac. Also plantain.**
burns — **Aloe.**
colic — **Catnip, chamomile, peppermint.**
constipation — **Aperients such as dandelion root, yellow dock.**
cough — **Garlic syrup, demulcents.**
dandruff — **Rosemary.**
diaper rash — **Honey, butternut, elm, chickweed.**
diarrhea — **Strawberry or blackberry leaves; mullein for adults.**
epilepsy — **Nervines, especially lady's bedstraw, valerian, skullcap, blue vervain, lady's-slipper.**
headaches — **Nervines; betony, skullcap, valerian.**
hemorrhoids — **Plantain, burdock, mullein, white water lily.**
insomnia — **Nervines.**
menopause — **Motherwort.**
menstrual cramps — **Peppermint, crampbark.**
overweight — **Diuretics, alteratives; yarrow, prickly ash.**
pimples or acne — **Burdock, yellow dock.**
ringing in the ears — **Violets, valerian, thyme, gill-over-the-ground.**
ulcers — **Meadowsweet.**
warts — **Castor oil, jewelweed, bloodroot.**

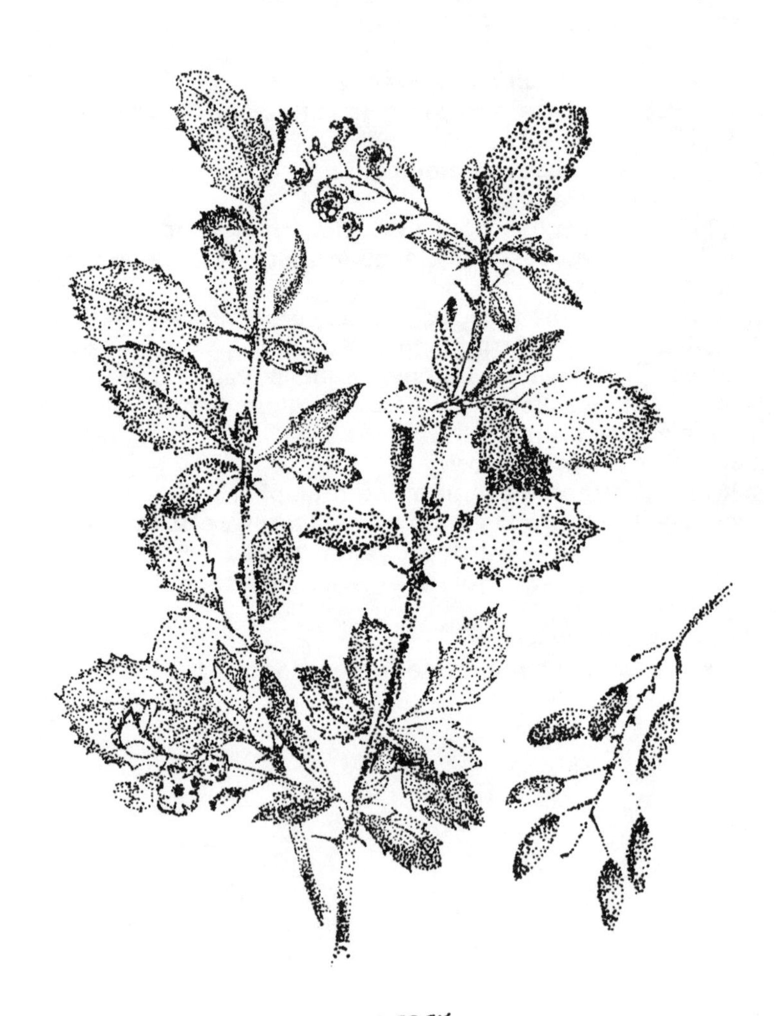

COMMON BARBERRY

Glossary

Note: These definitions are given in reference to herbalism. Many of these words are used as nouns (instead of as adjectives) when describing medicinal use. Various words have additional meanings not cited here.

acute — brief and severe, in contrast to chronic.
ad lib — as frequently as desired.
alimentary — pertaining to the digestive tract.
alterative — tending to alter body chemistry. No longer used in common medical terms, but the original meaning implied the return to healthy body conditions.
amenorrhea — without menstrual flow.
analgesic — relieving pain.
anodyne — relieving pain.
annual — a plant that comes up from seed each year.
anthelmintic — capable of killing worms.
antidote — a substance capable of counteracting the harmful effects of another substance.
antibilious — reducing excessive flow of bile; normalizing to liver function.
antiperiodic — countering periodic fevers that come and go, especially malaria, but now used by herbalists for all fevers.
antiscorbutic — relieving scurvy through high vitamin C content.
antiseptic — a substance which kills germs.
antispasmodic — relieving cramps and spasms.
antithrombotic — preventing blood clots.
aperient — having a gentle laxative effect. Derived from the Latin for "to open."
aromatic — with a pleasing smell; aromatics are often combined with bland or less pleasant herbs.
arthralgia — pain in the joints.
astringent — contracting and tightening. From the Latin for "to draw together."
axil — the angle between a leaf stem and the main stem.
bacteriostatic — preventing bacterial growth.

biennial — every two years. A biennial plant lives for two years, with flowering and setting of seed usually occurring in the second year.
calyx — the outermost parts of the flower; sepals.
capsicum — red pepper, a member of the nightshade family.
cardiac — pertaining to the heart; cardiac remedies normalize heart function.
carminative — expelling intestinal gas, reducing flatulence.
catarrh — inflammation of the mucous membranes.
cathartic — purging, especially evacuation of the bowels.
caustic — burning, harsh.
chlorosis — iron deficiency, characterized by a yellowish complexion.
cholagogue — increasing the flow of bile.
chronic — of long duration.
chutney — a spicy condiment, usually with a mix of sweet and sour.
colitis — inflammation of the colon.
congenital — denoting a condition present at birth.
cress — any of several plants of the mustard family with pungent-tasting leaves.
curative — healing. Many of the drugs prescribed by doctors are only palliative.
cutaneous — pertaining to the skin.
cyanotic — with bluish complexion, from lack of oxygen.
decoction — an extract obtained by boiling.
delirium tremens — tremor and nervous dysfunction caused by excessive alcohol consumption.
demulcent — soothing, especially to mucous membranes.
diaphoretic — inducing perspiration.
dicot — a plant having a seed with two halves; word is the short form of dicotyledon.
digitalis — heart stimulant, from the foxglove plant.
digits — toes and fingers.
dilated — expanded, widened.
distended — swollen.
diuretic — increasing the flow of urine.
douche — the cleansing of a body cavity, commonly the vagina, with a medicated solution.
dropsy — a once-used term for edema.
dysentery — diarrhea accompanied by inflammation of the bowels, often caused by microorganisms.
dysmenorrhea — painful menstruation.
dyspepsia — indigestion.
edema — swelling caused by retention of fluid in the tissues.
emesis — vomiting.

emmenagogue — stimulating menstrual flow.
emollient — soothing, especially to the skin.
endocarditis — inflammation of the membranes that line the cavities of the heart.
enuresis — bedwetting.
epigastric — of the upper abdomen; over the stomach.
erysipelas — an acute infection of the skin, caused by specific streptococcus bacteria.
escharotic — caustic.
exanthema — eruptive diseases, such as measles and chicken pox.
excoriated — with the skin abraded.
expectorant — discharging the phlegm or mucous that clogs the breathing passages.
farinaceous — starchy, made of flour.
febrifuge — reducing fever.
fibroid — fibrous, as in a uterine tumor.
flush — to redden; the ruddy complexion often accompanying a fever.
fomentation — a warm ointment, poultice, or dressing.
fungicide — a substance that exterminates fungus growth, as in athlete's foot or yeast infections.
gastric — pertaining to the digestive process in the stomach.
generative — capable of producing or reproducing.
gluten — the protein mass remaining when flour is washed of starch.
granulation — the early healing tissue, irregular in form, found in ulcers and wounds.
hematemesis — vomiting of blood.
hemostatic — arresting heavy bleeding; a styptic or astringent.
hepatic — affecting the liver; in herbal terms, promoting normal liver function.
hyperemia — an excessive accumulation of blood in a body part.
hyperglycemia — excessive blood sugar.
hypoglycemia — lack of adequate blood sugar.
infusion — an extract or tea made by steeping herbs in hot water.
laxative — a substance for relieving constipation.
larynx — the upper part of the wind pipe, where vocal cords are found.
legume — a plant family that produces seeds in pods; includes various peas and beans.
leucorrhea — a mucous discharge from the vagina.
lumbago — recurring lower back pain.
macerate — to soften or separate into parts by steeping in a liquid.
madder — a dark rose or red color; a dye from the root of the Rubia (or madder) family.
materia medica — Latin for "medical material."

menorrhagia — excessive menstrual flow.
mesenteritis — inflammation of the interior abdominal tissues that support the colon.
miasmic — noxious, decaying, poisonous, especially referring to swamps once thought to breed malaria.
mitral — the valve between the two left chambers of the heart.
monocot — a plant having a seed of one kernel, like corn; word is the short form of monocotyledon.
mordant — in dyeing, a substance that fixes the dye so it won't run.
mucilaginous — gummy and gelatinous.
myocarditis — inflammation of the heart tissue.
nervine — restorative to the nervous system.
neuralgia — sharp pains along a nerve path.
neuritis — nerve inflammation; continuous pain.
ophthalmia — inflammation of the eye.
palliative — relieving or lessening without curing.
palmate — in the shape of a hand or palm.
palpitation — unusual or rapid heart beat.
papule — pimple.
pectoral — pertaining to the chest or lungs.
pemmican — dried meat made into a cake or loaf with other dried foods, fat and berries — used by the Indians.
perennial — every year; botanically, growing from the same root year after year.
pericarditis — inflammation of the sac that surrounds the heart.
peritonitis — inflammation of the interior lining of the abdomen.
pharynx — the section of the throat between the mouth and esophagus.
phlegmatic — sluggish in temperament; not easily excited.
pinnate — resembling a feather.
plaster — an adhering substance applied to the outside of the body for healing purposes; often of a caustic or drawing nature.
plethoric — overfull.
potash — lye made from wood ashes.
potherb — herb used for edible greens, cooked.
poultice — a soft, moist mixture of herbs and material wrapped with cloth, applied to external parts of the body for soothing
prolapsus — a fallen or out-of-place condition, as with a uterus.
prophylactic — protecting from disease; preventive.
puerperal — pertaining to the 40 days following childbirth.
purge — to cleanse by emptying the bowels.
purine — uric acid.
purpuric — purple or brownish-red, as in skin spots.
rank — excessive growth, usually offensive.
refrigerant — reducing the body temperature.

renal — pertaining to the kidneys.
resolvent — reducing swelling.
ret — to soak in water until soft parts fall away, leaving only the fibers.
rigors — chills.
rose hips — the crimson fruit of the rose, which appears after blooming.
sallow — yellowish and sickly, in reference to complexion.
sanguine — cheerful, often with a ruddy complexion.
sciatic nerves — the nerves running from the base of the spine down the backs of the legs, including many of those in the pelvis.
scorbutic — causing scurvy, a deficiency of vitamin C.
scrofulous — pertaining to infection of the lymph glands, especially in the neck.
sedative — calming.
serous — of a watery nature; secreting serum.
shrub — a bushy, woody plant.
shrub — a beverage made with fruit, sugar, and vinegar.
species — in botany, a distinct plant with distinguishing characteristics, identified by a given Latin name; usually grouped with similar plants in the same class or family. Plants (and animals) can interbreed only within a species.
sputum — expelled mucous; spittle.
stimulant — temporarily quickening the functions of the body as a whole, or of various parts of the body.
stomachic — a substance that affects the digestive tract, including appetite.
styptic — causing the cessation of bleeding; highly astringent.
sudorific — causing perspiration.
syrup — a thick, sweet liquid often used as a vehicle for medication.
thrombosis — a blood clot in a blood vessel.
tincture — an herbal solution made with alcohol, usually stronger than an infusion.
tinnitus — ringing in the ears.
tonic — strengthening various body functions.
trauma — sudden, violent injury.
tuber — a large, fleshy root; a potato is a tuber.
umbels — flower stalks, spreading from a common central point, as with an umbrella.
urethra — the tube through which urine is passed.
uterine — pertaining to the uterus; promoting the natural processes of the uterus.
vehicle — a substance with little medicinal property that is used as a medium to carry the active agent.

vermifuge — expelling worms; also used for other parasites in addition to worms. See anthelmintic.
vertigo — loss of balance; dizziness.
vulnerary — promoting the healing of wounds.
weed — a plant growing wild, without cultivation, or where it is not wanted, as in lawns or gardens.
wineglassful — two fluid ounces.

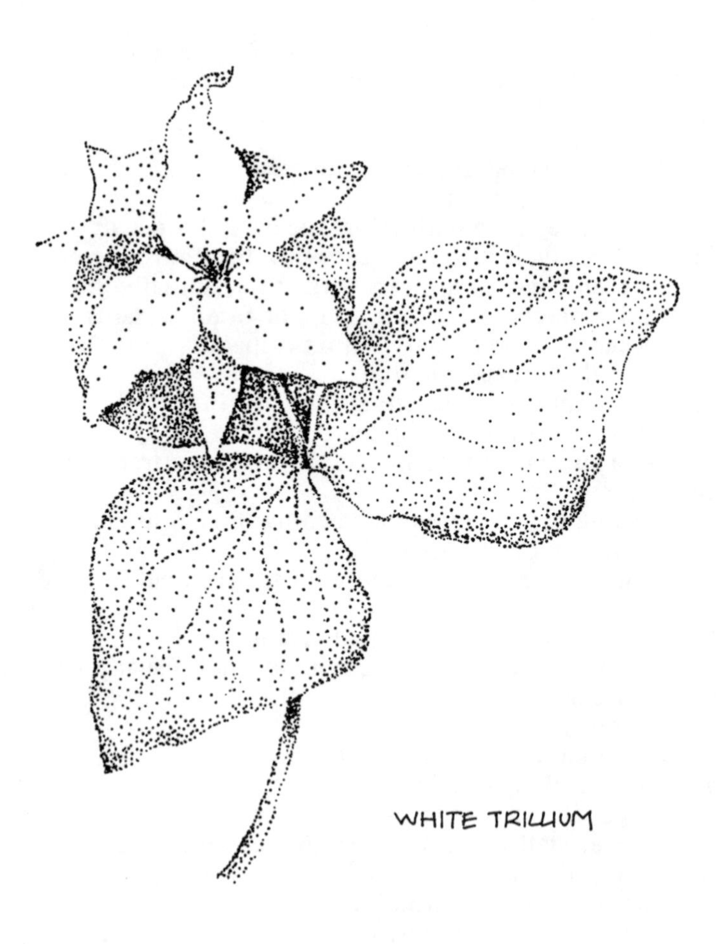

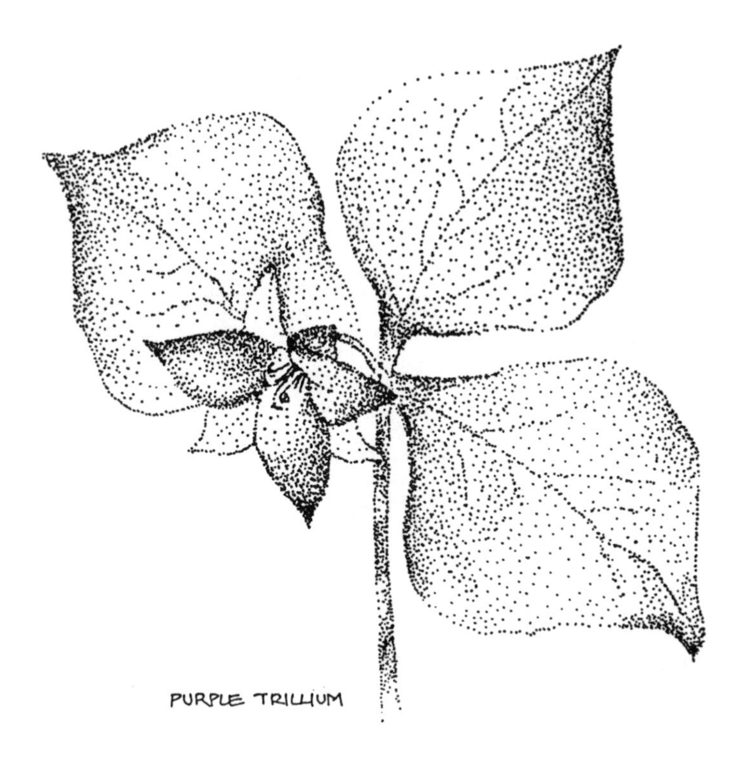

Index

Index

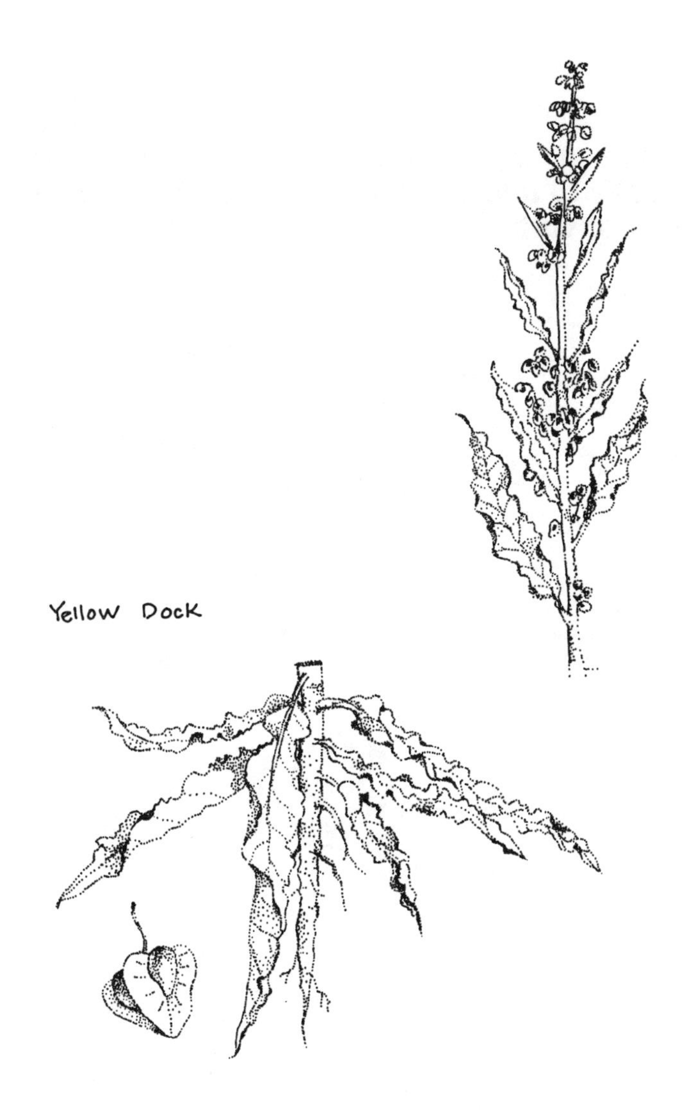
Yellow Dock

Upper Access Publishers selects nonfiction books to improve the quality of life. Please call or write for our catalog.

Upper Access Publishers
One Upper Access Road
P.O.Box 457
Hinesburg, Vermont 05461
802-482-2988
1-800-356-9315